# JOHNS ⊕ CREEK
## BAPTIST CHURCH

# THE FIRST 2⊕ YEARS
## 1993 - 2013

### BARBARA D. BROWN &
### DAVID T. BROWN

*Dave Brown*

*Barbara Brown*

*Bill Self*

**Wasteland Press**
www.wastelandpress.net
Shelbyville, KY USA

*Johns Creek Baptist Church:*
*The First 20 Years: 1993-2013*
by Barbara D. Brown & David T. Brown

First Printing – September 2013
ISBN: 978-1-60047-910-6
Library of Congress Control Number: 2013950420

Printed in the U.S.A.

0   1   2   3   4   5   6   7   8   9

*We dedicate this book to the congregation that was, is and will be Johns Creek Baptist Church.*

*~ The History Committee: Barbara Brown, Dave Brown, Mary Lou Parrish, Nancy Skidmore*

# CHRIST'S CHURCH

It is right that His Cross crowns her steeple
And that Grace holds her doors open wide;
As the Truth of God's Word guides her footsteps
Through the faithful who gather inside.

There is Joy in the sound of her Music
When all hearts beat together as one;
Giving glory to God there in Heaven
And Praise to Christ Jesus, His Son.

It is good that she thinks of Salvation
While sharing the blessed bread and wine;
Remembering His death there at Calvary
And the Love of our Savior Divine.

"It is finished," He said to His Father
As His mission on Earth was complete;
And the wonder of Holy transcendence
Made new birth for each Soul now replete.

It's that promise that He will not leave her
Whatever may tempt her to fail;
And new vision perceived through God's wisdom
Which assures her that she will prevail.

It's through death on the cross, JESUS suffered;
Souls' freedom from sin has been won.
And GOD's grace through the gift of His SPIRIT
Who commissions the Faithful as One.

~ Mary Lou Parrish, 2013

# CONTENTS

Appendix continued...

# FOREWORD

"It's Been a Good Day"

~ Dr. Bill Self

It was a good day when Carolyn and I started our ministry at the Chamblee/Johns Creek Baptist Church. I had taken an early retirement after 26 years as Senior Pastor of the Wieuca Road Baptist Church in Atlanta. One day I received a phone call from L. H. Johnson who had served with me at Wieuca Road as Executive Pastor for over ten years before he retired. He was now a member of the First Baptist Church of Chamblee. Dr. David Sapp had served Chamblee for ten years as Senior Pastor and had accepted a call to serve a church in Virginia. L. H. asked me if I would be interested in talking with the church about being their interim pastor while they looked for Dr. Sapp's successor. I gave him a positive reply, and he immediately informed the church leaders.

I was invited to supply the pulpit on the first Sunday of May (1991), and I accepted. Later that week I had lunch with Tommy Boland, Phil Brown, and Richard Eason to discuss the details of the interim arrangement. I knew after that lunch that there was something special about the Chamblee church. Though small in number and facing a declining population in the community, their leaders had a "life wish" for the church and the leadership ability to make it happen.

It was not long after the interim had begun that we started talking about the relocation. While Dr. Sapp was still pastor, the church had voted to relocate with no specific place in mind. I learned that he had led them through the difficult decision-making process to relocate, and had started conversations with Technology Park and the Dunwoody Baptist Church about relocating to a 16-acre tract of land that Technology Park intended to donate to the

Dunwoody church for a new church start. Because of the friendship of Dr. Sapp with Dr. Daniel Vestal, then pastor of the Dunwoody Baptist Church, it would be possible to work out arrangements for the Chamblee church to move to the Johns Creek community and absorb the mission church Dunwoody had started in the area.

During this time, leaders of the church began to talk with me about becoming the pastor of the relocated congregation which would be known as the Johns Creek Baptist Church. Carolyn and I struggled with the decision; other opportunities were presenting themselves, and we were trying to discern God's will in the situation. I had lunch with the Pulpit Committee to discuss the possibility of my becoming the pastor of the new church. The future was becoming clear. Later, after a discussion with the Pulpit Committee held at the home of the Chair, Tom Jack, it was agreed that I would permit the committee to present my name to the church. They voted to extend a call, and one month from my sixtieth birthday I became the pastor of the First Baptist Church of Chamblee which would later become the Johns Creek Baptist Church.

I was impressed with the quality of the Chamblee church and with their leadership. It was evident that they were well-organized. Much of their organization had been put into place when the church was much larger, and it was suited for a larger congregation. Though their finances were suffering from the decrease in population, they were extremely well-managed and maturely administered. The church had been led by Dr. Sapp through the Southern Baptist struggle with fundamentalism to adopt a moderate position; they ordained women to the diaconate, as well as the gospel ministry. They were among the first churches to identify with the Cooperative Baptist Fellowship. They had not sacrificed any of its Baptist heritage but had fought to preserve a mature understanding of Baptist life. I found a church that knew who it was, that was united in its commitment to the gospel, and appreciated its Baptist heritage. Also, the leadership in the congregation had the ability to make the move happen. After much prayer, Carolyn and I decided to accept the challenge.

When word spread about the future of the Chamblee church, we began to be noticed by those who were interested in becoming a part of the newly relocated church. Several families from the Johns Creek area began worshiping with us in Chamblee, while others came to us who were planning to move their residence to Johns Creek, as well as many people who had been at Wieuca Road.

We immediately began to make specific plans for the move. The most obvious was the need for a building. The firm of CDH Partners was employed to develop the site plan which consisted of four buildings. The first building included a chapel for worship and some basic space for religious education and administration. The second building was more educational space for adults and children. The third building was the largest—it included a gymnasium which was to be used for worship, dining, and recreational activities; office space; and a foyer for the fourth building, the sanctuary.

As these plans were being developed, the church had its annual picnic on the property in Johns Creek. It was a joyous occasion. The property was farmland with an old barn on it. The neighborhood was yet undeveloped. There was no traffic light at the corner of McGinnis Ferry Road and Highway 141, both two-lane highways. Forsyth County did not have sewer and water to the site. There was no residential development on the Forsyth side of McGinnis Ferry (the boundary between Fulton and Forsyth counties). We were in the country! As we described how the site would be developed with the four buildings, enthusiasm began to grow. Several remembered a meeting on the property earlier while Dr. Sapp was pastor that concluded with a prayer session asking God to lead the church to the property, and to help us develop it for His glory. They sensed that they were seeing God at work in the life of the church; this prayer was being answered.

There was much work to be done. We needed to sell the Chamblee property, design and develop the buildings for the new property with a special eye to the first building. Also, the organization would have to be reconfigured to fit the new community and the new buildings. The Chamblee church did not have the resources to do this without a capital funds campaign and cooperation from our bank. We set about to accomplish these tasks.

This work was accomplished in record time. However, special note should be made of the challenges that confronted the new congregation other than the buildings and finance. The hard questions were: What kind of congregation would we be? Would the old church from Chamblee and the new church members from Johns Creek integrate? How would we organize ourselves? What kind of worship would we have? What kind of religious education would we offer? How long would it take for the new congregation to mature?

The first Sunday at the new site was glorious. The church was filled to overflowing with people, a good mix of the Chamblee and Johns Creek people. When we extended an invitation to unite with the church, the aisles were filled with people—so filled that we could not absorb all of them. We had to stop the invitation and ask those who could not get to the front of the church to wait until the following week...and they did!

We were off to a great start. However, the real work was just beginning--the work of turning a crowd into a congregation. It is easy to draw a crowd but it is very difficult to turn them into a congregation, a church. Each person brings his/her own idea of what a church should be. This is usually the church of their dreams, or of their childhood, or a celebrated church in another city that they want to reproduce. A new church is a target for any and all heresies, both organizational and theological. We were no exception.

Earlier my wife and I had taken a hard look at the Sunday School program and had an idea that would become a radical new approach that would become the Johns Creek Adult Sunday School model. We saw the religious education work of the church as essential to our task of making disciples and building community.

The concept was developed while we were still in Chamblee. Larry Jones, Minister of Education, and Tom Jack, Director of Sunday School, working with Carolyn and me and the Sunday School leadership, began pilot groups in May 1992 in preparation for the move to Johns Creek. Intentional words like community, care groups, seminar leaders and appropriate curriculum were all dealt with along the way. Our commitment was to provide premier quality education, to create an environment of caring for fellow members and improved communication, as well as to develop new units, larger groups and an avenue for significant growth. We had the JCBC Adult Sunday School model in place when it came time to move. Later, when Dr. Michael McCullar came as Minister of Education, he brought an added dimension of teaching and curriculum excellence that helped to elevate the program even further.

As a standard-bearer for Sunday School programs in the Cooperative Baptist world, other churches have adopted this unique model, or some modified form of it. Although I am basically a preacher, it seemed to me that the long-term strength of the church would be well served if we started, as most Baptist churches have done, with the Sunday School. This has been one of the keys for turning a crowd into a congregation.

Another key has been worship. All church members have definite opinions on how a church should worship. Because the new congregation was made up of people from diverse backgrounds and generations, we had many suggestions of how we should conduct ourselves on Sunday mornings. Every conceivable form of worship had its proponents from high church liturgical to emergent and radical contemporary. Each worship style had its special kind of music that appealed to their taste. Some lobbied to discard all formality, or anything that looked like the past, including the organ and piano; others pushed for the exact opposite--nothing sung or played in church written after 1850. It seemed clear that to divide the church by worship styles with separate worship for each style would divide the church permanently. We may have several times to worship, but we would be together on *how* we worship. We were also determined that whatever form we used would be to worship God, not to entertain the people.

Most Baptists learned to worship at Billy Graham revivals or at the Ridgecrest Baptist Assembly. So this became our norm, with some variation toward both the contemporary and the highly liturgical. Although this did not satisfy all, it did give us a starting place, a place of reference. For the most part, this has helped us develop a sense of community, of church. Later, because the parents of youth asked for a special worship service especially designed for youth, we made that adjustment. Before we entered the permanent sanctuary in 2007 in a special study conducted by the Alban Institute, the church made it clear that they wished to have one service of worship and to continue essentially the same style of worship.

No church can develop properly without a strong pulpit ministry. Johns Creek Baptist has always valued a strong pulpit. The sanctuary is built with that in mind--with the pulpit virtually in the center of the room. "The preaching of the Word of God *is* the Word of God." This coupled with strong religious education has helped the church to mature.

During this time, many Baptist churches were taking the word "Baptist" out of their names. It seemed clear to our leaders that we should leave "Baptist" in our name and on our signage. It was a matter of truth in advertising. When people came to worship, they needed to know who we were. Our worship and mission would show the type of Baptists we are.

After the fourth building was completed in 2007, the church had a debt of approximately $19 million which we could afford in that economy. At this time, I felt as though my mission with the church was completed. However, I was particularly concerned that the usual method of pastoral transition used by Baptists would not work for our church. Also, the great recession had hit the nation and the economy was very uncertain. So after much prayer and study, I presented a Pastoral Transition Proposal to a study committee. This was later presented to the church for ratification. This plan guaranteed that the church would have continued leadership while the Pulpit Search Committee sought a new pastor. The transition would be smooth. They approved the plan, and it has provided a very smooth pastoral transition. I did not want to leave until the debt was reduced enough to be included in the budget. As of this writing, this has been accomplished.

Johns Creek Baptist has been unusually blessed. It is an old church (established in 1875) with a bright new future. This journey has been the best years of our lives for Carolyn and me. We have sought to be faithful and effective during our watch, and we go into retirement with the knowledge that the future for Johns Creek Baptist Church is as bright as the promises of God.

Carolyn and I can truly say, "It has been a good day," as we see our people worshiping with joy and exultation in the presence of God, and it is with confidence that we affirm that He has truly sent us. We know that these years have been worthwhile. "It has been a good day," when we see that the crowd has matured into a congregation, that they are developing through a program of positive religious education and not indoctrination, and that they are capable of struggling successfully with every new issue that they will face. It is truly "a good day" when it becomes clear that the people have developed a desire for true worship of the living God, and have not turned worship into a time of religious entertainment thus cheapening the gospel for which Jesus died. It is "a good day" to see that the buildings of the original site plan have been constructed and are well-financed, and the stewardship program of the church is maturing the church's understanding of stewardship as it relates to their mission in the world. The first 20 years of our history have provided a road map for the future, ensuring that they too will be "good days."

~ Dr. Bill Self

# PREPARING FOR
# A TRANSPLANT

Relocating our church is a lot like transplanting a big tree or plant that has lived in one place a long time. Given its current conditions, if left there, it will die. For it to survive, careful changes must be made.

It must be evident that the tree is not doing well in its present environment. Every effort must be made to improve conditions to enable the tree to survive in its current location. When the circumstances cannot be changed dramatically enough to save the tree, a difficult decision ensues: either move the tree to a healthier environment so it can continue to grow, or do nothing and let the tree slowly die. For the tree to live, a location where it will have the greatest possibility of re-establishing itself and continuing to grow must be found.

The tree must be prepared for the trauma associated with a move. Cutting the roots and pruning the canopy will cause significant shock to the tree. It will need time to adjust to the change in order to support the future healthy growth of deep roots and strong branches.

Questions regarding the environment of the new location such as drainage, needed sunshine, and health of the soil must be carefully answered in advance. The new location must be prepared. The correct size hole, the proper mix of nutrients in the soil, the precise requirements of fertilizer and moisture must be calculated in advance--all of the things necessary to insure the tree's ability to thrive in its new home.

Finally, once in its new location, the tree will require continual care through the years to come, providing all those things needed to insure healthy growth in being the tree it was created to be.

~ Beth Ann Boland, Deacon,
First Baptist Church of Chamblee, 1991

# JCBC ORIGINAL LOGO

October 17, 1993 – August 10, 2013

## JOHNS CREEK
### BAPTIST CHURCH

**Logo Symbolism**

The suggestion of a cross in the globe logo symbolizes our Christ centered ministry. Enveloping the globe form, it communicates the nurturing care of God as characterized through the gift of salvation through Christ. Stylistically the cross could represent a crossroad either figuratively in the life of the church at large, its individual members and prospects, or literally as the intersection of McGinnis Ferry Road and Highway 141. Furthermore, the road is symbolic of Christ as the "Way."

The globe itself symbolizes our vision for world missions. Also, the sphere is a "perfect" form and symbolic of wholeness or completeness, and like God, it has no beginning and no end.

The highlighted area of the globe over the center of the cross is symbolic of Christ as the "Light."

# INTRODUCTION

*"Hats off to the past; coats off to the future for there is work to be done!"*

~ Dr. William L. (Bill) Self

What are your first memories of this church?

For some, memories extend back to when the church had a different name and location, First Baptist Church of Chamblee.

My first memories are from Chamblee in 1956, when standing on the front pew in "the old white building," this four-year old gazed in wonder as our young pastor, Dr. Cecil Sherman, baptized my daddy. My name is David Brown and, as a member of the history committee of Johns Creek Baptist Church, I have been given the privilege of facilitating your journey through the following pages; but many of the words are not my own.

Our church's history committee consists of three more senior members, Barbara Brown (Chair), Nancy Skidmore and Mary Lou Parrish. Together, they have tirelessly dedicated the past three years to researching and compiling the details contained within. Researching all available data, the committee interviewed and worked in conjunction with members in past and present positions of leadership, along with past and current staff members gathering all varied forms of information historically available to form the contents of this document. Barbara, Nancy and Mary Lou have been relentless in their pursuit of a document suitable for the occasion of the 20th anniversary of our church. Each one of them has overcome great personal adversity over the past three years: Mary Lou, chronic illness; Barbara lost her mother, had several medical issues, and was recently diagnosed with chronic leukemia; and Nancy, who recently spent weeks in the hospital with surgery and respiratory distress, lost her husband, Charles (former Minister of Education of First Baptist

Chamblee) last Thanksgiving Day. These are deeply devoted and caring members of our church. The strongest, most driven of all, is Barbara Brown. This book is her dream and all credit for the publication rests with her. I'm certainly no historian. The committee recruited me because I've loved this church my entire life; I love people; I like telling their stories; and I've had a few of them published along the way, simple as that. The three ladies on our committee are the historians.

The period prior to the relocation to the church's current location was filled with uncertainty. In order for First Baptist Chamblee to survive, changes had to be made. Such changes for a church with a 115-year history took people with vision. In February 1990, because of their love of this church, the wise members took their dreams, made decisions to take actions, and followed through for the necessary changes to transplant the church from Chamblee to Johns Creek.

As you read in the Foreword written by Dr. Bill Self, he was called by First Baptist Church of Chamblee to be their pastor beginning December 8, 1991. Nineteen days after Dr. Self became their pastor, the property of the current Johns Creek Baptist Church location was deeded to the congregation. On January 22, 1992, the title for 15.84 acres was presented to the church from Technology Park/Atlanta. As Dr. Self has stated, "We immediately began to make specific plans for the move. The most obvious was the need for a building." The "building" to which Dr. Self refers becomes a four-phased construction process to create the facilities. Within months action was taken to create plans for what would be the first of four phases of construction. Fourteen years later all of the buildings are complete.

The history committee has taken the liberty of asking you as the reader to imagine each of the aforementioned phases to be a "season" of growth for our church. There are transplanting references throughout the book alluding to the care that must be taken with undertaking such a task. Accordingly, we have labeled each phase "Spring, Summer, Fall and Winter." (How can we be in the suburbs of north Atlanta and not begin our story in the Spring?) There are chapters within the book titled the same and each reference the phase of growth during those years. As you read Dr. Bill Self's Foreword, summarizing the story of his ministry at Johns Creek, you will also read our new pastor Rev. Shaun King's Epilogue as he shares his vision for the future. Following Shaun's words, there is an Appendix containing reference details for your interest and pleasure.

In the autumn of 1993, members of First Baptist Church of Chamblee, Georgia, moved from the property they had occupied for over one hundred years to pursue an exciting new opportunity for ministry in southern Forsyth County. Embracing their new community, they changed the name of their church to Johns Creek Baptist Church.

Our church has a long and storied past.

Their story began in 1875. Corinth Baptist Church combined congregations with the Olive Leaf Baptist Church, continuing to be known as Corinth Baptist Church until 1920. In 1891, the membership relocated to a new site on New Peachtree Road and established a cemetery on the grounds. The church established a rich history of ministry and community involvement remaining at this location over the next 100 years prior to the relocation to Alpharetta. In 1917, the church property was incorporated in the newly formed military company know as Camp Gordon. Soldiers training for service in France during World War I worshipped there. When the city of Chamblee was incorporated in 1920, the name of the church was changed to Chamblee Baptist Church. In 1941, Chamblee High School burned and our church became home to the Chamblee students while the school was rebuilt. As World War II began, Lawson General Hospital (Army) was built a few blocks away from the church, allowing the church the opportunity to minister to the families of soldiers being cared for at Lawson General Hospital. In 1950, the church name was changed to First Baptist Church of Chamblee.

In the early 1950s the post-war growth boom came to the Atlanta area and First Baptist Church of Chamblee. Over the next

20 years, the church launched three major construction projects to expand their facilities to accommodate the growth of their membership. The subsequent 20 years held a series of ups and downs in the church as the demographics largely changed in the area affecting its ministry.

Having seen declines in vital areas of growth by late 1989, it became clear to the leadership of First Baptist Chamblee that in order to survive, relocation would be necessary. Following a vote of the membership edifying the decision by a sufficient majority, a plan to relocate was put into action. The church agreed that the target area to move would be a minimum of 15 miles north of interstate highway I-285, between the boundaries east of interstate highway I-75 and west of interstate highway I-85.

During the studies for the move, Chamblee pastor Dr. David Sapp had a casual meeting with Dr. Daniel Vestal, then pastor of Dunwoody Baptist Church. Dr. Sapp shared the church's vision with Dr. Vestal, pondering how the church could realistically reach its goal.

The Dunwoody Baptist Church pastor explained that their church had been trying to establish a church in the Johns Creek area and were struggling. Sitting on 1,900 acres in Atlanta's fastest growing northern corridor, Technology Park at Johns Creek had set into motion a dynamic, thriving community since its inception in 1985. The Dunwoody Baptist mission had been meeting in an office in the Johns Creek area for almost two years and only had 17 members to date. Further, Dr. Vestal explained that Technology Park had offered their church 15 acres of property on McGinnis Ferry Road, the southern boundary of Forsyth County. There was only one caveat to the offer. They must begin construction within a two-year time frame of establishing a mission in the designated area. The time on the offer of the property was rapidly coming to a close with no realistic chance at beginning construction as required by the developer. Realizing it was geographically ideal for the vision of First Baptist Chamblee's church, Dr. Vestal suggested to Dr. Sapp that their little mission could be the answer to the church's relocation.

Armed with this information and the full cooperation of Dunwoody Baptist, their mission church in Johns Creek, and Technology Park, First Baptist Church of Chamblee put the project in motion. The Johns Creek mission was closed and membership to First Baptist Chamblee was offered to all of its members. Several of their congregation joined First Baptist Chamblee and remain current members of Johns Creek Baptist Church.

Following Dr. Sapp's resignation in the spring of 1991 to follow God's call to lead a church in Virginia, and prior to the relocation, First Baptist Chamblee called Dr. Bill Self to be its pastor in December of the same year.

Many logistical tasks were completed over the following two years as the time for relocation neared. Provisions had to be considered for the future ministry to the area, the church's kindergarten program, and the sale of the property. The cemetery was not to be sold but sustained as the responsibility of the future Johns Creek Baptist Church.

In an effort to strive to continue the provision of outreach for local and international people in the Chamblee area once the church relocated, First Baptist Church of Chamblee, Dunwoody Baptist Church, Wieuca Road Baptist Church, and First Baptist Church of Doraville formed the "Chamblee-Doraville Ministry Center." The Cooperative Baptist Fellowship provided the funds to hire a pastor and staff for the Chamblee-Doraville Ministry Center.

The operation of First Baptist Chamblee's kindergarten program was taken over by First Baptist Church of Doraville.

The property was placed for sale and sold (albeit, the sale wasn't completed within the two year-window but thereafter). The sanctuary building of the property remains a church. The name is now "Iglesia de Dios, Pentecostal, M. I. (Pentecostal Church of God, International Movement)" and is a hub of Hispanic American worship each week. The educational facilities that were on the property are now a for-profit college, Interactive College of Technology. The school has acquired all contiguous properties that have become available, and currently has an expansion project underway. The former educational building is their home campus. They have seven satellite campuses in Georgia, Texas and Kentucky. Additionally, they work in conjunction with Morehead State University to offer accredited Bachelor's degrees.

The cemetery on the property was improved to include parking for visitors, sidewalks to and from the parking areas, a substantial memorial facing New Peachtree Road with relevant bronze plaques, and a granite monument of respect for all those interred within. Johns Creek Baptist Church still owns and maintains the First Baptist Church of Chamblee cemetery.

This little band of a few more than 200 active Baptist pioneers from Chamblee ventured forth to re-establish their church less than 20 miles to the north of its former home. Ranging in age from innocent children to experienced octogenarians, the membership came with a "life wish" for their church. Charged with a directive from their pastor, Dr. Bill Self, that "this church will rise as high as the life wish of its people with the direct intervention of God;" they came, and their legacy of dedication and commitment to Christ lives on. This small group of Christians took occupation of the property on Sunday, October 17, 1993. Twenty years later the church still provides bus transportation for people in the Chamblee area to attend weekly worship services at the new location.

Near a community named for a creek, in a deeply moving worship service, they asked God to bless this church and its future for service in His kingdom. This is the story of the church's first 20 years.

# SPRING
## (Phase I: 1990 – 1997)

"In September 1904 deacons J. W. Warren and B. T. Sheffield were elected. Both were ordained in November. Warren was forty-seven years old when he became a deacon. John Warren, a good-natured, jolly man, was held in high esteem by his neighbors and friends. He worked hard to provide well for his family."
- *A Century In North DeKalb, the story of First Baptist Church, Chamblee, Georgia, 1875 – 1975.*

"A good-natured, jolly man...." Does this sound like any of the ladies or gentlemen you have met at Johns Creek Baptist Church? I'd like to begin by introducing you to the unofficial greeter of Johns Creek Baptist Church. It's likely some of your first memories of our church are of meeting him. Good-natured, happy people welcoming you into the church, not only the first time, but every time you enter. It's our heritage.

John Warren (1857 – 1940) and his wife Emily (1860 – 1925) were members of Corinth Baptist Church in Chamblee. They moved from Conyers, Georgia, at the insistence of John's sister, Elizabeth ("Betty") Warren Johnson and because of her excitement of a new church in Chamblee, Corinth Baptist, that was being formed by a group of women meeting in a local blacksmith's shop. The Warren family bought a farm just down the road from Bert Johnson's blacksmith shop on Chamblee-Tucker Road and rode to church each Sunday in a horse-drawn buggy. Mercer University's Atlanta campus now resides on a portion of John and Emily's family farm along with Warren Elementary School. Six Warren daughters and one son were Corinth members. The children were baptized under a cedar shed built over Hutchensen's spring, the source of water for the original Corinth Baptist Church building. Three of the children would relocate and move their church memberships. The four others, all daughters, would remain active members throughout their lives. Their daughter Ola (1886 – 1956) would later marry M. G. (Glenn) Henderson (1886 – 1982). Glenn and Ola would have six sons.

Shortly following Ola Henderson's fortieth birthday, their fifth son was born on March 23, 1926. They named him Fred. Young Fred was registered on the cradle roll of Chamblee Baptist Church. (Chamblee had become a city in 1920, and at a church conference in January 1920, Corinth Baptist Church had changed its name to Chamblee Baptist Church. It would change again in 1950 to First Baptist Church of Chamblee.) As Fred Henderson grew, he inherited several characteristics from his grandfather.

Like his grandfather, "he worked hard to provide well for his family." In 1959, Fred and his wife Lillian opened a lawn mower sales and repair business on Buford Highway in Chamblee. Thirty years later, as the demographics of the area were changing, Fred recognized a similar decline in his business and his church. Many of the customers of his business and many of the church's members were moving north to the suburbs, farther and farther away. Fred saw the need for change. He served on the Strategic Task Force to relocate the church. Like his grandfather who had moved from Conyers to Chamblee to be a part of an exciting new church, Fred and Lillian moved from their home in Chamblee to Forsyth County to be near their beloved church when First Baptist Chamblee moved a little more than 16 miles north of its original location and became Johns Creek Baptist Church. In time, they also relocated their business a little more than 16 miles northeast of its original location.

Fred still has the original cedar corner posts that served as anchors for the long since fallen shed that covered the spring where his mother, aunts and uncles were baptized in the nineteenth century. Along with former First Baptist Church of Chamblee pastor Dr. Don Parker and their sons, Fred removed the church bell from "the old white building's" belfry prior to the demolition of the old structure.

The bell rests safely in the halls of Johns Creek Baptist Church. It stands ready to ring again.

Like his grandfather John W. Warren, "a good-natured, jolly man," Fred Henderson greets guests and members alike each Sunday upon their entrance. He's always there with a word of encouragement, making you feel welcome. He's the youngest 87-year old you'll ever meet, and if by chance you haven't met him, he'll be in the church lobby next Sunday morning looking for you. This is a friendly place!

Thanks to vision and love for one another through Christ, a couple of hundred men and women like Fred felt the Holy Spirit moving within their church 20 years ago. They made tough decisions and followed them up with committed actions, and the doors of their beloved First Baptist Church of Chamblee still swing open as Johns Creek Baptist Church, welcoming all in the name of Jesus in the new millennium just as their predecessors of Corinth Baptist did a century ago.

Because of demographic changes within the community, First Baptist Chamblee's attendance was dwindling, and there were concerns for their financial situation. Dr. David Sapp was the pastor. February 21, 1990, First Baptist Church of Chamblee's deacons recommended the appointment of a strategic task force regarding the future of the church. Exactly one month later on March 21, a vote was taken in the church, and the recommendations of the task force were approved. The work began! Dr. Sapp led the church through the difficult decision-making process to relocate. The original resolution for the church to move profoundly stated, "We choose to live rather than die." While Dr. Sapp was pastor, the church had voted to relocate between I-75 and I-85 at least fifteen miles north of I-285. During a casual visit with his friend and fellow pastor Dr. Daniel Vestal (then pastor of Dunwoody Baptist Church), a relocation opportunity became available. Technology Park located in the Johns Creek area of north Fulton and south Forsyth counties had allocated land for four churches in their long-term development plans. According to Vestal, Dunwoody Baptist Church had been struggling to succeed with a startup mission church in the Johns Creek area. He further explained, for them to receive the gift of land from developers, they had to start construction within 24 months of forming their mission church. Dr. Vestal told Sapp he didn't believe their Johns Creek mission church could meet the time constraints set by the developers. First Baptist Chamblee started conversations with Technology Park and Dunwoody Baptist Church about relocating to a 15.84-acre tract of land that Technology Park had originally intended to donate to the Dunwoody church for them to establish a new church. Logistics included the closing of Dunwoody Baptist's Johns Creek Mission church and consequently offering membership to all the mission's members in First Baptist Chamblee. Because of the friendship of Dr. David Sapp and Dr. Daniel Vestal and their diligent efforts to find a solution for both congregations' needs, arrangements were made for the Chamblee church to move to the Johns Creek community and absorb the mission church Dunwoody had started in the area. Many from the original Johns Creek Mission Church were accepted into the membership of First Baptist Chamblee. Many of them remain current members and serve in positions of leadership of Johns Creek Baptist Church.

On March 6, 1991, Dr. David Sapp resigned to accept a call to a church in Virginia. His final service as pastor of First Baptist Chamblee was March 31, 1991. Prior to Dr. Sapp's departure on March 24, a vote was taken and approved to accept the gift of land as suggested by Dunwoody Baptist Church from Technology Park/Atlanta. The conclusion of his ministry signaled the start to an exciting new future for the church. Dr. Sapp will always be remembered for his guidance and leadership in this bold step taken by the members of First Baptist Church of Chamblee.

There was nothing on the new property but an old barn. And while the barn was to be destroyed in the near future, that didn't stop the fun-loving members of one Sunday School class from laying claim to it! Claud Eason had been out "scouting around" the old barn and found an old piece of lumber that he thought just might make a good sign for their Sunday School class, the Progressive Class. Fellow member and artist Hugh Johnson painted the sign, and Claud went out to the barn and nailed it on a post, "FUTURE HOME OF THE PROGRESSIVE SUNDAY SCHOOL CLASS ---," tightly securing their claim on the old barn! This was an exciting time for the church! In what has been described to me by one who was in attendance as a "deeply moving day," several members of the church gathered on the property while Dr. Sapp was still pastor and prayed together that God would bless the future of Johns Creek Baptist Church.

In May, Dr. Self accepted the church's call to serve as Interim Pastor.

On August 11, 1991, a Pastor Search Committee was elected. The members of the committee were: Tom Jack, Chair; Edith Bond, Phil Brown, John Dixon, Harold Hyde, Jerry Hyde and Cecelia Prator. On November 17, a vote was held to call Dr. Self as pastor, and December 8, 1991 was Dr. Self's first Sunday as Pastor. On August 16, 1992, the Installation Service was held to install Dr. William L. Self as the 21st Pastor of the First Baptist Church of Chamblee, Georgia.

On December 27, 1991, the property at Johns Creek was deeded to the congregation, and on January 22, 1992, the presentation of the title of 15.84 acres was made to the church from Technology Park/Atlanta.

Within six months, CDH Partners, a team of architects, engineers, interior designers and planners, were employed to develop the site's plan. This integrated and collaborative company's plan consisted of four buildings to be constructed in four phases. The first included a chapel for worship with space for religious education and administrative offices. The second building was additional religious educational space. The third building included a multi-use gymnasium that would be used as a center for temporary worship, dining, additional administrative offices, as well as typical use recreational activities. The third building would also include the foyer for the fourth and final building, the permanent sanctuary.

On October 25, 1992, less than one year from having the property deeded to the congregation and in accordance with the guidelines of the donor Technology Park/Atlanta, ground was broken for the construction of Johns Creek Baptist Church.

On March 28, 1993, the final "Homecoming" was held for all current and former staff members, members, former members, and friends of First Baptist Church of Chamblee. It was a grand day! Following worship there was "dinner on the grounds." So many tales of times gone by, remembering friends from the past and not letting them be forgotten; *Auld Lang Syne* in the truest sense of the lyrics of sixteenth century Scotsman Robert Burns. It was a day for the ages for all who loved First Baptist Church of Chamblee.

On May 19, 1993, the first vote was taken and passed on a Mission Statement of Johns Creek Baptist Church. Subsequent votes to change the Mission Statement have been taken and passed twice since: February 22, 1995 and January 31, 2007. The 2007 Statement is still in use. The current Mission Statement may be found in the Appendix of this document along with its predecessors.

The fortieth anniversary of one of the greatest success stories of First Baptist Church of Chamblee missions outreach programs happened in July of 1993, when a celebration of her youth was held for the church's own legendary Camp Rutledge. A humble civilian conservation corps (C.C.C.) camp built during the Roosevelt administration served as the home for a two-week annual mission camp for children ages nine through seniors in high school. Camp Rutledge is located about an hour east of Atlanta within the boundaries of Hard Labor Creek State Park in Rutledge, Georgia. The annual camp took place during the second and third weeks of July. Camp Rutledge had a great spiritual impact on hundreds, perhaps thousands of campers and staff members' lives as they shared in its experience through the years. Many attendees have attested that, while at Camp Rutledge with its old rustic setting, they experienced Christ's love through the leadership of our church, and this event did more to influence the camper's Christian walk than anything else in many of their lives. For most, rarely a week passes that sweet memories of Camp Rutledge don't come to mind. Words can't explain what the leadership and campers experienced on the grounds of the camp; everyone should have a "Camp Rutledge." The fortieth anniversary celebration was not only a physical success, but a time of spiritual renewal for all of those in attendance.

The next ten weeks were a blur as the move to Johns Creek neared. Bittersweet moments came to all as the First Baptist Chamblee congregation prepared to part with the place that had been home for the last century. The week of October 3-10, 1993 held the final Sunday night, midweek and Sunday morning services in the church.

The goal of the new JCBC congregation was to relocate and occupy the new building on McGinnis Ferry Road within one year from the date of breaking ground for construction. Phase I of the project, consisting of the chapel for worship with space for religious education and administrative offices (27,600 square feet), was complete and the congregation's goal was achieved! On Sunday morning, October 17, 1993, at 9:30 a.m., a ribbon-cutting ceremony took place, followed by the first worship service in the new church at 10:50 a.m. Dr. Self described the two events: "The first Sunday at the new site was glorious. The church was filled to overflowing with people, a good mix of the Chamblee and Johns Creek people. When we extended an invitation to unite with the church, the aisles were filled with people—so filled that we could not absorb all of them. We had to stop the invitation and ask those who could not get to the front of the church to wait until the following week...and they did!"

On Sunday, October 31, Dr. David Sapp returned to preach a Service of Celebration. The following Sunday, November 7, Dr. Self preached the Service of Dedication.

Other exciting things were happening in our metropolitan Atlanta community at the same time. Dr. Self attended the meeting of a Steering Committee with Mercer University for the Feasibility Study of locating a seminary on its Atlanta campus. Johns Creek Baptist Church supported the later founding of the McAfee School of Theology at Mercer University from its inception.

The following days, weeks, months and years would be a continual series of "firsts" for the church. On October 20, 1993, the first missions and music midweek sessions of Johns Creek Baptist began. The sessions included preschool, children, middle school and youth programs. On November 14, the first new members' reception was held. On December 1, the first parent/child dedication service was held. William Darcy Flowers and Christopher Lee Winn were dedicated. On December 12, the Chancel Choir joyfully presented its first Christmas program, *A Johns Creek Christmas*. On December 19, the first church-wide Christmas party was held.

With the advent of 1994 came three new ministries within the church: the Women's Ministry – Louise Wiley, Chair; the Men's Ministry – Keith Compton, Chair; and the Senior Adults' Ministry – Vivian Gay, Chair. Then on January 16 (three months following the first service at the new location) our church felt its first wonderful "growing pains!" The decision was made to add a second Sunday morning worship service for the convenience of the growing membership and the large number of guests. Later in January a number of members indicated that they had missed the Sunday evening services that were a part of the old church in Chamblee so it was decided that services would be held the first three Sunday nights in March, 1994 with guest speakers filling the pulpit. The guest speakers and the corresponding dates were as follows: Dr. Frank Harrington on March 6, Dr. Don Harp on March 13, and finally, Dr. Peter Rhea Jones on March 20. In the weeks following the trial evening services were discontinued. It was discovered the evening services weren't missed as much as originally believed! We enjoyed having Sunday evenings for family time.

Additional "firsts" for the church followed. On Sunday, March 27, *Celebrate Life!*, our first Easter drama presentation, was presented by the Chancel Choir. The following Thursday, Johns Creek Baptist Church had its first annual Maundy Thursday Communion Service. On April 3, 1994, Easter Sunday saw the church host three worship services. The first Johns Creek Easter Egg Hunt was held the prior day and was deemed such a success that it has become an annual event.

During the summer of 1994, our list of "firsts" grows. First use of the Child Development Centers as it is opened. First Graduate Recognition Sunday was held, recognizing eight local graduates. The service later became an annual event. The first Men's Ministry breakfast was held. Christian humorist Randy Hollings provided entertainment for the men's event. On June 12, the first college Sunday School class was offered. The first Vacation Bible School was held at the church during the week of August 1 – 5 with 130 children enrolled. The first four-week Johns Creek Concert Series is offered. As the summer ended, we reached a new high attendance total for Sunday School of 507; of note, 35 cars were parked along then two-lane McGinnis Ferry Road because the parking lot was full!

The autumn of the year brought further exciting growth. Organized and led by Carolyn Self, the first Mothers' Fellowship & Support Group began weekly meetings on September 14.

The First Women's Ministry Brunch was held on Saturday morning, September 24, 1994. This first brunch led to the establishment of an annual eagerly anticipated and very well attended Women's Banquet each autumn.

The following day a goal that had been established two years prior by joint churches to care for the area of Chamblee and Doraville was realized. In an effort to strive to continue the provision of outreach for local and international people in the Chamblee and Doraville areas once the church relocated to Johns Creek, First Baptist Church of Chamblee, Dunwoody Baptist Church, Wieuca Road Baptist Church and First Baptist Church of Doraville formed the "Chamblee-Doraville Ministry Center." The Cooperative Baptist Fellowship provided the funds to hire a pastor and staff for the Center. With great joy, the Chamblee-Doraville Ministry Center was dedicated and opened on September 25, 1994.

On the following Wednesday, September 28, 1994, Dr. Michael McCullar began his service at Johns Creek Baptist Church as Minister of Education and Administration. Michael is a native of Birmingham, Alabama. He holds degrees from the University of Alabama-Birmingham, New Orleans Baptist Theological Seminary, and Oxford Graduate School. He later served the church for many years as Executive Pastor and recently transitioned to the position of Formations Pastor and as we celebrate the 20th anniversary of the church, he has recently celebrated his 19th year of service here. His leadership accomplishments are many. He is the author of multiple books including *Sessions with James, Sessions with Corinthians, Sessions with Timothy & Titus, The Basics of Theology, A Christian's Guide to Islam,* and co-author of *Building Blocks for Sunday School Growth* and *Sessions with Mark.* Though he is an accomplished wordsmith and executive, his passion within the church is for missions and religious education. Michael serves as consultant to the Cooperative Baptist Fellowship in the areas on Sunday School and Missions. His mission involvement includes over thirty trips to twelve countries. When recently asked for input regarding those passions, he responded as follows:

> *"Johns Creek Baptist Church has been a mission's congregation from its earliest incarnation. Long a supporter of denominational cooperative missions, Johns Creek Baptist Church created a unique model in the mid-1990s that would soon be emulated by many other churches. Johns Creek Baptist Church has continued impressive support of global missions through the Cooperative Baptist Fellowship, while implementing opportunities for members to become directly involved locally, nationally and internationally.*
>
> *During these 20 years, missions giving and participation has increased exponentially. Johns Creek Baptist Church has fielded mission teams in eight states, ten countries and countless local endeavors.*
>
> *Johns Creek Baptist Church began with a unique and non-traditional approach to adult Sunday School. The Johns Creek Baptist Church Adult Sunday School Model came together in order to meet the needs of a soon-to-be thriving suburban area populated by people who*

*would not be natives. The primary focus of the new model would be to provide Christian community and to become a family-away-from-family for members and participants.*

*To achieve this foundational goal the groups were called communities rather than classes, were loosely age-graded to provide flexibility, and were led by community leaders rather than teachers. In this model, teachers would teach and facilitate rather than serve multiple roles.*

*An added bonus was the element of rotation, which saw teachers rotate from community to community leading the same seminar. Care and ministry was assigned to care group leaders within each community, a facet of the Johns Creek Baptist Church Model that allowed for specific gift and skill sets to be employed across the Sunday School.*

*Johns Creek Baptist Church began with four adult groups and over the years has expanded to over twenty. In 2000, Smyth and Helwys published the first "Sessions" book, a line of New Testament studies first created for use in Johns Creek Baptist Church Adult Sunday School. Presently there are 15 books in the Johns Creek Baptist Church line, with a goal of covering the entire New Testament by the end of this decade.*

*Johns Creek Baptist Church has long been a national model for church growth, discipleship and non-traditional adult Sunday School. Our model has assisted numerous churches in invigorating Sunday School, Christian education and adult learning."*

Following Dr. McCullar's arrival, two Sunday School sessions began on October 2, 1994.

The Georgia Dome was the site for a Billy Graham Crusade from October 26-30. Susan Hudson served as the coordinator for five weeks of classes on witnessing for a group of JCBC volunteers to qualify to serve as counselors during the Crusade. During the same week, the first Fall Festival took place culminating with a "High Attendance Sunday" that saw 637 in Sunday School.

January of 1995 saw the ministry budget increase 100% from the previous year, records broken twice on consecutive weeks for Sunday School attendance, and groundbreaking for a new parking lot. Throughout the balance of the winter months growth occurred. Men's Ministry fellowship/breakfast began meeting on a weekly basis. The first annual Youth (grades 6-12) *DiscipleNow* weekend happened on February 17-19.

On March 13-25, 1995, Dr. and Mrs. Self led a group of 26 people on a tour of the Holy Land. One of the people on the trip was Edith Bond. After decades of membership, Beth Ann Boland, Cecelia Prator, Celeste Massey and Edith had become the first four women to be ordained deacons at First Baptist Church of Chamblee on September 30, 1990. Edith and her husband Howard had raised their children in First Baptist Chamblee and knew the impact the church had made on the lives of her children. When asked of her first visit to the proposed site for the new Johns Creek church, Edith laughed aloud and exclaimed, "NOTHING was out here." Yet she marveled at how the people came and brought so many children into the life of the new church. When the tour group reached the Garden of Gethsemane and it was time for prayer, Dr. Self turned to Edith and asked her to lead them. At this sacred site, Edith explained she felt the Holy Spirit leading her, and she believes her time of prayer was perhaps the most important moment in her walk with Christ. Still a regular church and Sunday School attendee today, when asked of her prayers for the church, Edith (92) quickly responds, "I've prayed every day since we relocated from Chamblee for the Lord to send teachers prepared to teach the beautiful children coming to our new church." She then adds, "The Lord has blessed us; the Lord has blessed us!" Indeed "the Lord has blessed us," for just six weeks after her return from the Holy Land, the Lord answered Edith's prayers with a Minister to Preschool and Children named Jill Jenkins.

The spring of 1995 was brimming with activity beginning April 1. The Women's Ministry had a spring brunch featuring guest speaker Elizabeth (Mrs. Joe Frank) Harris, former first lady of Georgia. On the same day the Men's Ministry sponsored a workday at the First Baptist Church of Chamblee, keeping the old property in presentable condition as a buyer was sought. On Sunday, April 9, the Chancel Choir and the Music Ministry did two presentations of the Easter musical, *Joy Comes in the Morning*. At the close of the month on April 30, a special Money Management seminar was held with Danny Joiner of Wells Fargo serving as guest speaker.

The following Monday, May 1, 1995, Jill Jenkins began her service at Johns Creek Baptist Church as Minister of Preschool and Children. Jill is a native of Huntington, West Virginia. She is a graduate of Marshall University and Southern Baptist Theological Seminary. Earlier this year Jill celebrated her 18th anniversary of service to Johns Creek Baptist Church. Today, as Children's Pastor, she guides all of the ministries and programs for children for the church. Jill is a nationally respected conference facilitator and speaker for parents and Sunday School leaders throughout the country. Asked recently to share her thoughts on the children's programs of Johns Creek Baptist she replied:

> *"The last 20 years have seen many changes in the preschool and children's ministry of Johns Creek Baptist Church. When we began in one building, the phase 1 chapel building, we had children crammed in every available space, including closets! Though it was difficult to keep up with the space demands of ministry to these wee ones, the volunteers were faithful in meeting their demands for time, hugs, love, and lessons about Jesus. "Flexible" has been the word emblazoned on the tee shirts of all the workers in those areas. You never knew where you might be moved to help out each week, or what room would have to be quickly set up or how supplies would materialize to get the job done. These were nerve-*

racking, impromptu early days. "Winging-it" was found to be one of the most valuable spiritual gifts.

Since those days, when we might grow by 200 between one Sunday and the next in our area, we now have trained, seasoned teachers who are very willing to teach and minister to the needs of their age groups. We focus on the teaching aspect of ministry more than the activities (though we do have those as well).

Feeling that one of our main tasks is to advise and equip parents in the spiritual nurturing of their children, we provide classes that involve parents such as "How to Lead a Child to Christ," spiritual development of preschoolers and first graders; "Getting Ready to Become a Christian" classes; "New Christians" classes; and "Created by God." Also, each new Christian is given an age-appropriate workbook for parents to guide their child through this very important time.

Family fellowship times are offered with Outdoor Movie Night, Angel Breakfast, Muffins for Mom, Donuts for Dad, Trunk or Treat, and Family Egg Hunt. We hope that children will build lasting relationships with family and friends at church.

Summer brings us extra time to have fun, to learn, and additional times to learn about God through summer camps. We offer a variety of camps through the children's ministry, as well as our recreation ministry. Vacation Bible School, Day Camp, Spanish, Fine Arts, preschool camps, music, drama and crafts are a part of what we host at the church. We annually take the older boys and girls to an overnight camp which, in the most recent years, has been one called Passport Camp. There, children's lives are changed as they see how God works throughout the world and in their lives.

The faith development of our children is supplemented by what we offer on a weekly basis through

*Sunday School and Team Kid on Wednesdays. Parents are the primary influence on their children's faith development, and we are here to bolster them in their effort. It is of the utmost importance of everything we do.*

*Kids are our future at Johns Creek Baptist Church and together we all make a difference! The Children's Ministry of Johns Creek Baptist Church exists to help children to develop spiritually, mentally, emotionally and socially into all that God wants them to become.*

*Our prayer is that every child encounters God each time he comes to church. And we are committed to making that happen!"*

Before the end of the month on May 24, we voted and approved the acquisition of temporary buildings to be used for Sunday School meeting facilities.

The summer of 1995 saw the regular array of activities led by another successful Vacation Bible School and the tradition of the two-week period for church camp for the youth at Camp Rutledge.

On August 13, the first Teacher Preparation Day (special age group seminars for those involved in religious education) was held. This has since become an annual event. Later in the week on August 19, Dr. William Hendricks presented a special seminar to the church on the book of *Revelation* and the Second Coming of Christ. Under the supervision of Jill Jenkins the first children's "Getting Ready" class was offered to children from grades 1-5 for those asking about becoming Christians. "Getting Ready" has been implemented on a regular basis since this time. The summer was topped off by having a record attendance of 678 in Sunday School on August 27!

On Sunday September 3, 1995, approximately 600 members and guests attended a church picnic and concert held on the grounds of Johns Creek Baptist. On Saturday morning, September 23, the Men's Ministry Kickoff Breakfast was held. The guest speaker was former Atlanta Falcons quarterback Steve Bartkowski. The following morning (September 24) Johns Creek Baptist Church began offering three morning worship services, as well as an adult "Early Bird" Sunday School class. On October 17, the second anniversary of the move to the Johns Creek location, the church added 36 new members to the roll. Later that month, in order to manage our growth, temporary modular units consisting of 5,760 square feet of usable space were delivered and installed to serve as additional Sunday School space. On November 12, former United States Ambassador to the United Nations, Andrew Young, spoke for our Stewardship Banquet held at the Gwinnett Civic Center. The theme of the evening's events was *Faith Under Construction,* and the goal for the event was for 500 families to pledge. As the year came to a close, the first "Drop & Shop" Children's event was held on December 9, enabling parents to "drop" their children at the church for supervised and planned activities on Saturday from 9 a.m.-noon so the parents could "shop!" The event was a rousing success and has become an annual event. On December 10, the Music Ministry and the Chancel Choir presented Handel's *Messiah.*

January of 1996 was an eventful month in the life of Johns Creek Baptist Church. Having installed temporary Sunday School housing just two months prior, the church was putting the space to good use! On consecutive Sunday mornings, attendance records for Sunday School were handily broken with a 23 percent increase over a record set just four months prior! Johns Creek Baptist Church was growing! As a result, on January 31, 1996, building plans were presented for approval to the church for Phase II of JCBC's long-term facility, and the church voted to move forward as planned. Within a week on February 6, groundbreaking was held on the Atlanta campus of Mercer University for their new School of Theology. On March 10, in support of the Phase II plan, the *Faith Forward* campaign was launched; Tom Jack served as Chair of the campaign.

The remainder of the spring of 1996 was filled with excitement. On March 24, Leslie Morgan successfully directed the first JCBC Children's choir presentation of *Hans Bronson's Gold Medal Mission.* This has become an annual event. On Sunday, April 7, we set a record with worship attendance of 1,712! Later in April on the 28th, a *Faith Forward* campaign event was held at the Gwinnett Civic Center seeking financial support for Phase II construction. The goal for pledges of $2,200,000 for *Faith Forward* was exceeded; the congregation pledged $2,488,582!

On June 9, Johns Creek Baptist Church hosted a wonderful program celebrating the 3,000th anniversary of the city of Jerusalem. The event was co-sponsored by the Consulate General of Israel and the National Conference of Christians and Jews.

June 23, 1996 was a particularly special day for Johns Creek Baptist Church. The day was proclaimed "Cecil Sherman Day," a day of celebration in honor of Dr. Sherman's retirement from the position of Coordinator of the Cooperative Baptist Fellowship. But Cecil Sherman was so much more than that to many of us in JCBC's congregation. You see, 40 years ago in 1956, a young pastor fresh from the seminary accepted the call of a small Baptist congregation in Chamblee, Georgia. Cecil Sherman moved to Chamblee and served as the pastor of First Baptist Church of Chamblee from 1956 – 1960. As his title Coordinator of Cooperative Baptist Fellowship indicates, Cecil ventured far from his humble beginnings as Chamblee's 15th Pastor. Yet, whether he was a pastor in Georgia, North Carolina or Texas; whether he was Coordinator of Cooperative Baptist Fellowship, or whether he was a renowned seminary professor and author (as he would later become), we always felt like he was one of us. Wherever Cecil went, regardless of where God led him, First Baptist Chamblee always considered him one of theirs and went right along beside him. Cecil Sherman's reality is that he will go down in Baptist history books as a person who shaped Baptist history. It was a great day together for old friends, as well as new friends for Cecil. It was an honor to have him in our church's life, and it was good to have him home.

The rest of the summer of '96 was equally eventful. July 1996 brought "firsts" for more than our church; July brought the world to Atlanta as our city hosted the Centennial Summer Olympic Games. Following our first ever Adult Vacation Bible School on the 7th and

8th of the month, many from our church volunteered, watched and help host the world until the closing ceremonies on August 4. On August 21, a vote was held and passed to proceed with construction of Phase II -- JCBC's long-term facility plans (35,400 square feet) consisting of worship center renovation and expansion, new educational classrooms, 300 additional parking spaces, purchase of eight additional acres of adjacent property, and improvement of the First Baptist Church of Chamblee cemetery (a Johns Creek Baptist Church property).

Less than one month later on September 15, 1996, ground was broken for the Phase II project. The congregation's goal was again to occupy the new facilities within one year from this date. Later in September, on the 21st, former Atlanta Falcon and electrifying All-Pro NFL football star, Billy "White Shoes" Johnson, was the guest speaker for the Men's Ministry Fall Breakfast.

In November a new deacon's ministry three-part program was formed to include Care Ministry, New Member Ministry, and Growth Ministry. On November 10, there was a church-wide brunch with an emphasis on stewardship featuring a special musical guest, Oliver Sueing. On November 27, 1996, property owned by the church, known as "Missionary Manor" located on 3322 Hood Avenue, Chamblee, Georgia 30341 (adjacent to First Baptist Church of Chamblee), was sold.

On December 8, the Music Ministry of the church and the combined Chancel and Youth Choirs presented the Christmas musical event, *Festival of Light*. Then on December 22, the first Birthday Party for Jesus was held.

Sunday School attendance records continue to be broken with the arrival of the New Year! On February 2, 1997, a record was set by having 945 present only to have it broken the following week by 17 with 962 in attendance. March 23 saw the attendance reach another new peak with 977 present for Sunday School.

On Easter Sunday, March 30, 1997, Johns Creek Baptist Church had 2,288 in worship, the largest number in the church's history!

In March of 1997, the William L. Self Lectureship at Mercer University's McAfee School of Theology was established to promote the practice of faithful and effective preaching of the gospel. The purpose of the lectureship is to enlighten and inspire those whose calling is to preach the gospel of Jesus Christ. The lectures seek to instill in students and pastors a passion for better preaching by providing worthy models and by offering seasoned instruction and encouragement. Each year the lecture series will feature a nationally recognized preacher. The series is named in honor of our former senior pastor, William L. Self, who has distinguished himself with a national reputation as a gifted preacher, pastor, author, lecturer, motivational speaker and innovator in church growth. Dr. Self achieved considerable acclaim by leading Atlanta's Wieuca Road Baptist Church to a place of prominence in Georgia and the nation. As pastor of Johns Creek Baptist Church in Alpharetta, his leadership and substantial influence brought this church to the vanguard of fast-growing churches. On March 17-19, 1997, the first annual "William L. Self Preaching Lectures at McAfee School of Theology" were held on the campus of Mercer University's Atlanta campus; Dr. Self was the inaugural speaker.

April 23 had a vote come before the church to spend $60,000 for furnishings for the Phase II project.

In the spring of 1997, Fred Henderson and Claude Head ordered 25 yards of concrete to erect a substantial sign. The concrete was delivered to 5303 New Peachtree Road, Chamblee. There the sign would serve as identification for the First Baptist Church of Chamblee cemetery, which rests to its rear. There would be twin bronze plaques on the rear of the sign; the first to serve as timeline of the church, and the second, a more descriptive history of the cemetery. Their instructions of where to pour the concrete came from former beloved First Baptist Chamblee historian and member Mrs. Paul ("Bertie Lou") Pierce; together Fred and Claude who died recently would erect the sign on the old Corinth Baptist Church's cornerstone of 1891. Corinth Baptist is the parent church of First

Baptist Chamblee and the grandparent church of Johns Creek Baptist.

On May 4, 1997, in accordance with the church's Phase II plan for growth, the dedication of the First Baptist Church of Chamblee Cemetery was held. A granite monument was erected in honor of the dedication.

With Profound Gratitude and in Memory of the Faithful Christian
Witness of

CORINTH BAPTIST CHURCH
CHAMBLEE BAPTIST CHURCH
FIRST BAPTIST CHURCH OF CHAMBLEE

Located on This Site
1891 TO 1993


*"Your Labor in the Lord is not in vain"*
*I Corinthians 15:58*


In Loving Memory Placed by

JOHNS CREEK BAPTIST CHURCH – Alpharetta

Successor to

FIRST BAPTIST CHURCH OF CHAMBLEE

1996

# STAFF
## 1991 – 1997

## 1991

| | |
|---|---|
| Pastor | David Sapp/ |
| | Bill Self |
| Minister of Education | Larry Jones |
| Minister of Music | David Schwoebel/ |
| | Warren Fields, Interim |
| Church Administrator | L. H. Johnson, Interim |
| Organist | Bob Cash |
| Pastor's Secretary & Receptionist | Nancy Singleton |
| Education Secretary | Clyta Forrester |
| Financial Secretary | Ruth Humphrey |

## 1992

| | |
|---|---|
| Pastor | Bill Self |
| Minister of Education | Larry Jones |
| Minister of Music | Warren Fields, Interim |
| Church Administrator | L. H. Johnson, Interim |
| Program Intern | Traci Johnson |
| Organist | Bob Cash |
| Pastor's Secretary & Receptionist | Nancy Singleton/ |
| | Barbara Brown |
| Education Secretary | Clyta Forrester |
| Financial Secretary | Ruth Humphrey |

## 1993

| | |
|---|---|
| Pastor | Bill Self |
| Minister of Education & Administration | Larry Jones |
| Minister of Music | Warren Fields, Interim/ |
| | Greg Walton |
| Minister to Children | Jennifer Law |

| | |
|---|---|
| Program Intern | Traci Johnson |
| Program Associate | Pat Griffin (Volunteer) |
| Organist | Bob Cash |
| Pianist | Chester King |
| Pastor's Secretary | Barbara Brown |
| Education Secretary/ | Clyta Forrester/ |
| position changed to | |
| Program Secretary | Darlene Sprowls |
| Financial Secretary | Ruth Humphrey/ |
| | Helen Wilson |
| Maintenance | Rich Gotowka |

# 1994

| | |
|---|---|
| Pastor | Bill Self |
| Minister of Education & | |
| Administration | Larry Jones/ |
| | Michael McCullar |
| Minister of Music | Greg Walton |
| Minister to Children | Jennifer Law |
| Program Associate | Pat Griffin (Volunteer) |
| Minister to Students | Rick Wheeler |
| Organist | Bob Cash |
| Pianist | Chester King |
| Pastor's Secretary | Barbara Brown |
| Program Secretary | Darlene Sprowls |
| Financial Secretary | Helen Wilson/ |
| | Diana Mercado |
| Maintenance | Rich Gotowka |

# 1995

| | |
|---|---|
| Pastor | Bill Self |
| Minister of Education & Administration | Michael McCullar |
| Minister of Music | Greg Walton |
| Minister to PS/Children | Jill Jenkins |
| Program Associate | Pat Griffin (Volunteer) |
| Minister to Students | Rick Wheeler |
| Organist | Bob Cash |
| Pianist | Chester King |
| CDC Director | Louise Walker |
| Pastor's Secretary | Barbara Brown |
| Program Secretary | Darlene Sprowls |
| Financial Secretary | Diana Mercado |
| Maintenance | Rich Gotowka |

# 1996

| | |
|---|---|
| Pastor | Bill Self |
| Minister of Education & Administration | Michael McCullar |
| Minister of Music | Greg Walton |
| Minister to PS/Children | Jill Jenkins |
| Program Associate | Pat Griffin (Volunteer) |
| Minister to Students | Don Deavers |
| Business Manager | Mark Sauls |
| CDC Director | Keri Cook |
| Organist | Bob Cash |
| Pianist | Chester King/ Paula Wamsley |
| Pastor's Secretary | Barbara Brown |
| Program Secretary | Darlene Sprowls |
| Financial Secretary | Diana Mercado |
| Maintenance | Rich Gotowka & Ben Hall |

# 1997

| | |
|---|---|
| Pastor | Bill Self |
| Minister of Education & Administration | Michael McCullar |
| Minister of Music | Greg Walton/ |
| | Leslie Morgan, Interim |
| Minister to Children | Jill Jenkins |
| Minister to Preschool | Joye Smith |
| Minister to Students | Don Deavers |
| Business Manager | Mark Sauls |
| CDC Director | Keri Cook |
| Organist | Bob Cash |
| Pianist | Paula Wamsley/ |
| | Nannette Howard |
| Pastor's Secretary | Barbara Brown |
| Program Secretary | Darlene Sprowls |
| Publisher | Jo Anne Jackson |
| Financial Secretary | Diana Mercado/ |
| | Glenda Tilton |
| Receptionist | Debra Smith/ |
| | Jean Tracy |
| Maintenance | Rich Gotowka & Ben Hall |

# SUMMER
## (Phase II: 1997 – 2000)

"All God's creatures got a place in the choir
Some sing low, some sing higher,
Some sing out loud on the telephone wires
And some just clap their hands, or paws, or anything
      they got now."

~ Bill Staines

You could almost feel music in the air during the summer of 1997! Johns Creek Baptist Church and all its "creatures" were about to have plenty to hum, whistle and sing about. The Lord was at work in our church.

Over the next three years all of the dreams, plans and organization of the previous seven would lead to growth in every area of Johns Creek Baptist Church! The historical "Spring" season (1990 – 1997) was filled with the details involved in laying and solidifying the new church's foundation. As a result, Johns Creek Baptist's "Summer" season became a time of manifestation. During the "Summer" of our first 20 years from June of 1997 through the end of August in 2000, our actions of the past manifested themselves with tremendous growth. We added 600+ new members to the church; we baptized 300+ people, and the weekly giving of our congregation enabled the doubling of the church budget. Our church had a lot to "Make a Joyful Noise" about!

On June 15, the Children's Ministry led by Jill Jenkins held the first "Passport Camp." This successful and much anticipated event continues as an annual summer event for grades 3-5.

The next goal of the JCBC congregation was to occupy Phase II of their long-term facilities plan within one year from the date of breaking ground. Less than ten months after breaking ground, Phase

II was occupied. Phase II consisted of 35,400 square feet of new educational classrooms for all ages, worship center renovation and expansion, three hundred additional parking spaces, the purchase of eight additional acres of adjacent property, and additional improvements to the recently dedicated First Baptist Church of Chamblee Cemetery (a Johns Creek Baptist Church property). On Sunday morning, July 13, 1997, the doors were opened and the people came! Within a month of moving in to Phase II another attendance record was broken. On August 2, there were 1,110 people in Sunday School! Johns Creek Baptist now has 14 active, growing adult Sunday School communities and a new youth class called "Sixers," a ministry specifically tailored for sixth grade kids.

The months of September and October of 1997 were also of great consequence for Mercer University. On September 16, Mercer University held the dedication service for their new School of Theology. A month later, Johns Creek Baptist Church hosted Mercer's evangelism conference on October 17-18. On October 21, First Baptist Church of Decatur hosted the dedication of Mercer University's newly established McAfee School of Theology.

Johns Creek Baptist held the church's first "Spiritual Renewal" weekend on Saturday and Sunday, September 27-28. Seven years later, beginning in 2004, this event goes on to become an annual event as an important part of the spiritual maturing process for our church. Dr. Phil Lineberger, Senior Pastor of Sugar Land Baptist Church located in suburban Houston, Texas, was the inaugural Spiritual Renewal pulpit guest. As you will read, Dr. Lineberger returns to lead the church again in seven years.

In October our first JCBC pictorial directory was published. On November 12, John Creek Baptist held its first ever "Big Tent Event." Frank Boggs, internationally- acclaimed bass soloist and the first recording artist for WORD Records, provided special music for our Stewardship Sunday service.

The new Sunday School rooms were filling up and reaching new records as the church ushered in 1998; attendance climbed to 1,295 on the 11th of January.

The following month Dr. Self was honored as the keynote speaker at the Cooperative Baptist Fellowship/Georgia's annual meeting in Athens.

On May 1, 1998, Glenn Crosthwait began as Minister of Music. A native Texan, Glenn moved with his family to Johns Creek Baptist from Mississippi. He studied at Hardin-Simmons University in Abilene, graduating with both Bachelor's and Master's degrees in Music. He also has a Master in Music from Southwestern Baptist Theological Seminary and completed additional work at London's Royal College of Music. Glenn, currently Worship Pastor, recently celebrated his 15th anniversary of service with Johns Creek Baptist Church earlier this spring. Asked to summarize his success with the music program, Glenn humbly replied:

> *"In April 1998, 29 choir members came to a called choir rehearsal to meet and rehearse with Glenn Crosthwait, the prospective Minister of Music. On the first Sunday in May of that year, a new course was set for the music ministry of Johns Creek Baptist Church. This small but very dedicated group led worship, often singing two or three services per Sunday. A small room served as rehearsal space, robe storage and music library. Soon rehearsals were moved to the Fellowship Hall. As excitement and numbers grew, "Take the Rail Out" Sunday was celebrated when 57-choir members sang in worship and could no longer fit behind the rails of the platform in the sanctuary.*
>
> *As the church expanded, the choir also enjoyed a larger choir room in Phase III and now a wonderful choir suite in Phase IV. The Sanctuary (formerly Chancel) Choir personifies their theme of "More Than Music, We Are Family" in ministry, caring for the needs of choir members who are in the hospital or experiencing challenging life circumstances. Enrollment and attendance are three to four times what they were in*

*1998. But far more important than the numbers are the spirit of family and the spirit of ministry that the choir possesses. The choir as a whole and individually are worship leaders at each Sunday service and special event.*

*The orchestra began as a small but talented ensemble with limited instrumentation. They played only once per month. Through the years the orchestra has grown in numbers, in instrumentation, in quality, and in frequency of playing. They now play every Sunday except in July, and for all major events. The orchestra is blessed to have both talented adults and youth. Several of our youth are outstanding players in other organizations such as the Atlanta Youth Symphony Orchestra, Atlanta Youth Wind Symphony, and Georgia All-State Band.*

*Our custom-built Ruffati organ and Bösendorfer piano are dedicated to the Phase IV Sanctuary and are played by organist Bob Cash and pianist Glen Sloan. These superior musicians provide leadership for choir rehearsals, orchestra and worship experiences. Their dedication and talent reaches out to the church and community alike as they build a worshipful presence for weddings and funerals.*

*In December 1998, the Music Ministry presented its first "Christmas at Johns Creek." With full orchestra, lighting, and choir in formal wear singing all music from memory, it was a new challenge. The "Christmas Party" in August was also new and seemed untimely in the warm weather, but with the amount of music to be learned, it proved to be a much-needed addition. Today, "Christmas at Johns Creek" is a much anticipated community outreach. People from across the city and around north Georgia make it a part of their Christmas tradition.*

*Another special event, "Celebrate America!," is held the last Sunday of June each year. It is the second most-attended Music Ministry event. In this presentation God is worshiped and all that He has given us in this country is celebrated. Other special events vary year to year, but each has an intentional focus of worship and celebration.*

*Master's Singers, formerly known as Senior Singers, are an active group of more mature adults. They rehearse on Monday mornings and, in addition to enjoying fellowship and music together, they go out into the community monthly to sing at senior centers and assisted living homes.*

*The very active Children's Music Ministry has been led by talented leaders through the years, teaching children to sing and worship through music. Currently, Beth Irwin leads this vital ministry. Beth has many years experience loving and teaching children through music. The children present at least one musical per year with drama and costumes. They also sing in worship and other special events such as "Christmas at Johns Creek" and the Angel Breakfast.*

*Music for youth blends with the Youth Ministry schedule meeting on Sunday evenings. Through the years the JCBC Youth's music ministry was led by talented musicians with a love for kids. At times, the Youth Praise band has played along with them. This group is for youth grades 6-12. They have sung in worship, the Gathering, and "Christmas at Johns Creek."*

*The Music Ministry of Johns Creek Baptist Church provides a unique sense of community for members of every age developing their God-given talents to reach out in leading worship and touching the community for Christ. It is our prayer to be "More Than Music, We Are Family."*

The history of the music ministry of our church has great depth within the ranks of some of its most tenured members. For instance, in the Sanctuary choir there are members who have over 60 years' experience singing in our choir and its predecessor, First Baptist Church of Chamblee. On many Sunday mornings, tenor Grant Curtis (89) can still be seen smiling as he "sings his heart out," praising the Lord. Grant's wife Dot was the former organist and Children's Choir Director at First Baptist Chamblee during the 1950s and '60s. Several of her primary choir and "Sunbeams" have reached retirement age and still sing in the JCBC Sanctuary Choir. Dot still sits in the congregation each Sunday, lovingly nodding her approval to her beloved Grant, as well as former students. Dick Wolf (82) and Norman Parker (79) continue to sit beside one another on the choir's legendary "back-row bass" section as they have since the 1960s at First Baptist Chamblee. Look for them during the worship service next Sunday; Dick and Norman will be the two directly in the center of the back row in front of the baptistry. Norman likes to point out that Dick is the one with the white hair. Dick just says, "I'm the one sitting on the right!" In Glenn's above quote, he refers to 29 members coming to a called rehearsal ... six or eight of those original 29 came from the loyal pool of people mentioned. Under the splendid and deeply caring leadership of Minister of Music Glenn Crosthwait and those who loyally serve alongside him, the JCBC choir, orchestra and music ministry participants have grown to number in the hundreds and serve the Lord each week in glorious song! Indeed, with a shared and long standing devotion to the ministry of music to Johns Creek Baptist, its members are ... "More Than Music, They Are Family!"

Just two days after Glenn's arrival, on Sunday, May 3, 1998, plans for Phase III (Family Life Center) of JCBC's long-term facilities plan was presented to the church. The staff and membership were busy; new members were coming to be a part of our church every Sunday.

On July 11-12, a reunion was held to honor the tradition of the church's beloved Camp Rutledge. Campers and staff members gathered on the holy grounds of Camp Rutledge for a great time of fellowship, remembrance and spiritual renewal for all participants.

Another new high attendance record was reached Sunday morning, August 23, with 1,490 people in attendance at Sunday School. Just one week later on August 30, 1998, there were 1,553 in Sunday School. Through the first eight months of 1998 our Sunday School saw the attendance increase an average of over 30 people per month! Additional temporary worship space accommodating an additional 150-200 people was established in the Fellowship Hall to help handle the increase in attendance during worship services.

Offering the opportunity for new members to come and join as the choir began their preparation for the 1998 Christmas program, the music ministry held the Chancel Choir's first annual "Christmas Party" for the choir on Wednesday, August 26, 1998. Fifteen years later under Glenn's leadership, the choir's "Christmas Party" in August signals their preparation is underway once more for the eagerly anticipated *Christmas at Johns Creek* in December.

Two months later, on Sunday, October 25, Johns Creek Baptist held its second annual "Big Tent Event." Horatio Alger Award recipient, author, philanthropist, and JCBC member Deen Day Smith was the guest speaker for our Stewardship Sunday service.

On November 18, 1998, a vote was held and passed to proceed with the planning for construction of Phase III, JCBC's long-term facility plans (78,000 square feet) which would consist of a multi-use gymnasium that would be used as a center for temporary worship, dining, and typical use recreational activities; additional administrative offices; and education space. Tommy Boland served as Chair of the Building Committee for Phase III. The third building would also include the foyer for the fourth and final building, the permanent sanctuary. Later in November, a *Johns Creek Cookbook* was introduced, sharing favorite recipes of members for the pleasure of everyone's palate. On November 22, a celebration was held commemorating the fifth anniversary in the Johns Creek location.

Under the leadership of Minister of Music, Glenn Crosthwait, the Chancel Choir and Orchestra presented the first annual Christmas musical event, *Christmas at Johns Creek*, on three different occasions on Saturday and Sunday, December 12-13. *Christmas at Johns Creek* is a much anticipated holiday event and has become a staple for not only the local community but throughout north Georgia.

On March 21, our church celebrated the launch of the *Faith Forward II* campaign in support of the Phase III building plan with a campaign goal of $5,000,000. Tom Jack served as Chair of the campaign.

On Easter Sunday (April 4, 1999) JCBC's morning worship attendance was 2,740.

The final building plans for Phase III are approved on August 4, 1999. On the 22nd a new adult Bible study began called "Express Sunday School." Dr. Self was elected inaugural Chair of the Board of Visitors of McAfee School of Theology at Mercer University. Johns Creek Baptist Church members Tommy Boland and Way Kidd also served on the Board of Visitors for the School.

In the following months two of our staff members had their work published. In September, Glenn Crosthwait had two choral works and three keyboard arrangements published. Dr. Self's book *Defining Moments* was published by CSS Publishing in October.

Johns Creek Baptist Church hosted an innovative Sunday School growth conference on Friday and Saturday, October 8-9. On October 17, 1999, groundbreaking ceremonies were held for Phase III (Family Life Center – 78,000 square feet). JCBC's third annual "Big Tent Event" Stewardship service was held on Sunday, October 31.

On December 31, 1999, Johns Creek Baptist Church concluded the century with a special New Year's Eve service celebrating the past and welcoming in the new millennium. Do you remember "Y2K?"

To "kick" off the New Year, our beloved Minister of Music Glenn Crosthwait tripped and fell off the stage, breaking his leg before the worship service. He healed fast and said if it had to happen, he was glad it happened AFTER the *Christmas at Johns Creek* program. Broken leg and all, Glenn never stopped singing!

On the first Sunday in May of 2000, the church held its first "Join the Church" day, and 25 members joined the church.

During the summer of 2000, the church began its Recreation and Activities program. Under the careful guidance of many dedicated and talented people it has flourished and become a vibrant part of the church's ministry to the community. The Activities Ministry of Johns Creek Baptist Church focuses on delivering the message of Christ to participants from two years of age all the way to senior adults. The emphasis is not just sports leagues, but "life leagues." With programs including SporTykes, Upward Sports, summer camps, golf and tennis outings, Vacation Bible School, fitness classes and ballroom dancing, this vital ministry touches thousands of community members.

As the summer of 2000 drew to a close, a new Johns Creek Baptist Church pictorial directory was published, and throughout its pages staff and membership of our beloved church were smiling more than ever!

# STAFF
## 1997 – 2000

### 1997

| | |
|---|---|
| Pastor | Bill Self |
| Minister of Education & Administration | Michael McCullar |
| Minister of Music | Greg Walton/ Leslie Morgan, Interim |
| Minister to Children | Jill Jenkins |
| Minister to Preschool | Joye Smith |
| Minister to Students | Don Deavers |
| Business Manager | Mark Sauls |
| CDC Director | Keri Cook |
| Organist | Bob Cash |
| Pianist | Paula Wamsley/ Nannette Howard |
| Pastor's Secretary | Barbara Brown |
| Program Secretary | Darlene Sprowls |
| Publisher | Jo Anne Jackson |
| Financial Secretary | Diana Mercado/ Glenda Tilton |
| Receptionist | Debra Smith/ Jean Tracy |
| Maintenance | Rich Gotowka/ Ben Hall |

### 1998

| | |
|---|---|
| Pastor | Bill Self |
| Minister of Education & Administration | Michael McCullar |
| Minister of Music | Leslie Morgan, Interim/ Glenn Crosthwait |
| Minister to Children | Jill Jenkins |
| Minister to Preschool | Joye Smith |
| Minister to Students | Don Deavers |

| | |
|---|---|
| Business Manager | Mark Sauls |
| CDC Director | Keri Cook |
| Organist | Bob Cash |
| Pianist | Paula Wamsley/ |
| | Nannette Howard |
| Pastor's Secretary | Barbara Brown |
| Program Secretary | Darlene Sprowls |
| Education Secretary | Aimee Nelson |
| Music Secretary | Sandra Hawk |
| Publisher | Jo Anne Jackson/ |
| | Lori Ambrose |
| Financial Secretary | Glenda Tilton/ |
| | Lynn Walls |
| Receptionist | Jean Tracy |
| Maintenance | Rich Gotowka/Ben Hall |

## 1999

| | |
|---|---|
| Senior Pastor | Bill Self |
| Executive Minister | Michael McCullar |
| Associate Pastor | Roger Williams |
| Minister of Music | Glenn Crosthwait |
| Minister to Adults | Steve Prevatte |
| Minister to PS/Children | Jill Jenkins |
| Associate PS/Children's Minister | Melissa Lewis |
| Minister to Youth | Ben Vogler |
| Business Manager | Mark Sauls |
| CDC Director | Keri Cook |
| Assistant CDC Director | Lenore Whitley |
| Organist | Bob Cash |
| Pianist | Nannette Howard/ |
| | Glen Sloan |
| Ministry Asst/Sr. Pastor | Barbara Brown |
| Ministry Asst/Education | Aimee Nelson |
| Ministry Asst/Music | Sandra Hawk |
| Ministry Asst/Children | Kristen Cochran |
| Publisher | Lori Ambrose |
| Financial Secretary | Lynn Walls |
| Maintenance | Rich Gotowka/ |
| | Ben Hall |

## 2000

| | |
|---|---|
| Senior Pastor | Bill Self |
| Executive Minister | Michael McCullar |
| Minister of Pastoral Care | Roger Williams |
| Minister of Music | Glenn Crosthwait |
| Assoc. Minister of Music | Lee Bates |
| Minister to Adults | Steve Prevatte |
| Minister to Youth | Ben Vogler |
| Minister to PS/Children | Jill Jenkins |
| Associate PS/Children's Minister | Melissa Lewis |
| Minister of Recreation | Clif Anderson |
| Business Manager | Mark Sauls |
| CDC Director | Keri Cook |
| Assistant CDC Director | Lenore Whitley |
| Organist | Bob Cash |
| Pianist | Glen Sloan |
| Ministry Asst/Sr. Pastor | Barbara Brown |
| Ministry Asst/Education | Aimee Nelson |
| Ministry Asst/Music | Sandra Hawk |
| Ministry Asst/Children | Kristen Cochran |
| Publisher | Lori Ambrose |
| Financial Secretary | Lynn Walls |
| Receptionist | Linda Cessna |
| Maintenance | Rich Gotowka/ |
| | Ben Hall/ |
| | Al Powell |

# FALL
## (Phase III: 2000 – 2007)

"For I know the plans I have for you," declares the
LORD, "plans to prosper you and not to harm you,
plans to give you hope and a future. Then you will
call on me and come and pray to me, and I will listen
to you. You will seek me and find me when you seek
me with all your heart."
                                        ~ Jeremiah 29:11-13 (NIV)

Johns Creek Baptist Church's staff was all smiles on September 18,
2000, as they moved into their newly completed office suites! The
following Sunday would be the last worship service in the original
sanctuary. Since opening in 1993, this sanctuary saw over 1,500
people come down its aisles to join the church. The original
sanctuary would now serve as a permanent chapel for the church.
Following the final Sunday morning service, an "Open House" was
held for the new Phase III facilities. The inaugural worship service in
the new Family Life Center was held on Sunday, October 1.

During a month long celebration of our denomination, our
community, our nation and our world, Johns Creek Baptist Church
would welcome pulpit guests commemorating the opening of our
Phase III facilities. October 8 was designated as "Community Day,"
and Dr. Self welcomed Dr. J. Robert White as our guest. Dr. White
has served as the Executive Director of the Georgia Baptist
Convention since January 1993. October 15 was designated as
"National Day," as well as our Phase III Dedication Sunday. The
church was honored to have fellow Baptist, native Georgian, and
former President of the United States Jimmy Carter as its special
guest speaker. October 22 was designated as "International Day,"
and Dr. Self welcomed Dr. Denton Lotz, General Secretary of the

Baptist World Alliance. Prior to serving with the Baptist World Alliance, Dr. Lotz was an American Baptist missionary to Eastern Europe during the Soviet period. The Baptist World Alliance is an alliance of 215 Baptist conventions worldwide, representing the international community of 110 million Baptists. Our month commemorating the opening of Phase III came to a close on October 29 as we held "Baptist Heritage Day." Dr. Daniel Vestal was our special guest for the occasion. Dr. Vestal served as Coordinator of the Cooperative Baptist Fellowship. This was a particularly memorable day for Dr. Vestal. It was just ten years earlier, while he was still the pastor of Dunwoody Baptist, during a casual lunch with friend and fellow pastor Dr. David Sapp, he became involved in the initial conversation that would lead to First Baptist Chamblee becoming Johns Creek Baptist Church.

Mercer University recognized Dr. Self, along with fellow Johns Creek Baptist members, Tommy and Beth Ann Boland, for outstanding service and commitment to the University, the denomination, the church and humanity at the James and Carolyn McAfee School of Theology luncheon on November 14. Mercer President Dr. R. Kirby Godsey presented Tommy and Beth Ann with the James P. Wesberry Award for Service to the Denomination, and Dr. Self with the Louie D. Newton Award for Service to Mercer University.

Later in November *Johns Creek Cookbook, Volume 2* was introduced, sharing favorite recipes of members for everyone's pleasure.

High attendance records continued to be established on the New Year's first Sunday! On January 7, 2001, there were 1,742 in Sunday School. On January 21, our multi-talented Minster of Music Glenn Crosthwait, along with organist Bob Cash and pianist Glen Sloan, presented *Keyboard Festival of Praise*.

On April 1, under the direction of Glenn Crosthwait, the Chancel Choir and Orchestra presented *The Story of Easter*.

On the first Sunday in May of 2001, the church held its second "Join the Church" day, and 36 members joined the church.

On Sunday, June 24, the first *Celebrate America!* was presented by the Chancel Choir and Orchestra. In what will become an eagerly anticipated annual event *Celebrate America!* is held the last Sunday of June each year. It is the second most-attended Music Ministry event. In this presentation God is worshiped and all that He has given us in this country is celebrated.

In July Dr. McCullar's book, *Sessions with James,* was published by Smyth & Helwys.

On August 21, Dr. Self made a difficult decision to cancel a group trip he was planning to lead to the Holy Land. One hundred twenty-five members and friends had placed deposits to reserve their scheduled trip for the following March. He said something just didn't feel right. Exactly three weeks later on what will forever be known as "9/11," something wasn't right; terrorists attacked America. On September 12 and 14 Johns Creek Baptist Church held special worship services for our country. The following Sunday's attendance was the highest in the history of the church.

The same month the church called Jim Walls to serve as Minister of Youth. During the writing of this book, and following more than eleven years in his position, Jim accepted a call as Associate Pastor of First Baptist Church of Augusta, Georgia. He was kind enough to offer his thoughts from his area of ministry for inclusion in the book. When asked about the youth and their programs at Johns Creek Baptist, Dr. Walls responded as follows:

> *"In 2002 the youth ministry team at Johns Creek Baptist adopted the following two statements.*
>
> *The first is a Statement of Philosophy:*
> *"Learning about Christ from the inside out and turning the world upside down with Christ's love."*
>
> *The second is our Mission Statement:*
> *"The Youth Ministry of Johns Creek Baptist Church exists to draw teenagers to Christ and to deepen*

*their personal relationship with Him. We will provide opportunities to actively nurture faith through worship, Bible study, fun fellowship, service, and missions in our church, community and throughout the world."*

Since 2001 and the adoption of these guiding statements, the youth ministry of Johns Creek Baptist has faithfully pursued making these statements a reality. When these were first adopted, much of what they outlined was a dream—a hope for the future of our ministry. In 2012, we can confidently say we have met many of these goals. Though the journey is not over, we are proud of where we are.

From 2001 through 2004, the youth ministry experienced rapid numerical growth, going from an average of 80 youth in attendance to almost 225. With this increase came the challenge of finding a place to put all these kids! So for three years, the middle school department was housed in the Fellowship Hall, with retractable walls and all! Though this time of transition was a challenge for our church, it prepared the way for the new youth space as the sanctuary was completed in 2007.

And though numerical growth was exciting in those early years, it does not compare to the opportunity for spiritual growth among our teenagers in recent years.

In 2000, the ministry opportunities for our youth included: Sunday School, Camp Rutledge, and a Ski/Bible retreat, along with some other fellowship events. In 2012, the annual calendar of youth ministry opportunity includes Sunday School, High School Camp (Student Life), Middle School Camp (Passport), Fall Retreat, Disciple Now or Faith in 3D, March Missions Madness, X-Games (Sunday evening youth activities), the Gathering (a youth worship experience), and an international mission trip to the Dominican Republic.

*Though it is inspiring to list all of these ministry events, it does not compare to the faith development of our youth in recent years. As a result of the significant investment of a large group of volunteers in ministry, our teenagers today have the opportunity to grow and deepen their faith in a way that truly impacts their lives. The emerging faith of our students is being demonstrated in meaningful ways. Many youth regularly meet together to hold one another accountable for living a life of faith. Several students have participated in and have taken leadership roles on their school campuses in various Christian and service organizations. A growing number of our youth have responded to God's calling into vocational ministry. Serving in missions and the local community has become a regular aspect of many students' lives. And the list goes on."*

During Dr. Jim Walls' time of leadership for JCBC's youth ministry, he had great impact on thousands of kids' lives for Christ. Before he moved, I asked him for just one who had been under his watchful eye throughout his entire time here. After a time of careful thought, he shared that he thought I should speak with Kep Pate. He is Kirby and Shan's son, and he has one sister, Callie. As I was writing this book, I waited to contact Kep until I was penning the part that would include his thoughts. Upon initial contact I learned he would be leaving the next day for a six-week mission trip to Edmonton, Canada. In the last paragraph of Jim's quote he says, *"Though it is inspiring to list all of these ministry events, it does not compare to the faith development of our youth in recent years.... Serving in missions and local community service have become a regular piece of many students' lives."* Because of his departure to serve in Augusta, Jim was likely unaware of Kep's mission journey to Canada; but because of *"the faith development of our youth in recent years,"* Jim knew the heart of the young man he was sending to talk with me.

In 1999, Kep accepted Christ and was baptized at Johns Creek Baptist. A few short years later he became a member in the 7th Grade Sunday School class of Deborah and Paul Peterson. While studying scripture each week under the Petersons' leadership, Kep developed friendships with seven fellow classmates. They were inseparable. Zach Ballance, Grant Brown, Michelle Godwin, Abby Jones, Mackenzie Kenny, Tristan Rice, Austin Ward and Kep have remained important to one another though miles have separated them. They attended five different colleges but as Kep explains, their kinship through Christ has no boundaries. They love one another and still hold their friendships as a vital part of who they are becoming in their Christian walk. Upon his return from Canada, Kep will leave and return to Clemson University and graduate with a bachelor's degree in visual arts in December 2013. Also, in affiliation with the Baptist Collegiate Ministries (formerly known as Baptist Student Union), he will be entering a nine-month program of service as a "Semester Missionary." In the fall of 2014, Kep plans to enter the seminary and pursue his Master of Divinity degree. He feels called to work with young people as a Minister of Youth. The Lord has touched countless young people through the ministry of Johns Creek Baptist Church, behold just one.

Beginning on January 1, 2002, the church year was changed from October 1 to September 30 to a more traditional calendar year schedule. On January 6, the first four-week special elective course was held for new Christians and those new to the Baptist denomination. A new attendance record was set on January 13 with 1,983 in Sunday School. The next day a new Senior Adult ministry was established called "Sixties Plus." On January 20, Minister of Music Glenn Crosthwait, Bob Cash and Glen Sloan presented *Keyboard Festival of Praise*. On January 23, 2002, a vote was held to proceed with *Faith Forward III* (Tom Jack, Chair) to raise $4,000,000 to reduce debt and therefore better position the church financially for proceeding with the Phase IV building.

On February 22, a "Celebrating Marriage" banquet was held. Dr. William (Bill) Coates was the speaker. Dr. Coates is Senior Pastor of First Baptist Church of Gainesville, Georgia.

On March 1-2, Johns Creek Baptist hosted the celebration of the 10th Anniversary of the Cooperative Baptist Fellowship. The Cooperative Baptist Fellowship is a fellowship of Baptist Christians and churches that share a passion for the Great Commission of Jesus Christ and a commitment to Baptist principles of faith and practice. The understanding of Baptist faith and practice is expressed by the emphasis on freedom in biblical interpretation and congregational governance, the participation of women and men in all aspects of church leadership and Christian ministry, and religious liberty for all people.

In March the church hosted the first Christian college fair to enable prospective students to consider their options for their future education. Five Baptist colleges were represented at the fair.

Dr. Self was honored to preach in historic Edinburgh, Scotland, the site of the International Congress Preaching (ICOP), on April 9-11, 2002. Appropriately, "Preaching in a Missionary Age" was the theme for this great interdenominational event sponsored by *Preaching* magazine. While some have thought that the age of missionaries—and thus the need for preaching in a missionary setting— has passed, reality is far different. Many of the nations once considered Christian are now the very mission frontiers of post-modern society. Likewise, some countries, previously the target of mission endeavors, now send missionaries to reach those people who once sponsored gospel proclamation. Other than our senior pastor, speakers for the three-day event included William Willimon, Lloyd John Ogilvie, William Augustus Jones, Jr., John MacArther, Peter Grainger, Edwin Young, William Hinson, David Jackman, Robert Leslie Holmes, John Huffman, Greg Scharf, and David Searle.

Back "across the pond" at Johns Creek Baptist on Saturday morning, April 20, the Men's Ministry breakfast hosted University of Georgia head football coach Mark Richt as its speaker. Everyone in attendance (even including the Tech fans) had a great time of

Christian fellowship! On April 28, under the direction of Glenn Crosthwait, the Chancel Choir and Orchestra presented *Psalms, Hymns & Spiritual Songs.*

In June Dr. McCullar co-authored with Bo Prosser *Building Blocks for a Growing Sunday School,* published by Smyth & Helwys.

On September 14, the church sent volunteers for the first time to help Habitat for Humanity. On the first Sunday in October a new annual tradition begins, Old-Fashioned Gospel Sunday.

On February 9, 2003, Minster of Music Glenn Crosthwait, Bob Cash and Glen Sloan presented *Keyboard Festival of Praise.*

On February 21, a "Celebrating Marriage" banquet was held. On March 19, "Operation Uplift" was started. Operation Uplift adds service men and women to the weekly Prayer List. In March of 2003, the first "Six Weeks of Commitment" program was held. Six Weeks of Commitment is a discipleship program where each participant commits to prayer, Bible study, bringing a guest, giving, sharing faith, and attending Sunday School and worship. On March 30, the church held its "Join the Church" day, and 32 members joined the church. In April a new pictorial directory was published. Its pages were filled with happy faces!

The testimonies of 42 senior adult members of Johns Creek Baptist are presented as editor Dr. Bob Lynn's *Journeys into Faith I* is unveiled on June 21. During the next ten years, nine additional *Journeys* were led by Dr. Lynn; hundreds participated.

When Bill & Carolyn Self celebrated their 50th wedding anniversary, they invited the members of the church married for 50 years or more to celebrate with them. They wanted to serve as an inspiration and example to younger couples that long marriages are possible, regardless of the problems and heartaches that come, couples can persevere and keep their marriages intact. On August 3, a reception was held in honor of all couples married for 50 years or more. This inspiring group of couples would come to be known as the "Golden Club."

On Sunday, August 17, there were 2,043 people in Sunday School, a 750% increase from the fall of 1993. "Join The Church"

Sunday was held, and 21 new members joined the church. On October 19, 2003, Johns Creek Baptist Church celebrated its 10th Anniversary.

On November 1, the first Singles Conference was held. Harold Ivan Smith was the speaker for the event. Noted author and speaker, Dr. Smith was a grief specialist on the teaching faculties of Saint Luke's Hospital, Kansas City, Missouri, and the Carondolet Medical Institute in Eau Claire, Wisconsin. In November another "Join the Church" day saw 18 additions to the church. Later in the month Dr. McCullar published *Basics of Theology*.

In January 2004, Johns Creek Baptist Church launched its website: www.jcbc.org.

On February 29, 2004, our second "Six Weeks of Commitment" discipleship program began.

In March Dr. Michael McCullar was recognized by the Cooperative Baptist Fellowship's Congregational Life Department for Outstanding Leadership in Christian Education. Later in the month, the Chancel Choir and Orchestra presented *Spring Celebration*.

In May the Youth Year-End Celebration became a church-wide event. On July 4, 2004, Dr. Self was the featured speaker on *Day1* (formerly known as *The Protestant Hour*) radio program for the first time. *Day1* is aired on more than 150 stations across the country. He became a regular speaker on their broadcasts.

The building plans for Phase IV (sanctuary) were presented and approved on August 18, 2004. Tommy Boland served as Chair of the Building Committee for Phase IV.

Johns Creek Baptist held the church's first annual "Spiritual Renewal" weekend on Sunday, September 19. This event became an important part of the spiritual maturing process for our church. Dr. Phil Lineberger, Senior Pastor of Sugar Land Baptist Church located in suburban Houston, Texas, was the pulpit guest. Dr. Lineberger was also the pulpit guest at our original Spiritual Renewal weekend in September of 1997. Upon his return to Johns Creek Baptist's pulpit, Dr. Lineberger said, "If y'all haven't needed any "renewing" for the past seven years, I must've done a good job back in '97; thanks for having me again!" It was a wonderful weekend of renewal.

In October Dr. McCullar's book, *Sessions with Corinthians*, was published by Smyth & Helwys. October 10 was "Mercer University Day" at Johns Creek Baptist Church. Mercer President Dr. Kirby Godsey was the guest speaker.

The first annual Halloween "Trunk or Treat" children's event was held on the church grounds on October 27. It superseded Fall Festival, and was a fabulous success! The entire church embraced "Trunk or Treat," and all were rewarded with thousands of smiles, giggles and even a few shrieks!

November's "Join the Church" Sunday saw 16 new members join our church.

On February 26-27, Johns Creek Baptist hosted a *Marriage Mechanics* weekend. The guest speakers were husband and wife team, Kirk and Gina Schreck, founders of Pinnacle Achievement. They speak to groups that want to improve relationships from the inside out. Gina is the author of several books including *Marriage Mechanics: A Tune Up for the Highway of Love!*

During the month of March 2005, and in support of the Phase IV (Sanctuary) plan, the *Faith Forward IV* campaign was dedicated and an "Information Sunday" was held in the following weeks. Tom Jack served as Chair of the campaign. Within the next 90 days, the *Faith Forward IV* capital campaign was launched and a three-year goal of $10,000,000 was set for the project. On March 11-12, the Women's Ministry held its Spring Retreat at Brasstown Valley Resort in Young Harris, Georgia. Author and gifted humorist Kim Bolton served as the guest speaker. Kim's delightful ability of blending humorous stories helped the Johns Creek ladies laugh, while being encouraged and renewed. This successful event goes on to be an eagerly anticipated annual event. On March 20, under the direction of Glenn Crosthwait, the Chancel Choir and Orchestra presented *Somebody's Praying Me Through*. Three services were held the following week on Easter Sunday to accommodate the large number of worshippers.

On May 5, 2005, David White was hired as Minister of Pastoral Care. Some years earlier in February of 1999, Johns Creek Baptist had grown to the point that our staff needed a new associate to help their fellow ministers love and care for the members. Roger Williams was hired as Associate Pastor. Dr. Michael McCullar smiled at the memory of going to Virginia to interview Roger for the position. He would typically take the candidate out to dinner to pursue his intentions of an interview, but this wasn't the case with Roger. Roger explained to Michael that he and his wife wanted him to come and have dinner at their house. Michael realized upon his arrival later at their home, that in fact, Roger and his wife Virginia were the ones conducting the job interview. He smiled broadly when he remembered at the end of their interview, Virginia looked him right in the eye and said, "We'll take it!" Not long after Roger's arrival at Johns Creek Baptist his position became known as Minister of Pastoral Care. David took over for Roger in May of 2005, and they worked in tandem as Roger eased into retirement. Recently David's role has evolved into the position of Connections Pastor, where caring remains at the forefront of what he does for the church. A few weeks ago, I had the pleasure of sitting down with David and casually talking about his role in the church. I was interested in numbers as he seems a never-ending blur of activity for others; but by the end of our visit I was reminded of an old story about theologian and Christian apologist, Friedrich von Hugel. In 1925, as von Hugel lay dying, he tried to speak but he was so weak that the family members couldn't hear what he was trying to say. One of them leaned close to his lips and heard him repeatedly whisper, "Caring is everything. Nothing matters but caring." When I asked David to give me something to include in the book, he agreed on the condition any credit be deferred. For David, "Caring is everything."

> *"There are only a few things I know with absolute certainty. This is one of them: Every human being on the planet has worth and value. No person is disposable. Every person I encounter deserves my acknowledgement*

*and my attention, no matter what. It is that world-view that ultimately brought me to serve as the Minister of Pastoral Care at Johns Creek Baptist Church following my friend Roger Williams in May of 2005. Regardless of what may appear on paper in the form of a job description, this office is not about crises management, hospital visitation, funeral planning, or the execution of an outreach plan.*

*Simply put: This office is about love.*

*It has been our job, more our pleasure really, to invest ourselves lovingly in the lives of the people around us. We are a shoulder to lean on when things are a little rough, or a lot rough, and we are a back to slap in times of joy and celebration. We strive to be a constant, consistent presence in the lives of those we serve in order to remind them that they are not alone ... ever ... no matter what it may feel like ... and that a continually evolving better version of themselves is always possible in Jesus Christ.*

*We do it quietly under the radar. As Paul put it, we try to avoid sounding like resounding gong or a clanging cymbal. To continue the 1 Corinthians 13 reference, the Apostle Paul writes that love is patient and kind. It does not envy. It does not boast. It is not proud. It is not rude. It is not self-seeking. It is not easily angered. It keeps no record of wrong.*

*That's the spirit of this office.*

*To really push the outer limit of "keeps no record," it's tough for me to quantify the work I've been privileged to contribute these past eight years.*

*It should be strongly stated, however, that Roger and I are not the only ones with shoulders and backs around here. We serve alongside deacons, Sunday School community care groups, and people who are otherwise simply friends to each other to deliver a special kind of love and belonging. We could not do it alone, nor should we.*

*I have had the honor of loving, supporting and standing alongside literally thousands of people along the way. I am fortunate that they have loved, supported and stood alongside me back. They are my friends. I love them."*

On May 24, the groundbreaking was held for our new neighbor, Emory Johns Creek Hospital. Dr. Self was on the program and led the invocation.

The summer of 2005 was filled with activities. A growing Vacation Bible School filled the church with the sounds of happy children during the first week of June. The last week of June concludes with the Youth, grades 8-12, attending their beloved Camp Rutledge.

Johns Creek Baptist held the church's second annual Spiritual Renewal weekend on Saturday and Sunday, September 17-18. This event continues to be an important part of the spiritual maturing process for our church. Dr. Calvin A. Miller, theologian, best-selling Christian author of more than 40 books, and professor of preaching and pastoral ministry at Samford University's Beeson Divinity School, was the Spiritual Renewal pulpit guest. Dr. Self was so excited with the church's response to Dr. Miller at the end of the service he invited him back for 2006 on the spot, and Dr. Miller graciously accepted!

A unique decision was made to celebrate the start of the Phase IV construction. In lieu of the traditional groundbreaking to begin the project, two steel beams, painted white, were made available for every member of the church to sign prior to being installed in the permanent sanctuary. On October 2, 2005, thousands of signatures were placed on the beams prior to their erection in the new facility.

In November a series of parenting seminars began. The ministerial staff prepared and published a compact disc titled *The Twelve Days of Christmas: Devotional Reflections for the Christmas*

*Season.* The CD was made available at no charge for members and guests alike. On November 24, the Georgia Baptist Convention severed their long relationship with Mercer University.

Beginning on December 18, 2005, Dr. Self was honored to preach for 13 consecutive weeks on the Armed Forces Radio Network to all who serve at home or abroad.

A new pictorial directory is published in January 2006. It boasts smiles from cover to cover! Later in the month the Senior Singers (senior choir) changed its name to The Master's Singers. The Men's Ministry Breakfast kicked off a new program for Men's Small Groups. The study for all groups was Patrick Morley's book, *The Man in the Mirror.* The four individual groups would meet weekly on different days at different locations to accommodate busy schedules.

In February Johns Creek Baptist's own Minister to Children was nationally recognized. Jill Jenkins was presented the Cooperative Baptist Fellowship's Jack Naish Distinguished Christian Educator of the Year award. The award is named for Jack Naish, a beloved mentor to many, a life-long learner, and devoted minister of education.

On February 22, the Chancel Choir changed its name to the Sanctuary Choir. A week later the third "Six Weeks of Commitment" discipleship program began. Six Weeks of Commitment is a discipleship program when each participant commits to prayer, Bible study, bringing a guest, giving, sharing faith, and attending Sunday School and worship.

On March 19, under the direction of Glenn Crosthwait, the Sanctuary Choir and Orchestra presented *An Evening of Praise.* The first "March Missions Madness" youth weekend is held on March 25-26, with 52 young people involved. Focusing on their role in the missions of the church, this annual event has grown to now host more than 250 participants.

April 30 was "Mercer University Day" at Johns Creek Baptist Church. Mercer President-elect Bill Underwood was the guest speaker. Later in May we helped host the China Bible Exhibit at

Second Ponce de Leon Baptist Church. The Exhibit was only seen at three venues across the nation. On June 21-23, Johns Creek Baptist Church sent 50 volunteers to Atlanta's World Congress Center to help staff the registration of the Cooperative Baptist Fellowship's General Assembly.

Johns Creek Baptist held the church's third annual Spiritual Renewal weekend on Saturday and Sunday, September 16-17. This event remains an important part of the spiritual maturing process for our church. Dr. Calvin A. Miller returned at the request of Dr. Self for a second consecutive year as the Spiritual Renewal pulpit guest.

On October 22, Tommy Boland was recognized for his service of 50 years as church treasurer. Later in the month Minister of Pastoral Care David White was honored as a Gardner-Webb Distinguished Graduate, and Dr. McCullar's latest, *Sessions with Timothy & Titus,* was published by Smyth & Helwys. Contained in the November 2006 issue of *Baptists Today* was an article featuring our senior pastor, "A Conversation with Bill Self."

Over the past year since the two beams were signed signaling the start of construction for Phase IV, the site had been filled with activity. On November 1, 2006, the steeple and cross were erected on the new sanctuary. On the following Saturday the church held a 12-hour church-wide prayer event in the chapel. Then on Sunday, November 5, an open house event was held to tour the new (still unfinished) sanctuary, giving anyone that chose an opportunity to observe and even sign the walls and stage!

The New Year was a whirlwind of activity as we prepared to enter our new sanctuary. In accordance with the first sentence in our new mission statement, "We exist to reach up through the worship of God," the spiritual focus of 2007 was on worship. On January 7, "The Gathering" was launched! The Gathering is a new and exciting place for Youth grades 6-12 to worship on Sunday mornings. On the 21st the Youth began a Discipleship group and met on Sunday evenings. Minister of Pastoral Care David White was ordained for ministerial service on January 28. At a church conference on January

31, the new Mission Statement, Statement of Core Beliefs and Core Values were approved as written.

February was an exciting time for Johns Creek Baptist Church. Our new sanctuary was almost ready. Following a Sweetheart Dinner on the 10th and an Activities Breakfast on the 24th, all that's left ... was for the paint to dry.

# STAFF
## 2000 – 2007

## 2000

| | |
|---|---|
| Senior Pastor | Bill Self |
| Executive Pastor | Michael McCullar |
| Minister of Pastoral Care | Roger Williams |
| Minister of Music | Glenn Crosthwait |
| Assoc. Minister of Music | Lee Bates |
| Minister to Adults | Steve Prevatte |
| Minister to Youth | Ben Vogler |
| Minister to PS/Children | Jill Jenkins |
| Associate PS/Children's Minister | Melissa Lewis |
| Minister of Recreation | Clif Anderson |
| Business Manager | Mark Sauls |
| CDC Director | Keri Cook |
| Assistant CDC Director | Lenore Whitley |
| Organist | Bob Cash |
| Pianist | Glen Sloan |
| Ministry Asst/Sr. Pastor | Barbara Brown |
| Ministry Asst/Education | Aimee Nelson |
| Ministry Asst/Music | Sandra Hawk |
| Ministry Asst/Children | Kristen Cochran |
| Publisher | Lori Ambrose |
| Financial Secretary | Lynn Walls |
| Receptionist | Linda Cessna |
| Maintenance | Rich Gotowka/ |
| | Ben Hall/ |
| | Al Powell |

## 2001

| | |
|---|---|
| Senior Pastor | Bill Self |
| Executive Pastor | Michael McCullar |
| Minister of Pastoral Care | Roger Williams |
| Minister of Music | Glenn Crosthwait |
| Assoc. Minister of Music | Lee Bates |
| Minister to Adults | Steve Prevatte |
| Minister to Youth | Ben Vogler/ |
| | Jim Walls |
| Minister to Children | Jill Jenkins |
| Associate PS/Children's Minister | Melissa Lewis/ |
| Minister to Preschool | Tammy Sullivan |
| Minister of Recreation | Clif Anderson |
| Business Manager | Mark Sauls |
| CDC Director | Keri Cook |
| Assistant CDC Director | Lenore Whitley |
| Hospitality Director | Pat Eubanks |
| Organist | Bob Cash |
| Pianist | Glen Sloan |
| Ministry Asst/Sr. Pastor | Barbara Brown |
| Ministry Asst/Education | Aimee Nelson |
| Ministry Asst/Music | Sandra Hawk |
| Ministry Asst/Children | Kristen Cochran |
| Ministry Asst/Youth, Rec | Laura Cruce |
| Publisher | Lori Ambrose |
| Financial Secretary | Lynn Walls |
| Receptionist | Linda Cessna/ |
| | Mary Smith |
| Maintenance | Rich Gotowka/ |
| | Ben Hall/ |
| | Al Powell |

# 2002

| | |
|---|---|
| Senior Pastor | Bill Self |
| Executive Pastor | Michael McCullar |
| Minister of Pastoral Care | Roger Williams |
| Minister of Music | Glenn Crosthwait |
| Assoc. Minister of Music | Lee Bates/ |
| | Kathy Sanson |
| Minister to Adults | Steve Prevatte |
| Minister to Youth | Jim Walls |
| Minister to Children | Jill Jenkins |
| Minister to Preschool | Tammy Sullivan |
| Minister of Recreation | Clif Anderson |
| Business Manager | Mark Sauls |
| CDC Director | Keri Cook |
| Assistant CDC Director | Lenore Whitley/ |
| | Amy Carroll |
| Hospitality Director | Pat Eubanks/ |
| | Juan Venegas |
| Organist | Bob Cash |
| Pianist | Glen Sloan |
| Ministry Asst/Sr. Pastor | Barbara Brown |
| Ministry Asst/Education | Aimee Nelson |
| Ministry Asst/Music | Sandra Hawk |
| Ministry Asst/Children | Kristen Cochran |
| Ministry Asst/Youth, Rec | Laura Cruce |
| Publisher | Lori Ambrose/ |
| | Karen Ducote |
| Financial Secretary | Lynn Walls/ |
| | Vickie Wright |
| Receptionist | Mary Smith/ |
| | Ava Goodin |
| Maintenance | Rich Gotowka/ |
| | Ben Hall/ |
| | Al Powell/ |
| | Joyce Woody/ |
| | Erika Arce |

## 2003

| | |
|---|---|
| Senior Pastor | Bill Self |
| Executive Pastor | Michael McCullar |
| Minister of Pastoral Care | Roger Williams |
| Minister of Music | Glenn Crosthwait |
| Assoc. Minister of Music | Kathy Sanson |
| Minister to Adults | Steve Prevatte |
| Minister to Youth | Jim Walls |
| Minister to Children | Jill Jenkins |
| Minister to Preschool | Tammy Sullivan |
| Minister of Recreation | Clif Anderson |
| Business Manager | Mark Sauls |
| Financial Manager | Tiffany Kitchens |
| CDC Director | Keri Cook/ Amy Carroll |
| Assistant CDC Director | Amy Carroll/ Tobye Bristow |
| Hospitality Director | Juan Venegas |
| Facilities Manager | Don Barber |
| Organist | Bob Cash |
| Pianist | Glen Sloan |
| Ministry Asst/Sr. Pastor | Barbara Brown |
| Ministry Asst/Exec Pastor | Teresa McKinley/ Kris Peters |
| Ministry Asst/Adults | Aimee Nelson-Ransom |
| Ministry Asst/Music | Sandra Hawk |
| Ministry Asst/Children | Kristen Cochran |
| Ministry Asst/Youth, Rec | Laura Cruce |
| Publisher | Karen Ducote/ Phyllis Tutterow |
| Financial Secretary | Vickie Wright |
| Receptionist | Ava Goodin |
| Maintenance | Rich Gotowka/ Ben Hall/ Al Powell/ Keylor Reyes/ Julia Castano/ Isela Ortiz |

## 2004

| | |
|---|---|
| Senior Pastor | Bill Self |
| Executive Pastor | Michael McCullar |
| Minister of Pastoral Care | Roger Williams |
| Minister of Music | Glenn Crosthwait |
| Assoc. Minister of Music | Kathy Sanson |
| Minister to Adults | Steve Prevatte |
| Minister to Youth | Jim Walls |
| Assoc. Minister to Youth | Jenny Folmar |
| Minister to Children | Jill Jenkins |
| Minister to Preschool | Tammy Sullivan |
| Minister of Recreation | Clif Anderson |
| Business Manager | Mark Sauls |
| Financial Manager | Tiffany Kitchens |
| CDC Director | Amy Carroll |
| Assistant CDC Director | Tobye Bristow |
| Hospitality Director | Juan Venegas |
| Facilities Manager | Don Barber |
| Organist | Bob Cash |
| Pianist | Glen Sloan |
| Ministry Asst/Sr. Pastor | Barbara Brown |
| Ministry Asst/Exec Pastor | Kris Peters |
| Ministry Asst/Adults | Beth McLaughlin |
| Ministry Asst/Music | Sandra Hawk |
| Ministry Asst/Children | Kristen Cochran |
| Ministry Asst/Youth, Rec | Laura Cruce |
| Publisher | Phyllis Tutterow |
| Financial Secretary | Vickie Wright |
| Receptionist | Ava Goodin/ |
| | Glenda Garner |
| Maintenance | Rich Gotowka/ |
| | Al Powell/ |
| | Keylor Reyes/ |
| | Brian Weeks/ |
| | Julia Castano/ |
| | Erika Arce/ |
| | Isela Ortiz |

# 2005

| | |
|---|---|
| Senior Pastor | Bill Self |
| Executive Pastor | Michael McCullar |
| Minister of Pastoral Care | Roger Williams/ |
| | David White |
| Minister of Music | Glenn Crosthwait |
| Assoc. Minister of Music | Perry McCain |
| Minister to Adults | Steve Prevatte/ |
| | Rickey Letson |
| Minister to Youth | Jim Walls |
| Assoc. Minister to Youth | Jenny Folmar |
| Minister to Children | Jill Jenkins |
| Minister to Preschool | Tammy Sullivan |
| Minister of Activities | Deedra Oates |
| Business Manager | Mark Sauls |
| Financial Manager | Tiffany Kitchens |
| CDC Director | Amy Carroll |
| Assistant CDC Director | Tobye Bristow |
| Hospitality Director | Juan Venegas |
| Facilities Manager | Don Barber |
| Organist | Bob Cash |
| Pianist | Glen Sloan |
| Ministry Asst/Sr. Pastor | Barbara Brown |
| Ministry Asst/Exec Pastor | Kris Peters |
| Ministry Asst/Adults | Beth McLaughlin |
| Ministry Asst/Music | Sandra Hawk |
| Ministry Asst/Children | Kristen Cochran |
| Ministry Asst/Youth, Rec | Laura Cruce |
| Publisher | Phyllis Tutterow |
| Financial Secretary | Vickie Wright |
| Receptionist | Glenda Garner |
| Sunday receptionist | Debbie Bramlett |
| Maintenance | Rich Gotowka/ |
| | Al Powell/ |
| | Keylor Reyes/ |
| | Brian Weeks/ |
| | Julia Castano/ |
| | Erika Arce/ |
| | Isela Ortiz |

## 2006

| | |
|---|---|
| Senior Pastor | Bill Self |
| Executive Pastor | Michael McCullar |
| Minister of Pastoral Care | David White |
| Minister of Music | Glenn Crosthwait |
| Assoc. Minister of Music | Perry McCain |
| Minister to Adults | Rickey Letson |
| Minister to Youth | Jim Walls |
| Assoc. Minister to Youth | Jenny Folmar |
| Youth Intern | Justin Bishop |
| Minister to Children | Jill Jenkins |
| Minister to Preschool | Tammy Sullivan |
| Minister of Activities | Deedra Oates |
| Activities Director | Tracy Morris |
| Business Manager | Mark Sauls |
| Church Administrator | Michele Deriso |
| Financial Manager | Tiffany Kitchens |
| CDC Director | Amy Carroll |
| Assistant CDC Director | Tobye Bristow |
| Hospitality Director | Juan Venegas |
| Facilities Manager | Don Barber |
| Organist | Bob Cash |
| Pianist | Glen Sloan |
| Ministry Asst/Sr. Pastor | Barbara Brown |
| Ministry Asst/Exec Pastor | Kris Peters |
| Ministry Asst/Adults | Beth McLaughlin |
| Ministry Asst/Music | Sandra Hawk |
| Ministry Asst/Children | Kristen Cochran |
| Ministry Asst/Youth, Rec | Laura Cruce |
| Publisher | Phyllis Tutterow/ |
| | Earah Harris |
| Financial Secretary | Vickie Wright |
| Receptionist | Glenda Garner |
| Sunday receptionist | Debbie Bramlett |
| Maintenance | Rich Gotowka/ |
| | Al Powell/ |
| | Brian Weeks/ |
| | Johnny Leon-Venagas/ |
| | Erika Arce/ |
| | Isela Ortiz |

# 2007

| | |
|---|---|
| Senior Pastor | Bill Self |
| Executive Pastor | Michael McCullar |
| Minister of Pastoral Care | David White |
| Minister of Music | Glenn Crosthwait |
| Assoc. Minister of Music | Perry McCain |
| Minister to Adults | Rickey Letson |
| Minister to Youth | Jim Walls |
| Youth Intern | Justin Bishop |
| Minister to Children | Jill Jenkins |
| Minister to Preschool | Tammy Sullivan |
| Activities Director | Tracy Morris |
| Church Administrator | Michele Deriso |
| Financial Manager | Tiffany Kitchens |
| CDC Director | Amy Carroll/ |
| | Tobye Bristow |
| Assistant CDC Director | Tobye Bristow/ |
| | Monique Brown |
| Hospitality Director | Juan Venegas |
| Facilities Manager | Fred Wolford |
| Organist | Bob Cash |
| Pianist | Glen Sloan |
| Ministry Asst/Sr. Pastor | Barbara Brown |
| Ministry Asst/Exec Pastor | Kris Peters |
| Ministry Asst/Adults | Beth McLaughlin |
| Ministry Asst/Music | Sandra Hawk |
| Ministry Asst/Children | Kristen Cochran |
| Ministry Asst/Youth, Rec | Laura Cruce |
| Publisher | Earah Harris |
| Financial Secretary | Vickie Wright |
| Receptionist | Glenda Garner |
| Sunday receptionist | Debbie Bramlett |
| Sound Coordinator | Matt Shealy |
| Maintenance | Rich Gotowka/ |
| | Al Powell/ |
| | Johnny Leon-Venagas/ |
| | Sam Hardy/ |
| | Erika Arce/ |
| | Isela Ortiz |

# WINTER
## (Phase IV: 2008 – present)

"For greater things have yet to come, and greater things are still to be done in this city. Greater things are still to be done here!"

~ Richard Bleakley, Aaron Boyd, Peter Comfort, Ian Jordan, Peter Kernaghan and Andrew McCann (Members of the Northern Irish group, *Bluetree* from their 2007 CD, *Greater Things*)

On December 27, 1991, the property at Johns Creek was deeded to the congregation. Following on January 22, 1992, the management of Technology Park/Atlanta presented the title of 15.84 acres to the church. A little over 15 years later, the members and guests of Johns Creek Baptist Church entered our new permanent sanctuary.

We were finally able to occupy the facilities our church had been working so hard to finish since the little group of members prayerfully left First Baptist Chamblee with a "life-wish" for the church. During the prior week, on Thursday, March 8, Dr. Self held a "Blessing of the Cross" service for the baptistry, and scripture was read in the sanctuary throughout the day on Saturday in preparation for our first service of worship. The sanctuary's first worship service was held on Sunday, March 18, 2007.

On the last Sunday in March we began a new Sunday School format allowing all of our members to meet together at one time at 9:45. Prior to this format change meeting times were staggered. Additionally, March was designated as "Missions Month" during which $27,000 was given to the Cooperative Baptist Fellowship's Global Missions Fund.

Dr. Self preached at the third International Congress on Preaching on April 17-19, 2007, in the historic English city of

Cambridge. The three-day conference drew ministers from throughout the United States, Canada, the United Kingdom, Australia, and a host of other nations. Among the featured speakers were Bishop N. T. Wright, the bishop of Durham and one of the most popular Christian authors of recent years; David Jeremiah, Senior Pastor of Shadow Mountain Community Church in San Diego and speaker for the national broadcast *Turning Point*; Calvin Miller, Professor of Preaching at Beeson Divinity School and best-selling author; and Alister McGrath, Oxford University professor and prolific author in the area of theology and science. Other scheduled speakers in Cambridge included: Dave Stone, Senior Pastor of Southeast Christian Church in Louisville, Kentucky, one of the nation's ten-largest congregations; J. Alfred Smith, Senior Pastor of Allen Temple Baptist Church in Oakland, California; Michael Milton, Senior Pastor of First Presbyterian Church in Chattanooga, Tennessee; Michael Quicke, Professor of Preaching at Northern Baptist Theological Seminary in Lombard, Illinois; Robert Smith, Professor of Preaching at Beeson Divinity School in Birmingham, Alabama; John A. Huffman, Senior Pastor of St. Andrews Presbyterian Church in Newport Beach, California; plus more than a dozen additional speakers and workshop leaders.

On April 11, an initial meeting was held with Susan Beaumont, consultant with the Alban Institute regarding assisting the church with strategic planning. For over three decades, the Alban Institute has been consulting with American congregations and their leaders. Alban consultants are people who understand how congregations work and strive to help them become centers of grace and transformation that make a difference in their communities.

On April 28, a special dinner concert was held featuring Kyle Matthews, prolific songwriter and Christian recording artist. His music company, See for Yourself Music, produces recordings, print music, and devotional materials that model Christian "edu-tainment" more than "entertainment." Matthews has served as a teaching resource for the Staley Foundation, the Gospel Music Academy, and the Samuel Project, a grant-funded mentoring program for students considering church-related vocations. A children's talent show was held in conjunction with his concert.

Johns Creek Baptist Church hosted a community-wide open house for the new sanctuary, youth and choir suites on May 6. In a solemn and moving service on the Sunday before Memorial Day, the church held its first day of recognition, honoring church members who had died since the beginning of 2006.

On June 18, the sanctuary's Ruffatti pipe organ arrived from Italy. While architects were drawing the plans for the sanctuary, Ruffatti Brothers, organ builders in Padua, Italy, began constructing the pipe organ that would reside at Johns Creek Baptist Church in Alpharetta, Georgia. This handcrafted instrument has 103-ranks, 5,656 pipes, and is controlled by a five-manual console. Wood pipes are made from African mahogany and all the metal is handmade in the Ruffatti factory for the other pipes. The 103 ranks of pipes are augmented by the latest digital technology, including a musical instrument digital interface (MIDI). Taking three years to construct, the Johns Creek Baptist Church Ruffatti pipe organ is one of the largest in the Southeast. One of only seven five-manual Ruffatti organs in the United States, each organ is completely assembled in the Ruffatti's factory prior to shipping to the site of its final installation. Every part of the instrument is checked and thus, never requires any structural work at the installation site. The manufacturer supervised the final installation of JCBC's organ. The Ruffati factory artisans traveled from Italy and Brazil to Johns Creek to supervise the final installation.

Acknowledging the future need for short- and long-term plans and with the desire to develop a vision for the coming years, the Pastors' Council of the church recommended the church begin a strategic planning initiative, employing the Alban Institute to assist in the effort. A steering committee for the initiative was formed, consisting of staff members Drs. Self and McCullar, and church members, Kevin Tolbert (Chair), Tom Jack, Deborah Peterson, Tommy Boland and Carole Smith. The committee's first meeting was held on August 15.

Johns Creek Baptist held the church's fourth annual Spiritual Renewal weekend on Sunday, September 16. This event has become an important part of the spiritual maturing process for our church. Dr. Tom Long served as the weekend pulpit guest. Dr. Long is the Bandy Distinguished Professor of Preaching & New Testament Emeritus, Candler School of Theology at Emory University.

On October 9, 2007, Emory University's Candler School of Theology surprised Dr. Self in the Sunday morning worship service with their annual "Distinguished Alumni Award." The award annually recognizes Candler alumni whose service to God, church, community, and their school has been made with distinction through particular areas of ministry. Dr. Self is honored to be the first and only non-Methodist to receive the award!

On October 21, the dedication service was held for the sanctuary's five-manual Ruffatti organ. Ruffatti is the international standard of excellence among pipe organ manufacturers. From simple beginnings five centuries ago come the sweet sounds of the Italian Ruffatti pipe organ we hear each Sunday. The tonal planning of our instrument is unique, and its creation took into consideration our musical needs, available space and the acoustic environment. The primary objective of the aesthetic design of the manufacturer was to blend our organ within the existing architecture for the best possible sound. We were honored to have Dr. Joyce Jones as our guest organist. Dr. Jones is the former Joyce Oliver Bowden, professor of music, professor of organ and organist in residence at Baylor University. Dr. Jones' performing and teaching abilities are universally recognized and honored within the community of organists throughout the United States and around the world; quite a few of these organists, in fact, have been her students. Our own beloved organist Bob Cash studied under her tutelage while attending Baylor University. Jones' most recent accomplishment is an award by the American Guild of Organists, a national professional association serving the organ and choral music fields. Jones was chosen by the 22,000 members of the guild as the Honoree of the Year for their organization. Dr. Jones is no stranger to dedicating the magnificent

Ruffatti instruments. Her accomplishments also include being the first woman to perform on the five-manual Ruffatti organ at the Crystal Cathedral, the first organist to play for the Grand Teton Music Festival, and the only female organist chosen to play with the San Francisco Symphony Orchestra at the inauguration of the five-manual Ruffatti organ in Davies Symphony Hall.

On November 2, Johns Creek Baptist hosted Mark Lowry in concert. Mark is known and loved around the world as a trusted voice in gospel music and beyond. Mark is a singer, storyteller, humorist, author and songwriter, whose lyric to *Mary Did You Know?* resulted in one of the most loved modern Christmas songs of this century. His legacy is forever sealed as an entertaining communicator who can make audiences think, laugh and cry. Mark has spent more than 20 years as the baritone singer for the Grammy-award-winning Gaither Vocal Band. He serves as the sidesplitting comedic sidekick for Bill Gaither through concert tours and the Gaither Homecoming video series and television airings.

Beginning in early 2007, a second drought struck North Georgia on the heels of an earlier five-year drought. River levels plummeted, causing lakes to fill up more slowly when water was released. The most basic needs for water were not being met. In conjunction, Johns Creek Baptist acknowledged the severity of the drought in small ways during this period. In an attempt to save water we baptized less frequently and ceased coffee service during Sunday School. Throughout 2007, rain levels remained historically low, prompting a special prayer service on November 10, humbly seeking guidance for the needs of the region.

Under the leadership of Glenn Crosthwait, the Sanctuary Choir and Orchestra presented the eighth annual Christmas musical event *Christmas at Johns Creek* on Saturday and Sunday, December 8-9. Participants and congregation alike were excited to hold this year's *Christmas at Johns Creek* in the new sanctuary!

In accordance with the second sentence in our new mission statement, "We exist to reach out through the sharing of our faith and our service to God," the spiritual focus of 2008 was on evangelism and missions.

In 2008, Johns Creek Baptist began its mission relationship with No Longer Bound. No Longer Bound is a residential recovery program for men battling addiction and their families. No Longer Bound was founded by Mike Harden in 1983. As a former Marine, Mike had returned from a tour of duty in Vietnam (1968-69) with a new battle to fight, a powerful addiction to cocaine. Mike found freedom from his addiction through a personal relationship and encounter with Jesus, and received the vision to start No Longer Bound. As it began, only three desperate men arrived to attend the program, but nonetheless they continued to believe and build. One by one, the men continued to arrive, seeking help from their addictions. As the program grew in size and success, it quickly became a home and refuge to those who had given up (or were given up on) by life. No Longer Bound moved from being a halfway house to a structured drug and alcohol program. The initial recovery commitment was six months of residential treatment, but as time has passed, the Regeneration Program was developed into a 10-month in-patient treatment center. Each year approximately 82 men come to No Longer Bound to overcome their addiction to drugs or alcohol. The program maintains a 50 percent (and above) graduation rate but focuses its benchmark on the individual success of each graduate.

On January 26, the Men's Ministry Kick-Off Breakfast was held at the church. Jeremy Lewis, director of the Cooperative Baptist Fellowship's rural domestic poverty ministry "Together for Hope," was the guest speaker. Launched in 2001, "Together for Hope" is a long-term commitment to working with people in 20 of the nation's poorest counties in Appalachia, the Mississippi River Delta, the Rio Grande Valley, South Dakota, and Alabama. The focus of the ministry is to affect change and break the cycle of economic disparity by establishing long-term relationships, listening, learning and walking alongside local leaders. The hope and goal is to transform individuals, churches and communities through Christ.

From January 30 – February 1, members of Johns Creek Baptist Church volunteered with registration and provided shuttle service for the New Baptist Covenant meetings at the Georgia World Congress Center. The New Baptist Covenant is an association of Baptist organizations formed to address poverty, the environment and global conflicts. Former United States Presidents, Jimmy Carter and Bill Clinton, both raised as Southern Baptists, proposed the establishment of a broadly inclusive Baptist movement to counter the public image as being predominantly tied to conservative cultural perspectives. Dr. Self was a guest speaker. Dr. Jimmy R. Allen is coordinator of the New Baptist Covenant and was organizer of the event. Dr. Allen is former President of the three-million-member Baptist General Convention of Texas (1972-1973). In the year 2000, he was cited as one of the "Ten Most Influential Texas Baptists of the Twentieth Century." He is former President of the Southern Baptist Convention (1978-1979). He launched the Missions Service Corps, an organization that now has more than ten thousand persons serving around the world. Dr. Allen, as national President of Baptists Committed, arranged and presided over the Convocation of Baptists in Atlanta that launched the Cooperative Baptist Fellowship. He served as Founding Moderator of the Cooperative Baptist Fellowship. As a television producer, he won an Emmy from the American Academy of Arts and Entertainment for the Best Special Program in the nation in 1988. Produced for ABC television, it was filmed in the People's Republic of China titled *China: Walls and Bridges*. Dr. Allen served as a Non-Governmental Observer at the United Nations (1962). He served on the Planning Conference for the first White House Conference on Civil Rights. In 1974, he received The Citation of Merit from the Government of Honduras for humanitarian service in the wake of a natural disaster. Dr. Allen successfully negotiated with the Nation of Israel on its human rights position on religious propagation. He was invited to testify before the Committee on Law and Justice of the Knesset of Israel. He led a fact-finding mission to Iran during the hostage crisis at the United States embassy in Teheran during 1979-80. Dr. Allen's book,

*BURDEN OF A SECRET*, is subtitled *'A Story of Truth and Mercy in a Family Faced with AIDS.'* He tells of struggles and discoveries of his family as a transfusion-related HIV virus caused the death of his two grandsons and their mother, a pastor's wife and nurse. The virus destroyed the lives of four of his family of eight, including another son who is gay. The call to the churches to banish fears and be supportive to the victims of HIV/AIDS is coupled with the examination of lessons learned from grief and dying. Dr. Allen lives in the north Georgia mountain community of Big Canoe. He is Chaplain Emeritus of the Big Canoe Chapel, a multi-denominational chapel in North Georgia, and remains a member of Johns Creek Baptist Church.

On February 8-9, Minister to Children Jill Jenkins and Minister to Youth Jim Walls presented "Created by God," a two-day study of human sexuality to students, grades 5-6, and their parents.

The first meeting of "Sweet Tea" was held on February 10, as well. Sweet Tea is a ministry for cancer patients, survivors, and caregivers. It was started by Juliet Weaver, Heidi Carr, Frances Gober, Shan Pate and Elizabeth Powell, all cancer survivors. As each of them was going through her own battle with cancer, they found that there are many support groups to help with the physical and psychological effects of battling cancer. What they all found to be missing was a spiritual support group. Juliet felt called to form a faith-based support group for those whose lives have been or are currently being affected by cancer. She approached the other women, and they gladly joined in to form the Sweet Tea Ministry. People who are affected by cancer are suffering at the point of need; they are scared, lonely, and searching for a way to connect with others. Sweet Tea meets those individuals at that point of need, and provides an atmosphere of hope and healing in a welcoming setting that allows them to share the love of Christ with others. Currently, Sweet Tea hosts quarterly events. The theme of the events focuses on the age-old tradition of "tea time"... a time to relax, inspire and socialize. An assortment of teas, tea sandwiches and pastries are served on beautiful vintage china which was donated by individual church members.

The event seeks to tenderly calm the thoughts and soothe the souls of those that come. It is a blessing for all who attend.

Later in the evening of February 10, Glenn Crosthwait, Bob Cash and Glen Sloan presented *Keyboard Festival of Praise*. It was during this event that our newly dedicated Fratelli Ruffati pipe organ was officially engaged in concert with the equally magnificent Bösendorfer Imperial Grand (model 290). The Bösendorfer Imperial Grand is one of the world's most sought-after concert grand pianos. At nine feet six inches long, the Imperial Grand is the largest production piano available. The legendary Bösendorfer sound is usually described as darker or richer than the less full-bodied sound of its counterparts. On the Imperial Grand, this characteristic tonal quality derives in part from the inclusion of nine additional bass notes below bottom "A" note on a traditional keyboard. Austrian piano manufacturer Bösendorfer pioneered the extension of the typical 88-key keyboard, creating the Imperial Grand which has 97-keys (eight octaves). The extra keys, all at the bass end of the keyboard, simply have the upper surface of the extra natural keys finished in matte black instead of white to differentiate them from the standard 88. Take the time following a service to have Glenn, Glen or Bob show you both of these magnificent instruments! Not only are they gifted virtuosos, they are historians, as well as loving custodians of each of these world-class instruments.

The dedication service for our new sanctuary was held on March 9, 2008. Many guests were in attendance. Dr. Self hosted Dr. Neville George Callam as our pulpit guest. Dr. Callam, General Secretary and Chief Executive Officer of the Baptist World Alliance, was born in St. Ann, Jamaica. He grew up in a home where he was raised as a Baptist Christian. He is a graduate of Harvard Divinity School. He has served as educator and media manager, theologian and ecumenist, pastor and church administrator. Beginning in 1985, Dr. Callam has been associated with the Baptist World Alliance. This global Baptist movement has membership in 121 countries comprising a community of 42 million and serving a worldwide Baptist family of 110 million. In 2007, he became the first person from the Caribbean to be appointed as the general secretary and chief executive officer of the Baptist World Alliance, thereby becoming the first church leader from the Caribbean to lead a Christian World Communion. Author or editor of seven books, the most recent being *Pursuing Unity and Defending Rights: The Baptist World Alliance at Work* (2010), Dr. Callam has made presentations at fora, symposia, seminars, workshops and services of worship in more than 70 countries. He was one of the electoral observers serving on behalf of the United Nations in the elections in South Africa in 1994, and saw Nelson Mandela become President of that country.

The focus of 2008 remained missions. March was designated as "Missions Month" with a goal for missions giving of $38,000; instead, $60,263 was given! The first "Exploring JCBC" was held on March 30. Exploring JCBC is a four-week class designed especially for new members. This class was formerly known as "New Member Orientation."

On April 15, Dr. Michael McCullar's book, *A Christian's Guide to Islam,* was published by Smyth & Helwys. In keeping with the church's mission focus of 2008 (and relative to the timing of Dr. McCullar's book release), a 14-member team from Johns Creek Baptist spent a week in Istanbul, Turkey (April 19-26), assisting England's Elam College at their new location for ministry training. Elam College is a British Christian school dedicated to educating and training individuals for evangelistic work among Muslims in the Middle East and around the world. Since that first trip, JCBC has sent two additional mission teams to assist Elam College in Istanbul. Our relationship with Elam continues.

On April 27, under the direction of Glenn Crosthwait, the Sanctuary Choir and Orchestra presented *May Jesus Christ Be Praised.* This was the first presentation by the Music Ministry to be professionally recorded and released on compact disc.

In its June issue the publication *CountyLine* published a complimentary article about JCBC's Sweet Tea Ministry! *CountyLine* is a magazine for the northeast half of Johns Creek and South Forsyth. It is considered the source for information on local schools, organizations, businesses, and the people who are making outstanding contributions in our community.

During the same month, Vacation Bible School had over 550 participants! In keeping with the 2008 focus on missions, the goal of this year's VBS offering from the children (mind you, this offering is pennies, nickels, dimes and quarters) was to collect enough change to purchase a water buffalo for a family in India ... at the end of the week, enough had been raised to buy four buffaloes, some pigs AND chickens!

Later in June of 2008, the church was ABUZZ with over 10,000 unexpected guests! A massive interconnected hive of honeybees had taken occupancy in every available nook in the third floor attic of the porte cochere closest to the sanctuary entrance. Having listened to Dr. Self preach for months during the construction of their home, our swarm is believed to be the only Baptist bees in the apiarist world. Professional beekeepers were consulted and after locating the queen, our little Baptist buzzing buddies were relocated a few miles away to a new apiary. Five years later they are still faithfully serving in the mission fields of northern Forsyth County. The beekeepers indicated our bees had happily enjoyed their time as members of the Johns Creek Baptist congregation, having produced many pounds of honey during their stay. The locally grown Johns Creek Baptist Church honey was also relocated to northern Forsyth County into the cabinets of the beekeepers' wives!

Recognizing the sudden downturn of the economy and in keeping with the focus for the church on evangelism and missions in 2008, beginning July 23 and continuing on a bi-weekly basis throughout 2008, Johns Creek Baptist Church held job networking group meetings to assist all who were seeking employment as the economic slowdown continued.

On August 10, the Fall Women's Ministry Kick-Off Luncheon hosted Grace Powell Freeman, Director of Global Missions Operations for the Cooperative Baptist Fellowship as their speaker. Through Freeman's insightful stories they heard how churches, communities, families, and the Holy Spirit continue to work in lives of people throughout the world.

Following an all day prayer vigil focused on personal spiritual growth, Johns Creek Baptist held the church's fifth annual Spiritual Renewal weekend on Sunday, September 7. This event continues to be an important part of the spiritual maturing process for our church. Anne Graham Lotz, author, evangelist and founder of *AnGeL Ministries,* and daughter of Billy Graham, was the Spiritual Renewal weekend's pulpit guest.

For the first time, on September 20-27, Johns Creek Baptist Church took a group of people on a mission trip to Brussels, Belgium. They went to help Arab Baptist Church with their efforts to build a loving community in Brussels. Loving communities transcend the message of the gospel; a beautiful example is the missionary couple leading such a community in the Arab Baptist Church in the Arab sector of Brussels, Belgium.

On October 4, Johns Creek Baptist Church collected and delivered over 3,000 books to the people of Perry (Marion County), Alabama. This effort was made in conjunction with the Cooperative Baptist Fellowship's rural domestic poverty ministry "Together for Hope." The hope and goal is to transform individuals, churches and communities through Christ.

On November 2, Johns Creek Baptist Church was honored to have Dr. Billy Kim as our pulpit guest. Dr. Kim was the first Asian elected as president of the 40-million-member Baptist World Alliance; he served from 2000 – 2005. Dr. Billy Kim, a global spiritual leader, advocate for the poor, and humanitarian was born in 1934, and was raised in what is now North Korea during a time where "war" and "home" were synonymous in his country. Born into a poor family and the eldest of three siblings, life in Korea was difficult for Kim and his family, especially during the long Korean War of the 1950s. He went to work as a houseboy for the U.S. military under Sgt. Carl Powers. Powers was responsible for changing Kim's life and introducing him to Christianity. "I was able to attend college in the United States because of the help of an American soldier I worked for," Kim said. "All he asked of me was to spread the word of Christ, human values and democracy around the world."

As the Christmas season approached, the church collected dozens of bicycles and donated them to North Fulton Community Charities' Santa Shop. On December 17, a special family Christmas concert was held featuring Kyle Matthews, prolific songwriter and Christian recording artist. Kyle first performed at Johns Creek Baptist in April 2007.

In accordance with the final sentence in our new mission statement, "We exist to reach in through Bible study and building Christian community," the focus of 2009 was on discipleship and personal growth. As of 2009, the Adult Sunday School communities numbered 21. On January 12, Dr. Michael McCullar and Minister to Adults Rickey Letson co-authored *Sessions with Mark,* published by Smyth & Helwys.

On January 28, a special business meeting was called and the Strategic Planning Report's recommendation was given to the church. Having begun in 2007, with 882 church members participating in the U.S. Congregational Life survey, administered by the Alban Institute, the comprehensive report outlined current strengths that the congregation believed needed to be preserved (the community model of Sunday School; the sustenance of a warm, loving community of care; world class oratory and integrity from the pulpit; excellence in our worship experience), and five new strategic priorities (leadership development, Christian witness and mission outreach, discipleship, children's ministry, and debt reduction) to pursue in the future. Church member Task Forces would develop plans within each area of interest. The recommendation was approved with a unanimous vote.

On March 1, our church celebrated the launch of *Faith for Future Generations* in support of the capital campaign for debt retirement with a campaign goal of $3,900,000. Tom Jack served as Chair of the campaign. Also in March, the first uniform single-topic focus (Discipleship) was implemented for every adult Sunday School community. On March 29, under the direction of Glenn

Crosthwait, the Sanctuary Choir and Orchestra presented *The Song of Easter*. On Easter Sunday over 2,400 attended the worship services.

The 2009 flu pandemic involving the H1N1 influenza virus was the worst outbreak of the illness since 1918. Johns Creek Baptist made every precaution to protect the congregation as the virus spread. This involved additional installations of hand sanitizing equipment, enhanced disinfection of door handles, stair rails, children's equipment and restrooms. This precaution has remained a part of the weekly maintenance of our facility for the well-being of all present.

Vacation Bible School had 735 in attendance! The goal of this year's offering from the children (again, mind you, this offering is pennies, nickels, dimes and quarters) was to collect enough change to purchase containers of fresh water for families in Malawi, a tiny land-locked country in southeast Africa. Nicknamed "The Warm Heart of Africa," Malawi is among the world's least developed countries. Their "warm hearts" touched the children and by week's end they had raised $4,420 for "Watering Malawi!"

In June Dr. McCullar's book, *Stewardship: A Way of Living*, was published by NextSunday Resources. On August 13, Dr. McCullar began his *FaithBlog*.

Johns Creek Baptist held the church's sixth annual Spiritual Renewal weekend on Sunday, September 13. Bill Curry, former Georgia Tech and NFL player, Super Bowl Champion, multiple-winner of SEC Coach of the Year (University of Alabama), and then current head football coach of Georgia State University, was the guest speaker. Coach Curry offered candid words of wisdom stating, "There are two pains in life – the pain of discipline and the pain of regret. The first is temporary. The other lasts forever. You alone decide which to endure."

In autumn 2009, we saw the first Sunday School session to take place offsite at our neighboring facility, Alta Senior Living. On the weekend of September 17-18, the 20th annual Senior Adult Retreat was held at the Georgia Baptist Conference Center in Toccoa. In the following months several social organizations were started to foster the relationships of individuals with common interests. These would include "JCBC Reads," a book club for avid readers, Hook & Needle Guild for those who like to do handiwork, *Connections* for mature singles (by choice or by chance), and WITs (Women in Transition), a support group for mature singles to share prayer needs, life experiences, laughter, fun times, and stories of faith.

At the October 21, 2009 church business meeting, the Pastoral Succession Resolution was presented. The resolution is explained in detail in a separate Appendix article titled "Strategic Planning Initiative."

On the cover of the November 2009 issue, the publication *CountyLine* published the cover article about the success and growth of the JCBC's Sweet Tea Ministry!

Upon welcoming the 2010 New Year, the church began a program with the emphasis of commitment to our everyday Christian walk. Called "Small Steps 2010," the program had quarterly focuses of scripture reading, fruits of the spirit, prayer and stewardship.

During a church business meeting on January 27, 2010, a comprehensive witness strategy called "The Force of 70," was presented and approved. This "Force" would address the strategic priority of organizing, enlisting and training church members for the effective sharing of the gospel through Christian witness and missions outreach. Dr. Bob Lynn, who served as coordinator of "The Force of 70," explained the recommendation was based on the scripture passage in Luke 10 where Jesus sends 70 disciples as an advance team to the villages in Galilee to announce that He is coming to proclaim the Good News. At the same meeting, after careful consideration over the past 90 days, the Pastoral Succession Resolution was approved by the church.

On February 25, Johns Creek Baptist welcomed Christian entertainer Mark Lowry. Mark first performed at Johns Creek Baptist in 2007.

On Friday evening, March 19, Sean and Leigh Anne Tuohy from Memphis, Tennessee, spoke in our church. Their courageous story of inviting a young man to live with them as a member of their family was the inspiration for the Academy Award winning movie *The Blindside*. On Good Friday the youth of Johns Creek Baptist presented their first deeply moving and reflective "Stations of the Cross," a 30-minute visual walk through the day of Christ's crucifixion.

At the church business meeting on April 21, 2010, the Strategic Planning Task Force recommended the approval of the Discipleship Task Force's three-year plan. The recommended themes for the coming three years were as follows: Year One (2011) – "Grow" (spiritual growth), Year Two (2012) – "Give" (invest in our church and community), and Year Three (2013) – "Go" (missions). The Small Steps program implemented in January 2010 supports this plan. The three-year plan was unanimously approved.

On May 3, Ed Rivers was hired as Recreation Director. Ed is a native of Riverdale, Georgia. He is a graduate of the University of Georgia with a Bachelor of Arts degree in Journalism (1985). When asked to express his thoughts on the Recreation Ministry at Johns Creek Baptist, he responded as follows:

> *"During the summer of 2000, the church began its Recreation and Activities program. The ministry kicked off with Upward Basketball in the Family Life Center, the centerpiece of the new Phase III building. The upstart program had 70 kids that first season.*
>
> *Under the careful guidance of many dedicated and talented people, this ministry has flourished and become a vibrant part of the church's ministry to the community. The Activities Ministry of Johns Creek Baptist Church focuses on delivering the message of Christ to participants from two years of age all the way to senior adults.*
>
> *The emphasis is not just sports leagues, but "life leagues." The team is dedicated to reflecting values such as these ---*

*"Similarly, if anyone competes as an athlete, he does not receive the victor's crown unless he competes according to the rules."*

*~ 2 Timothy 2:5*

*With programs including SporTykes, Upward Sports, Kindermusik, Summer Camps, Golf and Tennis Outings, Vacation Bible School, Fitness Classes and Ballroom Dancing, this vital ministry touches thousands of community members."*

On May 6, 2010, Johns Creek Baptist Church hosted the "Sons of Jubal" in concert. The Sons of Jubal is a male chorus composed primarily of ministers of music who serve in churches of the Georgia Baptist Convention. Their concert program is widely varied in content, provides for congregational participation, and features both the Jubal Brass and Jubal Handbells.

On August 8, the Sunday School year was kicked off with the roar of engines and a cloud of dust as a legendary Black Hawk helicopter landed on the Johns Creek Baptist soccer fields. The versatile Black Hawk has enhanced the overall mobility of American troops due to dramatic improvements in troop capacity. At Johns Creek Baptist we hope it helps inspire us to enhance our overall mobility to our community as we increase our Sunday School troop capacity!

Johns Creek Baptist held the church's seventh annual Spiritual Renewal weekend from September 10-12. Dr. Charley Reeb, a native Atlantan, was the weekend's pulpit guest. Dr. Reeb is the Senior Pastor at Pasadena Community Church in St. Petersburg, Florida, and is the author of two books.

On September 29, plans are presented for the renovation of the pre-school and children's area. October 20 sees the first online pledging software fully operational. The final Sunday of the month was the first ever "Spirit Day," when everyone wore their favorite team colors to church in support of our Recreation Ministry.

In accordance with the church's approval of the Discipleship Task Force's three-year plan 2011 is designated the year to "Grow." The membership is encouraged to read *The Story* during the calendar year. *The Story* is the Bible written like a story. The books, modified for adults, teens and children, were available from the church.

Tifton, Georgia native Clay Shiver was the guest speaker at the first annual Super Bowl Breakfast on February 6. Clay is a former American college and pofessional football player who was an offensive lineman in the National Football League (NFL) for three seasons during the 1990s. He played college football for Florida State University, where he was a member of a national championship team and earned All-American honors. Thereafter, he played professionally for the NFL's Dallas Cowboys.

On February 20, 2011, Dr. Self following God's leadership and, with the ongoing support of the Pastors' Council, announced his desire to initiate the church's pastoral succession plan. Dr. Self would continue to serve as Senior Pastor throughout the search process for the next Senior Pastor.

In March 2011, a new church pictorial directory was published. Smiles abounded from cover to cover! Even more beautiful smiles abounded on Sunday morning, March 7. This was the day for Johns Creek Baptist Church's first "Blessing of the Children" ceremony in worship. Tender, touching, sacred moments ensued. On Good Friday the youth again presented their deeply moving and reflective Stations of the Cross, a thirty-minute visual walk through the day of Christ's crucifixion.

On April 27, 2011, after 17 years, six months and ten days since opening in 1993, the first ever Johns Creek Baptist Church Senior Pastor's Search Committee was approved to begin our search for a new person to lead us. The committee members are: Tom Benberg, Phil Brown, Melissa Floyd, Danny Henderson, Tom Jack, Angie Kleckley, Sanford McAllister, Kirby Pate (Chair), and Trudy Woodard.

In conjunction with the National Day of Prayer, Johns Creek Baptist holds its first ever Prayer Walk. Comprised of twelve stations, the walk was self-guided and gave pause to remember, reflect and refresh our walks with Christ. Later in the month on May 22, a prayer vigil was held for the Pastor Search Committee.

In June, the newly formed "JCBC Biker's Club" took their first motorcycle ride together throughout the north Georgia mountains.

Following a five-hour prayer vigil for our spiritual renewal the Saturday prior, Johns Creek Baptist held the church's eighth annual Spiritual Renewal on Sunday, September 11. This event is an important part of the spiritual maturing process for our church. Dr. Robert Smith, Jr. was our pulpit guest for the weekend. Dr. Smith is an Associate Professor of Divinity, Beeson Divinity School, Samford University in Birmingham, Alabama.

On September 14, 2011, Beth Irwin joined the staff as Children's Music Director. The pre-school and grade school children of JCBC learn to sing praises to God, and they are led by loving volunteers and seasoned professional music teachers. For children ages 3, 4, and Kindergarten, our weePraise choirs combine motion, rhythm, and song. Children from grades 1 to 5 learn and perform more involved music that culminates in annual musicals, featured special music in worship, and participation in major events such as *Christmas at Johns Creek* and *Celebrate America!* iPraise and weePraise, which meet Wednesday evenings from 6:00-7:00, blend singing, acting, games and lots of fun into a unique musical experience. On the same day, the Pastor Search Committee oversaw the distribution, completion and collection of a Senior Pastor Survey to the JCBC congregation. September 25 was the first breakfast meeting of "New and Expecting Parents."

In October the staff solicited church members to write devotional articles to be included in the Advent devotional guide to be used in the coming season. October 2011 also saw Dr. Self's tenth book, *Surviving the Stained-Glass Jungle,* published by Mercer University Press.

Johns Creek Baptist hosted the Cooperative Baptist Fellowship of Georgia's annual meeting on November 6-7. On November 17-

19, the church sent numerous attendees to the New Baptist Covenant annual meeting at Second Ponce de Leon Baptist Church in Atlanta.

On Sunday, December 11, the first highly attended (over 250) JCBC "Angel Breakfast" was held. Before the end of the month, Dr. McCullar's *2012 Annual Bible Study Guide for Moderate Baptists* (on the Book of *James*) was published by Smyth & Helwys.

In accordance with the church's approval of the Discipleship Task Force's three-year plan 2012 was designated the year to "Give," a year of investment in our church and community. In January, in conjunction with the Force of 70, Johns Creek Baptist's YouTube channel (JCBC Video) filmed and posted the testimonies of twelve church members.

The congregation recognized Valentine's Day on February 12, by having the children wear red and declaring it "Healthy Heart" Month. On the 22nd, devotional guides for the season of Lent were made available to all for individual study. The 25th saw our own Sanctuary Choir combined with our community's own Johns Creek Symphony Orchestra to perform a concert from the works of Beethoven.

In March the church asked for special prayers for the Pastor Search Committee and the missions ministry. Church members gathered each Sunday morning of March between 9:00 – 9:30 and prayed with one another for these requests. On March 9, Dove Award winners Ernie Haase and Signature Sound were in concert in the sanctuary. Ernie Haase & Signature Sound is a Grammy nominated Southern Gospel vocal quartet founded in 2002 by Ernie Haase, former Cathedral Quartet tenor, and Garry Jones, former Gold City pianist. On the weekend of March 16-18, Johns Creek Baptist hosted Georgia's March Missions Madness for youth. There were over 250 participants! Our annual special "Missions Month" offering was $85,000.

On August 1, the Preschool Weekday Program was approved to begin in the fall of 2013. On August 12, to kick-off the new Sunday School year, "Soaring to New Heights," Drs. Self and McCullar decided to soar a little for themselves! Together in view of the church, they soared to new heights above Johns Creek in a hot air balloon (they both held on tightly)!

As September began, the Women's and Men's Ministry at Johns Creek Baptist each had expanded respectively to four and five small weekly meeting groups.

Our Women's ministry is all about fostering Christian friendships and seeking God's grace and peace in our everyday lives. We gather to study God's word and how it applies to us as friends, moms, wives, sisters, and women from all walks of life. We're all about "doing life together," supporting one another, and "leaning in" to each other's needs. Our Women's Ministry sponsors four weekly small groups where women can take advantage of deeper discipleship studies, build relationships and connect with ministry opportunities in the local area. Additionally, for 20 years JCBC offers a unique Mother's Fellowship group on Wednesday mornings where family, parenting and faith issues are discussed and explored.

Our Men's ministry empowers men to seek God in their everyday lives. Whether it's in the work place, family relationships or friendships, our five weekly small groups foster an environment of faith building and support through fellowship, prayer and Bible study.

The Adult Sunday School grew to 24 communities, one of which was meeting offsite. Johns Creek Baptist was continuing to grow!

Johns Creek Baptist held the church's ninth annual Spiritual Renewal on Sunday, September 9. The weekend brought Dr. Eugene Lowry a gifted musician and celebrated preacher to Johns Creek Baptist, where he led the captivated audience through histories, harmonies and humor with his presentation of *Faith & Jazz*, a blend of story-telling, explanation, and bursts of music. Dr. Lowry is the William K. McElvaney Professor of Preaching Emeritus, Saint Paul School of Theology in Kansas City, Missouri.

Later in September excitement abounded throughout Johns Creek Baptist Church. On September 23, 2012, the Pastor Search Committee presented the church with their candidate for our new

Senior Pastor, Rev. Shaun Michael King. He preached that morning in view of a call from the church. Upon the conclusion of the sermon and service, the church offered vote to approve Rev. King. He graciously accepted. He would begin on November 16, 2012, and his first sermon would be on January 6, 2013.

The World Series Breakfast meeting featured former Atlanta Brave Darrel Chaney as guest speaker. While everyone wore their favorite team's attire, Chaney gleefully informed the crowd he would have rather been watching the Braves play in the World Series. Most in the crowd agreed! Chaney led in a fun time of Christian fellowship ... even for those who weren't Braves fans!

On November 4, Karen Keyes was introduced as the Director of the Johns Creek Baptist Church Preschool Weekday Program. Karen has been working with preschool children as either a teacher or administrator for the past ten years. She feels it's extremely important to provide children with as many learning experiences as possible to foster their creativity and imagination. She absolutely loves being an early childhood educator.

The annual bike drive for North Fulton Community Charities' Santa Shop continued to grow as Johns Creek Baptist Church continues to give back to our community. From the humble beginnings our church gave a few dozen bikes, trikes and scooters during the Christmas season of 2008. In November 2012, the church joyfully contributed over 600 to this worthy community need. JCBC continued its 2012 mandate, "Give," on the following day as the church sent over 500 assembled shoeboxes with gifts and supplies for children in need to Operation Christmas Child for distribution. Operation Christmas Child is a focus of Franklin Graham's Samaritan's Purse global ministry.

On November 16, 2012, Rev. Shaun King began as Senior Pastor of Johns Creek Baptist Church.

On December 2, 2012, Dr. William L. Self preached his final sermon, *It Is Finished* (John 19:30), as Senior Pastor of the church. Following the service, Dr. Self was promoted to Senior Pastor Emeritus of Johns Creek Baptist.

In accordance with the church's approval of the Discipleship Task Force's three-year plan, 2013 is designated the year to "Go," a year of investment in missions.

On January 6, 2013, Rev. Shaun King preached his first sermon as Senior Pastor of Johns Creek Baptist Church titled *Intended for Intimacy*. This was the first sermon of a six-week series titled *Life on the Vine* (John 15:1-8).

January 2013 also saw logistical updates.

"Hospitality Hubs" were placed in church rotundas as information posts for guests' convenience. The guests' dinner became a quarterly event called the "Newcomer Meal."

New members' orientation is now called "JCBC 4D." JCBC 4D is a fully experiential newcomers' orientation class. The purpose of this four-week class is to allow newcomers (guests and new members alike) to discover who we are at JCBC and how they may become fully engaged in a life of purpose and mission with us. Here is a look at 4D, at a glance. Week 1: In this first session we make sure that every newcomer understands from the beginning what and who is "The Church's One Foundation." Week 2: We explore what it means to be a Baptist church. What are Baptists? If there are 30+ Baptist denominations alone, where does JCBC fit in? And why? Week 3: We begin to truly engage the individuals; newcomers will explore their own God-given gifts and will discover the numerous and exciting ways their gifts and passions can be used in vital ministries here at JCBC. Week 4: Week 4 is experiential. During this session, class members will take tours of the campus, and will specifically visit areas of interest.

On Sunday mornings, parking lot attendants and portico point people are used to direct guests and members on a regular weekly basis.

After 20 years of investments exceeding $50 million, the January payment of the church's long-term debt brought our outstanding balance to below $10 million.

During the Sunday morning worship of February 10, 2013, the Installation Service was held for Rev. Shaun King as the 22nd Senior

Pastor of Johns Creek Baptist Church. On February 17, 2013, Rev. Shaun King began a seven-week series of sermons titled *Seven Last(ing) Words* (Luke 23:34-46).

In conjunction with the Discipleship Task Force's three-year plan, 2013, having been designated the year to "Go," the Youth Ministry Spaghetti Luncheon held a fundraiser on March 3, to support a third Dominican Republic mission team from Johns Creek Baptist.

On March 31, 2013, Rev. King preached a non-series sermon titled *Fear Knot* (Mark 16:1-8).

On April 14, 2013, Rev. King preached the sermon, *Hidden Wholeness.* This was the first sermon of a 16-week series titled *Sermon on the Mount* (Matthew 5:1-11).

In June Dr. McCullar's book, *Basics of Theology,* was republished by Smyth & Helwys. His book is made available to Johns Creek Baptist Church members free of charge.

On August 4, Shaun introduced his next sermon series. In his message Shaun challenged the church to:

*"Never underestimate the power of a provoked imagination!"* He continues, *"A vibrant and living journey with Jesus Christ never ends. As followers, we are in a constant state of becoming. All the time. Always. If we pay close attention to the way Jesus encounters people in the Gospels, we find him doing the same thing again and again. He meets people right where they are, but then with grace and power, He beckons them to more. He bids them (regardless of who they are, or where they've been) to follow him to a new and next place in their adventure of faith. If we know nothing else, we know this: In Christ, there is never NOT a next. True for individuals. True for congregations. What would a new and next step of faith look like for you as a follower of Jesus? What would a new and next step of faith look like for us as a*

*congregation gathered in His name? Perhaps it's time to consider it. Perhaps time to intentionally imagine ... to deliberately discern ... the new and next call of Christ upon all of us. Perhaps it's time to iMAGiNEXT!*

The series lasts ten weeks and is titled *iMAGiNEXT ... because in Christ, there's never NOT a next* (Jeremiah 29:11-13, Isaiah 43:2-3a). This series culminates by leading the church to its 20th Anniversary Celebration Sunday on October 20, 2013.

On August 11, our church's website (www.jcbc.org) was completely rebuilt and launched during the worship service. At the same time, the church fully engages in social media with Facebook and Twitter accounts, and encourages all members to join in this cultural phenomenon for connection. In other words, "Like" us on Facebook and "Follow" us on Twitter!

On Wednesday, August 14, a special church conference was called to receive a recommendation from Deacon Chair Tom Waller for candidate Rev. Chris Moore to serve as Minister of Youth. Youth Council spokesperson Susan Grissom reported Chris, having worked with youth programs of a similar size (Bon Air Baptist Church, Richmond, Virginia), "is someone who understands and has done what we do here." When questioned, Shaun King explained he has known and cared about Chris since their days as classmates at Carson Newman College. He further describes Chris as a "great relationship person." The vote was unanimous in favor of calling Chris Moore.

On September 3, 2013, led by Director Karen Keyes, the Johns Creek Baptist Church Preschool Weekday Program opened. It was the first day of our brand new JCBC Preschool! We believe each child is a special gift from God, with unique gifts and abilities. Our school offers a warm, nurturing, Christ-centered environment where gifted teachers and enjoyable experiences are brought together to challenge students academically and to enhance their love of learning.

On Sunday, September 22, Rev. Chris Moore began as Minister of Youth. Tennessee native, Chris is a 1995 graduate of Carson Newman College where he majored in Religious Studies. In 2000, he was awarded his Master of Divinity degree from Southwestern Baptist Theological Seminary. Since graduating from the Seminary, Chris has served in two churches over the past 13 years. When asked to express the theme he lives by, Chris offered six words:

*"Love God, love people, follow Jesus."*

On October 8-11, the JCBC Preschool's week was dedicated to fire prevention. Fire Prevention Week was highlighted with the arrival of local fire trucks for the children to observe (and crawl all over)! On October 13, the Women's Ministry held its eagerly anticipated annual banquet with Jeanie Miley as guest speaker.

Then last, but not least ... on October 20, 2013, Johns Creek Baptist Church celebrates its 20th Anniversary!

So there's the story of the first 20 years of our church, but before I hand it over to Shaun to write what comes next, I'd like to wrap it all up with one last story.

On the first pages of this book I introduced you to the grandparents, great aunt, and parents of Johns Creek Baptist Church's beloved 87-year young unofficial greeter, Fred Henderson.

I'd like to tell you about another set of grandparents, parents, and grandchildren in our church.

When Susan was 16 years old, her pastor's wife Carolyn was her Sunday School teacher. Carolyn was also a mentor, and Susan loved her. After Susan graduated from Dykes High School, she attended Auburn University and studied to become a Pharmacist. After graduating and entering the workforce back home in Atlanta, she met her future husband John, a native of Mobile, Alabama. John and Susan began dating and fell in love. During their courtship, John asked Susan to be his wife, and they were married in Susan's home church in 1976 by the pastor of her youth. Life took them away from Susan's home church. Starting their family, Susan and John had two children, Courtney and Philip. They lived in Cherokee County where they found a new church and joined. The commute was becoming too taxing, so several years later they decided to move closer to Atlanta and chose Alpharetta for the location of their new home. During this time of relocation, Susan learned her childhood pastor and his wife, her beloved mentor Carolyn, were involved in a church relocation project of their own.

Twenty years ago, on October 17, 1993, Susan and John T. Hudson, along with their children Courtney and Philip, joined Johns Creek Baptist Church. Dozens of new members joined on the opening day, yet in a sentimental reunion of old friends, Dr. Bill Self, the same pastor who had married Susan and John in 1976, introduced the Hudson family first to the congregation that morning. Courtney transferred her letter from the same church as her parents. Dr. Self baptized her younger brother Philip on a later date. Courtney and Philip became active in the youth program of Johns Creek Baptist.

Courtney became involved in the youth group out in the trailers when we were building more buildings, Camp Rutledge, Discipleship Now weekends, camp counselor for Jill, helped with Vacation Bible School ... you name it. Soon she had graduated from Chattahoochee High School and off she went to attend college at the University of Georgia. Following graduation, she came back to Atlanta to work. Her younger brother Philip had a mentor named Alex. As life would have it, Alex and Courtney met and began dating. Thirty years following her parent's marriage, Courtney Hudson became Mrs. Alex Tetterton in 2006. Shortly after their marriage, Alex transferred his letter of membership to Johns Creek Baptist.

In a few short years Courtney and Alex began a family. Their sons, Hudson, 3, and Henry, 18 months, were dedicated in the church by Dr. Self.

On March 8, 2013, their daughter Presley was born. On Mother's Day 2013, Presley, in a tender and touching ceremony, was carried through the sanctuary and introduced to her Johns Creek Baptist family. Presley Tetterton was the first baby dedicated by our new Senior Pastor, Rev. Shaun King.

Whether from Fred Henderson's Aunt Betty Johnson, meeting with a few ladies in Bert Johnson's Blacksmith Shop, founding a church in the nineteenth century, or Presley Tetterton, being introduced to well over a thousand people 138 years later in the same church, everyone who has ever passed through our beloved church's doors has been loved.

Happy 20th Anniversary, Johns Creek Baptist Church!

# STAFF
## 2008 – 2013

### 2008

| | |
|---|---|
| Senior Pastor | Bill Self |
| Executive Pastor | Michael McCullar |
| Minister of Pastoral Care | David White |
| Minister of Music | Glenn Crosthwait |
| Assoc. Minister of Music | Perry McCain |
| Minister to Adults | Rickey Letson |
| Minister to Youth | Jim Walls |
| Youth Intern | Justin Bishop |
| Minister to Children | Jill Jenkins |
| Minister to Preschool | Tammy Sullivan |
| Activities Director | Tracy Morris |
| Church Administrator | Michele Deriso |
| Financial Manager | Tiffany Kitchens |
| CDC Director | Tobye Bristow |
| Assistant CDC Director | Monique Brown/ |
| | Tracy Brown-Morrison |
| Hospitality Director | Juan Venagas/ |
| Food Service Director | Arlene Hollier |
| Facilities Manager | Fred Wolford |
| Organist | Bob Cash |
| Pianist | Glen Sloan |
| Ministry Asst/Sr. Pastor | Barbara Brown |
| Ministry Asst/Exec Pastor | Kris Peters |
| Ministry Asst/Adults | Beth McLaughlin |
| Ministry Asst/Music | Sandra Hawk |
| Ministry Asst/Children | Kristen Cochran |
| Ministry Asst/Youth, Rec | Laura Cruce |
| Publisher | Earah Harris |
| Financial Secretary | Vickie Wright |
| Receptionist | Glenda Garner |
| Sunday receptionist | Debbie Bramlett/ |
| | Toni Draper |
| Sound Coordinator | Matt Shealy |
| Maintenance | Al Powell/ |

Johnny Leon-Venagas/
Adnan Zukanovic/
Sam Hardy/
Roberto Soto/
Erika Arce/
Isela Ortiz

## 2009

| | |
|---|---|
| Senior Pastor | Bill Self |
| Executive Pastor | Michael McCullar |
| Minister of Pastoral Care | David White |
| Minister of Music | Glenn Crosthwait |
| Minister to Adults | Rickey Letson |
| Minister to Youth | Jim Walls |
| Youth Intern | Justin Bishop |
| | Dan Stockum |
| Minister to Children | Jill Jenkins |
| Minister to Preschool | Tammy Sullivan |
| Activities Director | Tracy Morris |
| Financial Manager | Tiffany Kitchens |
| CDC Director | Tobye Bristow |
| Assistant CDC Director | Tracy Brown-Morrison |
| Food Service Director | Arlene Hollier |
| Organist | Bob Cash |
| Pianist | Glen Sloan |
| Ministry Asst/Sr. Pastor | Barbara Brown |
| Ministry Asst/Exec Pastor | Kris Peters |
| Ministry Asst/Adults | Beth McLaughlin |
| Ministry Asst/Music | Sandra Hawk |
| Ministry Asst/Children | Kristen Cochran/ |
| | Heidi Carr |
| Ministry Asst/Youth, Rec | Laura Cruce |
| Publisher | Earah Harris |
| Financial Secretary | Vickie Wright |
| Sunday receptionist | Toni Draper |
| Sound Coordinator | Matt Shealy |
| Maintenance | Al Powell/ |
| | Johnny Leon-Venagas/ |
| | Adnan Zukanovic/ |
| | Roberto Soto/ |
| | Winston Jennings/ |
| | Erika Arce/ |
| | Isela Ortiz |

## 2010

| | |
|---|---|
| Senior Pastor | Bill Self |
| Executive Pastor | Michael McCullar |
| Minister of Pastoral Care | David White |
| Minister of Music | Glenn Crosthwait |
| Minister to Adults | Rickey Letson |
| Minister to Youth | Jim Walls |
| Youth Intern | Justin Bishop |
| | Dan Stockum |
| Minister to PS/Children | Jill Jenkins |
| Activities Director | Tracy Morris |
| Recreation Director | Ed Rivers |
| Church Administrator | Nan Pope |
| Financial Manager | Tiffany Kitchens |
| CDC Director | Tobye Bristow |
| Food Service Director | Arlene Hollier |
| Organist | Bob Cash |
| Pianist | Glen Sloan |
| Ministry Asst/Sr. Pastor | Barbara Brown |
| | Peggy Stanley |
| Ministry Asst/Exec Pastor | Kris Peters |
| Ministry Asst/Adults | Beth McLaughlin |
| Ministry Asst/Music | Sandra Hawk |
| Ministry Asst/Children | Heidi Carr |
| Ministry Asst/Youth, Rec | Laura Cruce |
| Publisher | Earah Harris |
| Financial Secretary | Vickie Wright |
| Sunday receptionist | Toni Draper |
| | Debbie Iwasaki |
| Sound Coordinator | Matt Shealy |
| Maintenance | Al Powell |
| | Adnan Zukanovic |
| | Roberto Soto |
| | Winston Jennings |
| | Erika Arce |
| | Isela Ortiz |

# 2011

| | |
|---|---|
| Senior Pastor | Bill Self |
| Executive Pastor | Michael McCullar |
| Minister of Pastoral Care | David White |
| Minister of Music | Glenn Crosthwait |
| Children's Music Director | Beth Irwin |
| Minister to Adults | Rickey Letson |
| Minister to Youth | Jim Walls |
| Youth Intern | Justin Bishop |
| | Dan Stockum |
| Minister to PS/Children | Jill Jenkins |
| Recreation Director | Ed Rivers |
| Church Administrator | Nan Pope |
| Financial Manager | Tiffany Kitchens |
| Food Service Director | Arlene Hollier |
| Organist | Bob Cash |
| Pianist | Glen Sloan |
| Ministry Asst/Sr. Pastor | Peggy Stanley |
| Ministry Asst/Exec Pastor | Kris Peters |
| Ministry Asst/Adults | Beth McLaughlin |
| | Paige Edwards |
| Ministry Asst/Music | Sandra Hawk |
| Ministry Asst/Children | Heidi Carr |
| Ministry Asst/Youth, Rec | Laura Cruce |
| Publisher | Earah Harris |
| Financial Secretary | Vickie Wright |
| Sunday receptionist | Debbie Iwasaki |
| Sound Coordinator | Matt Shealy |
| Maintenance | Adnan Zukanovic |
| | Roberto Soto |
| | Erika Arce |

# 2012

| | |
|---|---|
| Senior Pastor | Bill Self |
| | Shaun King |
| Executive Pastor | Michael McCullar |
| Minister of Pastoral Care | David White |
| Minister of Music | Glenn Crosthwait |
| Children's Music Director | Beth Irwin |
| Minister to Adults | Rickey Letson |
| Adult Ministry Intern | Tara Brooks |
| Minister to Youth | Jim Walls |
| Youth Intern | Justin Bishop |
| | Dan Stockum |
| Minister to PS/Children | Jill Jenkins |
| Preschool Director | Karen Keyes |
| Recreation Director | Ed Rivers |
| Church Administrator | Nan Pope |
| | Richard Eason |
| Financial Manager | Tiffany Kitchens |
| Food Service Director | Mark Stamper |
| Organist | Bob Cash |
| Pianist | Glen Sloan |
| Ministry Asst/Sr. Pastor | Peggy Stanley |
| Ministry Asst/Exec Pastor | Kris Peters |
| Ministry Asst/Adults | Paige Edwards |
| Ministry Asst/Music | Sandra Hawk/ |
| | Sue Bowron |
| Ministry Asst/Children | Heidi Carr/ |
| | Juliet Weaver |
| Ministry Asst/Youth, Rec | Laura Cruce |
| Publisher | Earah Harris |
| Financial Secretary | Vickie Wright |
| Sunday receptionist | Debbie Iwasaki |
| Sound Coordinator | Matt Shealy |
| Maintenance | Adnan Zukanovic |
| | Roberto Soto |
| | Lamont Watkins |

## 2013

| | |
|---|---|
| Senior Pastor | Shaun King |
| Formations Pastor | Michael McCullar |
| Connections Pastor | David White |
| Worship Pastor | Glenn Crosthwait |
| Children's Music Director | Beth Irwin |
| Adult Ministry Intern | Tara Brooks |
| Youth Pastor | Jim Walls |
| | Chris Moore |
| Youth Intern | Justin Bishop |
| | Dan Stockum |
| Children's Pastor | Jill Jenkins |
| Preschool Director | Karen Keyes |
| Recreation Director | Ed Rivers |
| Church Administrator | Richard Eason |
| Financial Manager | Tiffany Kitchens |
| Food Service Director | Mark Stamper |
| Facilities Manager | Chuck Watson |
| Organist | Bob Cash |
| Pianist | Glen Sloan |
| Ministry Asst/Sr. Pastor | Peggy Stanley/ |
| | Rhonda Byrd |
| Ministry Asst/Exec Pastor | Kris Peters |
| Ministry Asst/Adults | Paige Edwards |
| Ministry Asst/Music | Sue Bowron |
| Ministry Asst/Children | Juliet Weaver/ |
| | Shelaine Cole |
| Ministry Asst/Youth, Rec | Laura Cruce |
| Publisher | Earah Harris |
| Financial Secretary | Vickie Wright |
| Sunday receptionist | Debbie Iwasaki |
| Sound Coordinator | Matt Shealy |
| Maintenance | Adnan Zukanovic |
| | Roberto Soto |
| | Lamont Watkins |

# EPILOGUE

I don't know who said it first.

I wish I could say it was I.

*"You are who you have been becoming."*

Sit with that thought for just a moment, will you? Let it marinate.

All of the experiences that have made up your life thus far; all of the encounters, the conversations, the losses, the gains, the failures, the successes; all of the hurts that have left scars and all of the healings that have given redemptive meaning to those scars. All of it has contributed (and contributes still) to the unfolding story of you.

*You are who you have been becoming.*

True for individuals.

True for congregations.

The preceding pages chronicle the first twenty years of life, love and ministry at Johns Creek Baptist Church. Marvelous is the unfolding story of us.

The story of *who we have been becoming.*

And who is that?

Answer: The living, breathing, body of the risen Christ. That is who.

Even the most casual glance into our history reveals it. We are a resurrection people. Period. Time and again, throughout significant seasons of challenge and change, our congregation was faced with making critical, risky, trajectory-shaping decisions. Decisions upon which, the very life-wish of the church hung in the balance. Through all of these seasons of change; at each gut-checking crossroad in the journey; the church has chosen to live, and live again.

This reality became crystallized for me one early spring morning when David White (JCBC Connections Pastor) and Fred Henderson invited me to visit the old Chamblee Cemetery. I had not been to the site and was eager to go. (Years ago, I had listened to Dr. Tom Long, professor of homiletics at Candler School of Theology. He spoke of a similar experience in which an elder member of that congregation had walked him out behind the church building after services, to visit their cemetery and to meet, in his words, *"the other members of the congregation."*)

So, being new to the story of Johns Creek Baptist, I too wanted to walk among those whose lives and shared story had been such a vital part of our becoming.

So we went. And we walked with great care among those who have now become part of a "great cloud of witnesses." As we sauntered through the rows of headstones and foot markers, we would stop respectfully at one resting place or another, as Fred regaled us with stories. Stories of people and persons, and the shaping influence of their lives upon the church I now serve as Pastor. He was introducing me to my other members.

Toward the end of our walk, we returned to the car, where Fred pulled out three cokes and three bags of salted peanuts. Standing there (snacking) beneath the canopy of tall trees with deep roots, I was humbled to consider just how deep the roots go.

Just a few yards away, on the western retaining wall of the cemetery proper, there is fixed a bronze marker. It summarizes the history of the congregation by a simple listing the various names we have known, and the corresponding dates when those names (for specific and deliberate reasons) changed. It was then that David wrapped words around it for me. He said, *"You know, Shaun, the thing that has always amazed me about this church is the courage it has always had to continually reinvent itself. When changes and challenges demanded it, they have always found a way to live and thrive and become something new."*

I have thought about those words a great deal, in these early days of learning, loving and leading.

It is true.

We are a resurrection people.

Who have we been becoming? We have been becoming the Body of Christ, visible in this world, continually overcoming the grave.

Perhaps these words of the great hymn, "The Church of Christ in Every Age," speak of the heritage and hope of Johns Creek Baptist Church.

The church of Christ in every age,
beset by change but Spirit-led,
must claim and test its heritage
and keep on rising from the dead!
*(The Church of Christ in Every Age, by Fred Pratt Green)*

THAT is who we have been becoming.
That is who we are becoming still.

There is something extraordinarily powerful about that part of who we are. There has been and continues to be a kind of congregational courage, long-braided into our DNA. It is the courage to *lean into*, and *live out of* the great mystery of our Lord's resurrection.

For this reason, I could not be more grateful to be called to lead the people of Johns Creek Baptist Church into our new and next season of becoming. Even now, as we rehearse our congregational narrative; as we tell our children about where we have been, and dream together about where we will go, I find myself grateful, humbled, and filled with extraordinary hope for our future.

Why?

Because of a conviction I hold as truth: In Christ, there is never not a next.

As followers of Jesus we are in a constant state of becoming.

All the time.

Always.

Just pay attention to the way Jesus encounters people in the Gospels, we find him doing the same thing again and again. He meets people (and peoples) right where they are, but then with grace and power, He beckons them to more. He bids them (regardless of who they are, or where they've been) to follow him to a *new* and *next* place of becoming, in their adventure of faith.

If we know nothing else, we know this: In Christ, there is never NOT a next.

On this, our 20th anniversary as Johns Creek Baptist Church, may we give thanks to God for who we have been becoming.

And who we are becoming still.

~ Rev. Shaun King

# ACKNOWLEDGEMENTS

Thirty-five years ago I was a representative vendor for a home appliance manufacturer at the Sun Belt Agricultural Exposition in Moultrie, Georgia. Home and agricultural products from all over the world were on exhibit for three days at an old airport in Moultrie. Crowds exceeded 250,000 folks from all over the South.

It was here I first met Jerry Clower, country comedian, recording star and member of 'The Grand Ol' Opry" in Nashville. He was attending the Expo as a celebrity representative for an agricultural equipment manufacturer. He and I had been randomly scheduled by the local FM radio station, WMTM, to share a 30-minute segment promoting our products. Mr. Clower was about 30 years older than I, and I paid him his due respect but he insisted I call him Jerry. During the breaks from our banter on the show, Jerry showed a genuine interest in me, asking about my parents, siblings, where I went to church, college, etc. When I told him I was a member of First Baptist Chamblee and went to Furman his eyes lit up and he laughed aloud exclaiming he thought I might be a "good ol' Baptist boy." He explained he was a good ol' Baptist boy himself. When our shared time on the radio concluded, he asked to come and see the product I was representing. I explained the features and benefits to him as he carefully listened to my conviction of the product's value. When I finished, he shared how he had actually "backed into show business," his background was in agronomy, and prior to his being involved in the entertainment industry he had run a "half-a-billion-dollar" organization called Mississippi Chemical Corporation.

I will never forget the wisdom he offered as we parted that October afternoon. He put his arm around my shoulder and said, "Dave, you'll likely amount to something down the road, and if you don't remember another thing from all that goes on at this Expo, remember this, Son. There is no limit to what can be done, if it doesn't matter who gets the credit."

The history committee offers humble thanks and gratefully acknowledges the following for their interest, input and help in the compilation of this document. First and foremost, without the support, encouragement and patience of our families, this book could not have been written. We especially thank our spouses, Pete Brown, Sheri Brown, and the late Charles Skidmore; Phil Brown, and Lee & Helen Brown. Special appreciation goes to the JCBC staff members who contributed to the book and clarified historical facts: Dr. Bill Self, Rev. Shaun King, Dr. Michael McCullar, Jill Jenkins, Glenn Crosthwait, Bob Cash, Glen Sloan, Dr. Jim Walls, David White, Ed Rivers and Richard Eason; support staff members Rhonda Byrd, Kris Peters, Vickie Wright, Earah Harris, and Peggy Stanley. Other church members who have assisted in this project are: Edwin Boland, Tommy & Beth Ann Boland, Edith Bond, Sandra Eason, Judy Bond Hansard, the late Claude Head, Grant & Dot Curtis, John Dixon, Pat Griffin, Fred & Lillian Henderson, Susan Hudson, Tom & Elizabeth Jack, Angie Kleckley, Ann Livingston, Bob Lynn, Norman Parker, Kep Pate, Kirby & Shan Pate, Mark & Lisa Sauls, Carolyn Self, Wayne & Esther Shaw, Alex & Courtney Tetterton (& Hudson, Henry & Presley), Tony & Brenda Turpin, Tom & Lynne Waller, Brad & Camille Ward, and Dick Wolf.

## TO GOD BE THE GLORY!

# JCBC FAMILY ALBUM

*March 23, 1991. We're building our new church here.*

*Plank from barn; Claud Eason secured it; Hugh Johnson painted it.*

*Looking over the property.*

*Looking over the property.*

*Fund raising for Phase I.*

*Groundbreaking Phase I.*

*Groundbreaking Phase I.*

*Groundbreaking Phase I, Robert McFarland,*
*Tommy Boland, Kristen Prator & Bill Self.*

*Dr. Self enjoys Homecoming in 1993 at Chamblee.*

*Construction of Phase I.*

*Affixing the cupola to Phase I.*

*Back view of Phase I.*

*First Sunday, October 17, 1993.*

*Ribbon cutting, Tommy Boland & Bill Self.*

*Jerry Hyde & Tom Jack discuss Sunday School logistics.*

*Mr. Harold & Ms. Elizabeth Smith.*

*(L-R) Greg Walton, Tommy Boland, Bill Self and Larry Jones.*

*Children's sermon.*

*New members in line to join church.*

*Groundbreaking for parking lot extension.*

*Groundbreaking of the parking lot extension.*

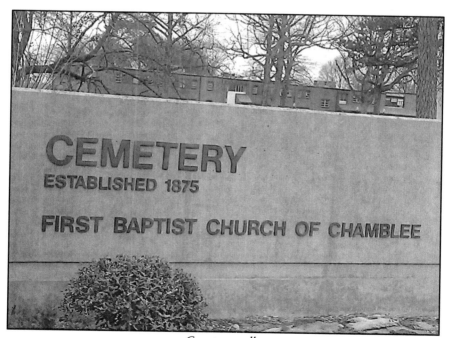

*Cemetery wall.*

*Obverse of Cemetery Memorial.*

*Dr. Cecil Sherman on June 23, 1996.*

*Big Tent Event, October 16, 1999.*

*Aerial view of Phases I & II (McGinnis Ferry Rd. on the right).*

*Side view of Phases I & II.*

*Groundbreaking Phase III.*

*View of Phase III basement, November 1999.*

*View of the rear portion of Phase II.*

*Steel beams from east side of Phase III, February 9, 2000.*

*Gym, March 15, 2000.*

*Eason, Tolbert, Prevatte and Pate at the*
*"Topping Out Ceremony", April10, 2000.*

*Gym floor, April 10, 2000.*

*Outside of the gym, April 10, 2000.*

*Outside angle – October 2000.*

*View from the south, April 10, 2000.*

*Same view from the south, October – 2000.*

*Dedication of The Family Life Center, October 15, 2000. President Jimmy Carter, guest speaker with Dr. & Mrs. Self.*

*Aerial view, Phases I, II & III, August 1, 2005.*

*View from courtyard, July 25, 2005.*

*July 25, 2005.*

*August 8, 2005.*

*August 31, 2005.*

*Footings being poured, November 1, 2005.*

*November 8, 2005.*

*November 13, 2005.*

*December 9, 2005.*

*December 9, 2005.*

*December 15, 2005.*

*Staircase, March 5, 2006.*

*Aerial, March 27, 2006.*

*Choir loft, April 23, 2006.*

*Balcony, April 23, 2006.*

*April 25, 2006.*

*May 7, 2006.*

*July 20, 2006.*

*July 24, 2006.*

*July 28, 2006.*

*Emily Sikes signing beam, October 2, 2006.*

*Olivia Sikes signing beam, October 2, 2006.*

*Signed beams installed in ceiling, June 1, 2006.*

*Steeple & Cross*

*Steeple & Cross*

*Steeple & Cross*

*Steeple & Cross*

*Steeple & Cross*

*Steeple & Cross*

*Steeple & Cross*

*Bill Self presents plaques of appreciation to Tom Jack and Tommy Boland.*

*Charlie Brown, Technology Park who made the original land gift.*

*CDH Partners, Inc. (L-R) Mel Manor, Karen Brown (architect of Phase IV), Mr. & Mrs. Bill Chegwidden*

*Jill Jenkins, Children's Pastor.*

*Children's sermon.*

*Children's sermon.*

*Bill Self preaching the first sermon in the new sanctuary.*

*David White, Connections Pastor with Bill Self.*

*Michael McCullar, Formations Pastor with Bill Self.*

*Bill Self with pulpit guest, Neville Callam,*
*General Secretary of the Baptist World Alliance.*

*Rev. Shaun King (with his family) on September 23, 2012.*

*Bob Prator presents Dr. Self (with Carolyn) the Senior Pastor Emeritus Resolution.*

*Edith Bond greets Dr. Self.*

*Kep Pate alongside Dr. Self.*

*Shaun King and Bill Self.*

*Presley Tetterton's dedication, Mother's Day, 2013.*

*Glenn Crosthwait, Worship Pastor.*

*Sanctuary Choir & Orchestra.*

*Bob Cash, Organist.*

*Glen Sloan, Pianist*

*Children's Choir singing in church.*

*Sanctuary Choir "Christmas Party", August 29, 2012.*

*Kids participate in KidQuake as they tell the Christmas story.*

*Dominican Republic Mission Trip, October 2012.*

*Dominican Republic Mission Trip, July 2013.*

*Dr. Michael McCullar leads worship in La Romana, Dominican Republic, July 2013.*

*JCBC's first Sunday afternoon mission outing.*

*MarchMissionsMadness2012.*

*MarchMissionsMadness2012.*

*MarchMissionsMadness2012.*

*MarchMissionsMadness2012.*

*Eggs for Ghana.*

*Kids In Support of Soldiers (ChapStick edition)*

*Tornado relief work, 2011.*

*PassportKids 2013.*

*2nd grade class shows their spirit on "Spirit Day 2011."*

*Basketball Camp, July 2011.*

*Easter Egg Hunt, 2013.*

*Trunk or Treat, 2011.*

*Gerry Caldwell with her pet 'possum, Louise at Trunk or Treat, 2011.*

*Trunk or Treat, 2011.*

*Bottom Photo – VBS 2013.*

*"Flat Shaun" with Logan Rice.*

*Sweet Tea.*

*Sweet Tea Coordinators.*

*Women's Fall Banquet, 2011.*

*Women's Fall Banquet, 2011.*

*Golf Outing, 2011.*

*Tennis Outing, 2011.*

*Men's Retreat, 2011.*

*Women' Retreat, 2013.*

*Claud & Mary Catherine Eason*

*Al & Sandy Stewart*

*Charles & Nancy Skidmore*

*Claude & Sylvia Head*

*Everett & Teresa Bennett*

*Monroe & Jeanette Dempsey*

*Grant & Dot Curtis*

*Doyle & Jan Chasteen*

*W.O. & Kathleen Brannan*

*Bob & Joyce Harris*

*Ed & Dot Waters*

*Jack & Delores Gillian*

*Jim & Carole Dill*

*Fred & Lillian Henderson*

*Don & Margaret Braswell*

*Tom & Elizabeth Jack*

*Hugh & Ollie Johnson*

*John & Louise Wiley*

*Myron & Syble Strickland*

*Tommy & Beth Ann Boland*

*Norman & Barbara Parker*

*Paul & Dorothy Herrington*

*2013 JCBC History Committee (L-R) Mary Lou Parrish, Barbara Brown (Chair),
Dave Brown, Nancy Skidmore*

# APPENDIX

# LISTS OF "FIRSTS"
(First time a regularly scheduled program or event was held.)

## 1991
12/8   Dr. Self's first Sunday as Pastor.

## 1992
5/2   First time new Sunday School format was tried using seminar leaders.

## 1993
February First year February was designated as "Family Month;" continued throughout Dr. Self's tenure.

10/17  First worship service at Johns Creek Baptist Church.

10/20  First midweek service at JCBC; preschool, children, middle school and youth programs (missions and music) began.

11/14  First new members' reception (held monthly, then on a regular basis as deemed appropriate) November First CBF foreign missions offering campaign.

12/1   First Guests' Dinner (initially held monthly, then on a regular basis. We eventually held luncheons after Sunday morning worship.)

12/19  First Baptist Women meeting at Johns Creek (later renamed Women on Mission).

    First Parent/Child Dedication service (William Darsey Flowers and Christopher Lee Winn).

    First annual church-wide Christmas Party (held on a Wednesday in mid-December).

## 1994

| | |
|---|---|
| 1/9 | First "Big Breakfast" during Sunday School hour. |
| 3/31 | First annual Maundy Thursday Communion Service. |
| 4/2 | First annual Johns Creek Easter Egg Hunt. |
| 6/5 | First annual Graduate Recognition Sunday (8 graduates recognized). |
| 6/11 | First Men's Ministry breakfast. |
| 6/12 | First College Sunday School class offered. |
| 8/1-5 | First annual Vacation Bible School held at JCBC. (130 children enrolled). |
| 9/14 | First Mothers' Fellowship & Support Group began (weekly); organized and led by Carolyn Self. |
| 9/24 | First Women's Ministry Brunch held. (We now have banquets each fall.) |
| Fall | First annual collection of coats/hats/gloves/scarves for local charities. |
| 10/29 | First annual Fall Festival held (now have Trunk or Treat). November First annual collection of Christmas Stockings in conjunction with Salvation Army. First "Adopt-A-Family" for Christmas. |

## 1995

| | |
|---|---|
| January | First collection for food pantries of local charities (held quarterly, then monthly). |
| 2/17-19 | First annual Youth (grades 6-12) *DiscipleNow* weekend. |
| 4/30 | First special seminar on Money Management held; Danny Joiner of Wells Fargo, speaker. |
| May | First international mission trip; 8 adults went to Prague. |
| Summer | First Youth mission project (in Atlanta). |
| 8/13 | First annual Teacher Preparation Day (special age-group seminars). |
| 8/20, 27 | First regularly scheduled Children's "Getty Ready" class for grades 1-5 (for those asking about becoming Christians). |

| October | First time designated as Stewardship Education month. |
| 12/9 | First annual Drop & Shop Christmas event: children's activities provided on Saturday, 9-noon. |

## 1996

| 2/6 | First Men's Ministry monthly luncheon held (at Piccadilly Cafeteria in Peachtree Corners). |
| 3/24 | First annual Children's choir presentation, *Hans Bronson's Gold Medal Mission.* |
| 3/31 | First annual Baby Olympics. |
| 4/16 | First Prime Time (covered dish dinner with program for Adults 50+). |
| 7/7-8 | First Adult VBS. |
| 12/22 | First annual Birthday Party for Jesus. |

## 1997

| 3/17-19 | First annual William L. Self Preaching Lectures at McAfee School of Theology; Dr. Self was inaugural speaker. |
| 6/15 | First Passport Camp (grades 6-12). |
| August | First annual collection of school supplies and backpacks for charities. |
| 9/27-28 | First Spiritual Renewal weekend (later became annual event) |
| October | First JCBC pictorial directory published. |
| 11/2 | First Stewardship Event with special entertainment, Frank Boggs ("Big Tent" event). |

## 1998

| 8/26 | First annual Chancel Choir Christmas Party. |
| November | First *Johns Creek Cookbook* published |
| 12/12-13 | First annual *Christmas at Johns Creek* presented. |

## 1999

| | |
|---|---|
| 6/26-7/4 | First mission trip to assist Elam College in England (now located in Istanbul). |
| 8/22 | First Express Sunday School (adult Bible study). |
| 9/14 | Seniors on Mission debuted. |

## 2000

| | |
|---|---|
| March | First "ONE" campaign (each church member was to bring one guest to church). |
| 5/7 | First "Join the Church" Day with 25 new members (held on regular basis.). |
| 10/1 | First worship service in Family Life Center. |

## 2001

| | |
|---|---|
| 1/21 | First *Keyboard Festival of Praise* presented by Glenn Crosthwait, Bob Cash and Glen Sloan. |
| 5/20 | First "Experience the Tithe" Day. |
| 6/24 | First annual *Celebrate America!* presented by Chancel Choir and Orchestra. |
| 9/30 | First New Member Orientation (4-week special elective for new Christians and those new to the Baptist faith; later became "Exploring JCBC;" held on a regular basis). |
| 10/15 | First Baptist Women's Fellowship group begins (morning and evening meetings). |

## 2002

| | |
|---|---|
| 3/10 | First Christian College Fair for high school students and parents (with 5 Baptist colleges participating). |
| 9/14 | First time to work with Habitat for Humanity. |
| 10/6 | First annual Old-Fashioned Gospel Sunday. |

## 2003

| | |
|---|---|
| March | First "Six Weeks of Commitment." |
| 5/4 | First Youth Year-End Celebration. |

| 5/11 | First time for "Muffins for Mom;" Mother's Day photos were taken. |
| 6/15 | First time for "Donuts for Dad;" Father's Day photos were taken. |
| 6/21 | First unveiling of *Journeys into Faith* (Vol. I), Bob Lynn, editor (adults wrote their testimonies through their Sunday School communities). |
| 11/1 | First Singles' Conference. |

## 2004

| January | First time JCBC went online with www.JCBC.org. |
| April | First started providing meals and fellowship at Memorial Drive Homeless Shelter. |
| 7/4 | First time Dr. Self was featured speaker on Day1 radio program. |
| 9/19 | First annual Spiritual Renewal Weekend: Dr. Phil Lineberger, guest preacher. |
| 10/27 | First annual "Trunk or Treat" (church-wide event, formerly Fall Festival). |

## 2005

| 3/11-12 | First annual Women's Ministry Retreat (offsite). |
| 7/3 | First "Casual Day" in church. |

## 2006

| 1/26-29 | First mission trip to Pearlington, Mississippi. |
| March | First time Missions Liaison assigned from each Sunday School community. |

## 2007

| 3/18 | First Sunday in the new permanent sanctuary. |
| 5/27 | First Memorial Day recognition of deceased church members in past year. |
| 8/15 | First Strategic Planning Initiative Steering Committee Meeting (see separate Appendix article). |

9/24-28    First of 3 mission trips to Weimar, Germany.

November First time to assemble shoe boxes for Operation Christmas Child, a ministry of Franklin Graham's Samaritan's Purse.

12/2    First annual Advent Lunch.

## 2008

2/7    First served meals to No Longer Bound (monthly, then twice a month).

2/8-9    First offered "Created by God" (for grades 5, 6 with parent), a study of human sexuality, led by Jill Jenkins and Jim Walls.

2/10    First quarterly "Sweet Tea" held for those affected by cancer.

3/6-9    First of 12 mission trips to Perry County, Alabama (CBF Rural Poverty Initiative).

3/30    First "Exploring JCBC" as on-going 4-week class.

4/19-26    First mission trip to Istanbul (to assist Elam College).

4/27    First professionally recorded CD of Sanctuary Choir and Orchestra (*May Jesus Christ Be Praised*)

7/23    First JCBC Job Search & Networking Group meeting.

9/20-27    First of 2 mission trips to Brussels (to assist the Arab Baptist Church).

11/22    First annual collection of bicycles for NFCC's Santa Shop.

## 2009

1/14-18    First mission trip to Presidio, Texas.

Spring    First time Adult Sunday School had single topic focus: Discipleship.

5/12-17    First mission trip to Plaquemines Parish, Lousiana.

7/28    First meeting of "JCBC Reads" bookclub.

Fall    First Sunday School session offsite (at Alta Senior Living).

11/1    First luncheon for Singles who were near or at retirement age (spawned Connections and WITs).

11/17   First meeting of Hook & Needle Guild.

## 2010

1/5     First meeting of Bridge Club.

2/25    First luncheon for Connections.

3/10-13 First of 4 missions trips to Haiti.
        First of 12 mission trips to Dominican Republic.

4/2     First time Youth presented "Stations of the Cross," a 30-minute visual walk.

August  New prayer room opened daily (7:00 a.m. to 8:00 p.m.).

10/31   First "Team Spirit" Day (members to wear team colors in worship service).

## 2011

2/6     First annual Super Bowl Breakfast; Clay Shiver, guest speaker.

3/7     First "Blessing of the Children" ceremony in worship.

5/4     First JCBC Prayer Walk (self-guided, 12 stations, in conjunction with National Day of Prayer).

6/11    First Biker's Club (motorcycles) ride (held twice a year).

9/25    First "New & Expecting Parents" Breakfast.

12/11   First "Angel" Breakfast for preschool families.

## 2012

3/9     First Parents' Night Out (Youth fundraiser to raise money for Dominican Republic mission trip).

4/15-29 First Peer Pressure seminar (grades 5).

4/28    First playground clean-up.

7/16-20 First JCBC Music Week (grades 1-6).

9/23    Rev. Shaun preached in view of a call.

## 2013

| | |
|---|---|
| January | First time Hospitality Hubs were placed in church rotundas. |
| | First time parking lot attendants are used weekly. |
| | First time portico point people are used. |
| | First "Newcomer Meal" (formerly guest dinner/luncheon/brunch). |
| | First "4D" classes, newcomer orientation, offered (formerly New Members' Orientation). |
| 1/6 | First Sunday Rev. Shaun King preached as Senior Pastor. |
| 5/12 | Rev. King's first Parent/Child Dedication (Presley Tetterton was dedicated). |
| 9/3 | First JCBC Preschool (Tuesday to Friday) opened. |

# TIMELINE

The purpose of this timeline is to provide an overview of when and how our current programs and activities evolved. It is not an unabridged diary of all the programs and activities that the membership of JCBC enjoyed these past twenty years. It would be impossible to include every activity, special seminar or event that occurred along the way. For example, listed elsewhere is a list of staff members who have served our church, though we have included here the start dates of current ministerial staff members only. Hopefully, this will help those who are currently involved in the life of the church to recall how our programs evolved. Hopefully, this will help those members who have moved away to recall the excitement our church enjoyed in these early years. Hopefully, this will help future members to appreciate the diligent work of our staff, church leadership and membership to get us to this point. Hopefully, if you have any criticism of this list or find omissions, you will volunteer to serve on the next history committee!

## 1990

| | |
|---|---|
| 2/21 | FBC/Chamblee Deacons recommended the appointment of a strategic task force regarding the future of the church. |
| 3/21 | Vote to approve the recommendation regarding the strategic task force (see separate Appendix article.) |

## 1991

| | |
|---|---|
| 3/6 | Dr. David Sapp resigned. |
| **3/24** | **Vote to accept gift of land as suggested by Dunwoody Baptist Church from Technology Park/Atlanta.** |
| 3/31 | Dr. Sapp's last Sunday as Pastor. |
| 5/5 | Dr. Self's first Sunday as Interim Pastor (Sunday School attendance 297). |
| 6/2 | Barn on Johns Creek property (deliberately) burned. |

| | |
|---|---|
| 8/11 | Pastor Search Committee approved: Tom Jack, Chair; Edith Bond, Phil Brown, John Dixon, Harold Hyde, Jerry Hyde, Cecelia Prator. |
| 11/17 | Vote to call Dr. Self to serve as Pastor. |
| 12/8 | Dr. Self's first Sunday as Pastor (Sunday School attendance 341). |
| **12/27** | **Property at Johns Creek deeded to congregation.** |

*[NOTE: Throughout the year Dr. Self attended meetings and hosted a luncheon for pastors to study the feasibility of an organization for moderate Baptists which became Cooperative Baptist Fellowship.]*

**1992**

| | |
|---|---|
| 1/22 | Presentation of title of 15.84 acres from Technology Park/Atlanta. |
| **5/20** | **Master plan for Phase I was unanimously approved (26,000 sq. ft.).** Tommy Boland, Chair of Building Committee. |
| 8/16 | Installation Service for Dr. William L. Self as 21st Pastor; Dr. Duke McCall preached. |
| **10/25** | **Groundbreaking for church at Johns Creek site. Beginning of "The Dream Is Now," capital campaign; goal: $300,000.** |

**1993**

| | |
|---|---|
| February | Designated as Family Month (Dr. Self based his sermons on family issues; continued throughout his tenure). |
| 3/28 | Last "Homecoming" at First Baptist Church/Chamblee. |
| 5/2 | First new Sunday School format tried (implemented in Adult 3, "Median Adults," for 8 weeks). |
| 5/5-6 | Dr. Self preached at National Congress on Preaching in Atlanta. |
| 5/6 | Article on homecoming and relocation in *Atlanta Journal & Constitution.* |

| 5/19 | Vote on Mission Statement of Johns Creek Baptist Church (see separate Appendix article). |
|---|---|
| 7/12-16 | 40th Anniversary of Camp Rutledge. |
| 8/18 | New church logo introduced. |
| 9/29 | Dr. Self attended announcement of Billy Graham Crusade in Atlanta. |
| 10/3 | Final Sunday evening service at First Baptist/Chamblee. |
| 10/6 | Final midweek service at First Baptist/Chamblee. |
| 10/10 | Final service at First Baptist/Chamblee; Lord's Supper served. |
| **10/17** | **9:30 a.m. Ribbon cutting at Johns Creek Baptist Church.** |
| | **10:50 a.m.   First service at Johns Creek Baptist Church.** |
| 10/20 | First midweek service at Johns Creek Baptist Church; preschool, children, middle school and youth programs (missions and music) began. |
| 10/31 | Service of Celebration – Dr. David Sapp preached. |
| 11/7 | Service of Dedication - Dr. Self preached. |
| 11/11 | Dr. Self attended meeting of Steering Committee with Mercer University Feasibility Study Committee regarding seminary.* |
| 11/14 | First new members' reception (held monthly, then regularly as deemed appropriate). |
| 11/21 | Hosted community Thanksgiving meal. |
| 12/1 | First Guests' Dinner (initially held monthly, then on a regular basis. We tried brunches, and then eventually held luncheons after Sunday morning worship services.) |
| 12/12 | Chancel Choir presented *A Johns Creek Christmas*. |
| 12/19 | First Parent/Child Dedication service (William Darsey Flowers and Christopher Lee Winn). First church-wide Christmas Party. (This became an annual event, held on a Wednesday in mid-December.) |

*NOTE: JCBC supported the founding of McAfee School of Theology at Mercer University from its beginning.*

## 1994

The following ministries were begun this year:

        Women's Ministry – Louise Wiley, Chair

        Men's Ministry – Keith Compton, Chair

        Senior Adults' Ministry – Vivian Gay, Chair

1/9        First "Big Breakfast" during the Sunday School hour.

**1/16**    **2 morning worship services began** (3 months after our first Sunday at new location).

2/3        Article on the church in *Baptists Today*.

2/21-25    Dr. Self preached at National Congress on Preaching in Newport Beach, California.

*[Note: Several people had missed Sunday evening services so evening services were held in the month of March with guest speakers. We discovered people didn't miss the evening services as much as they thought they did! We had come to devote that time to family.]*

3/6        Pulpit guest: Karl Heinz Walter, Baptist World Alliance.

p.m.      Pulpit guest: Dr. Frank Harrington, Pastor of Peachtree Presbyterian Church, Atlanta; music provided by Salvation Army Band.

3/13      p.m. Pulpit guest: Dr. Don Harp, Pastor of Peachtree Road United Methodist, Atlanta.

3/20      p.m. Pulpit guest: Dr. Peter Rhea Jones, Pastor of First Baptist Church, Decatur.

3/23      209 new members since October 17, 1993; 413 new members since December 1991.

3/27      Easter drama, *Celebrate Life!* Presented by Chancel Choir.

3/31      First annual Maundy Thursday Communion Service.

4/1        Hosted Community-wide Good Friday service with lunch.

4/2        First annual Johns Creek Easter Egg Hunt.

4/3        Easter Sunday: 3 worship services.

**5/9**      **JCBC Child Development Center opened.**

| | |
|---|---|
| 6/5 | First annual Graduate Recognition Sunday (8 graduates recognized). |
| 6/11 | First Men's Ministry breakfast. Entertainment by Christian humorist, Randy Hollingsworth. |
| 6/12 | First College Sunday School class offered. |
| 6/26 | Listening sessions on church budget to be designated as Ministry-Driven (6 segments are: Worship & Pastoral Care, Missions, Personal Growth, Music & Drama, Fellowship & Activities, Community Outreach). |
| 6/28 | Mercer University presented proposal to establish a seminary. |
| 7/11-15 | Camp Rutledge (88 campers and 27 staff & counselors). |
| 8/1-5 | First annual Vacation Bible School held at JCBC (130 children enrolled). |
| 8/7 | Johns Creek Concert Series (4 consecutive weeks). |
| 8/28 | Record Sunday School attendance: 507. (35 cars were parked on McGinnis Ferry Road.) |
| 9/14 | First weekly Mothers' Fellowship & Support Group began; organized and led by Carolyn Self. |
| 9/18 | Bob Cash recognized on 5th anniversary as organist. |
| **9/21** | **Campaign for parking lot expansion (114 spaces) began; $103,000 pledged.** |
| 9/24 | First Women's Ministry Brunch held; we now have banquets each fall. |
| 9/25 | Chamblee-Doraville Ministry Center dedication service. |
| 9/28 | Michael McCullar began as Minister of Education & Administration. |
| **10/2** | **2 Sunday School sessions begin.** |
| | Began using Embry National Bank (now United Community Bank) for additional parking; shuttle service provided to the church. |
| 10/26-30 | Billy Graham Crusade held at the Georgia Dome in Atlanta. Volunteers from JCBC attended the Crusade as counselors after attending witnessing classes for five weeks. (Susan Hudson was coordinator for JCBC.) |

| | |
|---|---|
| 10/29 | First Fall Festival held (became an annual event in one form or another). |
| 10/30 | Designated as "High Attendance Sunday" with 637 in Sunday School. |
| 11/13 | Stewardship Banquet at Holiday Inn Crowne Plaza Ravinia. Theme: *Ministries on the Move.* |

## 1995

Church budget of $1,200,000 was 100% increase over 1994 budget, and was over-pledged by $13,435.

| | |
|---|---|
| 1/8 | Record Sunday School attendance: 639. |
| 1/15 | Record Sunday School attendance: 648. |
| **1/29** | **Groundbreaking for new parking lot.** |
| 2/3 | Men's Ministry fellowship/breakfast began on weekly basis. |
| 2/17-19 | First annual Youth (grades 6-12) *DiscipleNow* weekend. |
| 3/13-25 | Dr. & Mrs. Self led tour of the Holy Land and Athens, Greece (26 church members went). |
| 4/1 | Women's Ministry event: brunch with guest speaker Elizabeth (Mrs. Jo Frank) Harris, former first lady. Men's Ministry work day at Chamblee church. |
| 4/9 | Two presentations by Music Ministry of Easter musical, *Joy Comes in the Morning.* |
| 4/30 | First special seminar on Money Management held; speaker, Danny Joiner of Wells Fargo. |
| 5/1 | Jill Jenkins began as Minister to Preschool and Children. |
| 5/24 | Church approved vote on temporary buildings for Sunday School. |
| 7/6-9 | Camp Rutledge (completed grades 3-5). |
| 7/9-13 | Camp Rutledge (completed grades 6-12). |
| 7/25 | Dedication of Arboretum for Harold Smith at FFA/FHA Camp/Covington, Georgia. |
| 8/13 | First annual Teacher Preparation Day (special age-group seminars). |

| | |
|---|---|
| 8/19 | Special seminar by Dr. William Hendricks of Golden Gate Baptist Seminary on the Revelation and the Second Coming. Men's Ministry Outing: Falcons preseason football game, Falcons vs. Cleveland Browns. |
| 8/20, 27 | First Children's "Getting Ready" class for grades 1-5 (for those asking about becoming Christians; now held on a regular basis). |
| 8/27 | Record Sunday School attendance: 678. |
| 9/3 | Church picnic and concert (casual dress appropriate); 550-600 attended. |
| 9/23 | Men's Ministry Kickoff Breakfast; speaker, Steve Bartkowski, former Falcons quarterback. |
| **9/24** | **3 morning worship services and adult "Early Bird" Sunday School began.** |
| 9/30 | Special seminars *Parenting with Power* (selection of two of three offered by professionals). |
| October | First designated as Stewardship Education Month. |
| 10/17 | 2nd anniversary in Johns Creek location; added 36 members to the church family this day. |
| **10/29** | **Added modular units for additional Sunday School space (5,760 square feet).** |
| 11/12 | Ambassador Andrew Young spoke at Stewardship Banquet at Gwinnett Civic Center. Theme: *Faith Under Construction.* Goal: 500 families to pledge. |
| 12/3 | Security system implemented for pre-school Sunday School. |
| 12/9 | First annual *Drop & Shop* Christmas event: children's activities provided on Saturday, 9-noon to allow parents a time to shop. |
| 12/10 | Chancel Choir presents Handel's *Messiah.* |

## 1996

| | |
|---|---|
| January | Chamblee property was sold to Interactive College of Technology. |
| 1/14 | Record Sunday School attendance: 806. |

| | |
|---|---|
| 1/21 | Record Sunday School attendance: 834. |
| **1/31** | **Building plans for Phase II (Education Building) approved (30,000 square feet).** Tommy Boland, Chair of Building Commitee. |
| 2/6 | Groundbreaking for Mercer University School of Theology. First Men's Ministry monthly luncheon at Piccadilly Cafeteria in Peachtree Corners. |
| 2/8-10 | Dr. Self was keynote speaker at CBF/Florida meeting. |
| 3/9 | Women's Ministry Spring Luncheon; speaker, Barbara Joiner. |
| **3/10** | ***Faith Forward* campaign introduced to support Phase II.** Tom Jack, Chair. |
| 3/24 | First annual Children's choir presentation, *Hans Bronson's Gold Medal Mission*. |
| 3/31 | First annual Baby Olympics. |
| 4/7 | Easter: record worship attendance: 1,712. |
| 4/16 | First "Prime Time" (monthly covered-dish dinner with program for adults 50+). |
| **4/28** | ***Faith Forward* event at Gwinnett Civic Center to support Phase II**. Goal: $2,200,000. Pledged: $2,488,582. |
| 6/9 | Hosted program celebrating 3,000th anniversary of the city of Jerusalem, sponsored by Consulate General of Israel and the Nation Conference of Christians and Jews. |
| 6/23 | Dr. Cecil Sherman Day at JCBC (upon his retirement from Cooperative Baptist Fellowship). |
| 7/7-8 | First Adult VBS. |
| 7/14 | Dr. Self attended "Call for Prayer" at Peachtree Presbyterian Church for the Centennial Summer Olympics Games, hosted by the City of Atlanta, 7/19 – 8/4. |
| 8/15 | Men's Ministry annual Falcons football outing (Falcons vs. Oakland Raiders). |
| **8/21** | **Vote to proceed with construction of Phase II** (35,000 square feet), worship center renovation and expansion, |

300 additional parking spaces, purchase of 8 acres of adjacent land, and cemetery improvement.

**9/15**    **Groundbreaking for Phase II.**

9/21    Men's Ministry fall breakfast; guest speaker, Billy "White Shoes" Johnson, former Atlanta Falcon.

November New deacons' ministry program formulated to include:

Care Ministry

New Member Ministry

Growth Ministry

11/10   Stewardship emphasis event: church-wide brunch with Oliver Sueing, special musical guest.

11/27   Property known as Missionary Manor, located at 3322 Hood Avenue, and adjacent to the Chamblee church, was sold.

12/8    Dr. Self recognized on 5th anniversary as Pastor. Chancel and Youth Choirs presents *Festival of Light.*

12/22   First annual *Birthday Party for Jesus.*

**1997**

2/2    Record Sunday School attendance: 945.

2/9    Record Sunday School attendance: 962.

3/17-19 First annual William L. Self Preaching Lectures at McAfee School of Theology; Dr. Self, inaugural speaker.

3/19   Vote to televise worship services on Prestige Cable (services televised until 6/8/2003).

3/23   Record Sunday School attendance: 977. Chancel Choir and Orchestra presented *Joy in the Morning…From Tragedy to Triumph.*

3/30   Easter: 3 services; record worship attendance: 2,288 (baptized 17 in 4-stall baptistry).

4/20-28 Dr. Self preached at International Congress on Preaching in Westminster Chapel, London.

4/23   Vote to spend $60,000 on furnishings for Phase II.

**5/4**    **Dedication of First Baptist Church/Chamblee Cemetery.**

| | |
|---|---|
| 6/15 | First Passport Camp (grades 6-12). |
| **7/13** | **Phase II opened (36,000 square feet).** |
| 8/24 | Record Sunday School attendance: 1,110 (14 adult communities). "Sixers" ministry started for sixth-graders. |
| 9/16 | Dedication service of Mercer School of Theology. |
| 9/27-28 | "Spiritual Renewal" weekend; Dr. Phil Lineberger, pulpit guest. |
| October | First JCBC pictorial directory published. |
| 10/16-17 | Hosted Mercer University Evangelism Conference. |
| 10/21 | Dedication of McAfee School of Theology at First Baptist Church, Decatur. |
| 11/2 | Frank Boggs provided special music at Stewardship Sunday (first "Big Tent" event). |
| 12/10 | Costs for Phase II increased from $4,357,000 to $4,550,000. |

## 1998

| | |
|---|---|
| 1/11 | Record Sunday School attendance: 1,295. |
| 2/9-11 | William L. Self Preaching Lectures at McAfee School of Theology. Guest lecturer: Barbara Brown Taylor, Professor of Religion & Philosophy, Piedmont College, Demorest, Georgia. |
| 3/6 | Dr. Self was keynote speaker at CBF/Georgia in Athens. |
| 5/1 | Glenn Crosthwait began as Minister of Music. |
| **5/3** | **Building plans for Phase III (Family Life Center) presented.** Tommy Boland, Chair of Building Commitee. |
| 7/11-12 | Camp Rutledge Reunion for campers and staffers (1954-1990). |
| 8/23 | Record Sunday School attendance: 1,490. Started using Fellowship Hall for Sunday morning worship services (for additional 150-200 people). |
| 8/26 | First annual Chancel Choir Christmas Party. |
| 8/30 | Record Sunday School attendance: 1,553. |

| 10/25 | Stewardship "Big Tent" event; guest speaker, Deen Day Smith. |

**11/18** **Vote to proceed with construction of Phase III and main foyer plus 430 parking spaces.**

November *Johns Creek Cookbook* published.

11/22 Fifth anniversary in Johns Creek location celebration.

12/12-13 First annual *Christmas at Johns Creek* presented by Chancel Choir and Orchestra (3 presentations).

## 1999

3/8-10 William L. Self Preaching Lectures at McAfee School of Theology. Guest lecturer: Dr. Fred Craddock, Bandy Distinguished Professor of Preaching & New Testament Emeritus, Candler School of Theology, Emory University.

**3/21** ***Faith Forward II* introduced to support Family Life** Center (goal $5,000,000); Tom Jack Chair.

4/4 Easter attendance: 2,740.

6/26-7/4 First mission trip to Elam College in Shackleford, England.

**8/4** **Building plans for Phase III approved.** Tommy Boland, Chair of Building Committee.

8/22 "Express Sunday School" (adult Bible study) began.

8/24 Dr. Self was elected inaugural chair of Board of Visitors of McAfee School of Theology at Mercer University. Church members Tommy Boland and Way Kidd also served on this Board.

9/1 Glenn Crosthwait published two choral works and 3 keyboard arrangements.

9/12 Bob Cash recognized on 10th anniversary as organist.

9/14 Seniors on Mission debuted.

9/19 Michael McCullar recognized on 5th anniversary as Executive Minister.

October Dr. Self's book *Defining Moments* published by CSS Publishing.

| | |
|---|---|
| 10/8-9 | Hosted innovative Regional Sunday School Growth Conference. |
| **10/17** | **Groundbreaking for Phase III (Family Life Center; 77,000 square feet).** |
| 10/31 | Stewardship "Big Tent" Event. |
| 12/11-12 | *Christmas at Johns Creek* presented by Chancel Choir and Orchestra (4 presentations). |
| 12/31 | Special New Year's Eve service at 6:00 p.m. for new millennium (remember Y2K?). |

## 2000

| | |
|---|---|
| 1/9 | Glenn Crosthwait fell off the stage before morning worship service and broke his leg! |
| 2/20-23 | Dr. Self preached at National Congress on Preaching in Orlando, Florida. |
| March | "ONE" campaign (each member is to bring one guest to church). |
| 4/3-5 | William L. Self Preaching Lectures at McAfee School of Theology. Guest lecturer: Dr. James Earl Massey, Dean Emeritus and Distinguished Professor-at-Large, Anderson University School of Theology, Anderson, Indiana. |
| 5/1 | Jill Jenkins recognized on 5$^{th}$ anniversary as Minister to Children. |
| 5/7 | First "Join the Church" Day (25 new members). Ordination of Melissa Lewis for ministerial service. |
| 8/23 | Church By-laws Revision approved. |
| September | JCBC pictorial directory published. |
| **9/18** | **Moved into new offices in Phase III.** |
| 9/24 | Last worship service in first sanctuary (now Chapel); open house in new building. |
| **10/1** | **First worship service in Family Life Center.** |
| 10/8 | Community Day; special guest: Dr. Robert White, Executive Director of Georgia Baptist Convention. |
| **10/15** | **National Day/DedicationSunday; special guest speaker: President Jimmy Carter.** |

| | |
|---|---|
| 10/22 | International Day; special guest: Dr. Denton Lotz, General Secretary of Baptist World Alliance. |
| 10/29 | Baptist Heritage Day; special guest: Dr. Daniel Vestal, Coordinator of Cooperative Baptist Fellowship. |

November *Johns Creek Cookbook, Volume 2*, published.

| | |
|---|---|
| 11/14 | Tommy & Beth Ann Boland received James Wesberry Award for denominational service, and Dr. Self received Louie D. Newton Award for Service to Mercer University. |

12/9-10 *Christmas at Johns Creek* presented by Chancel Choir and Orchestra (3 presentations).

## 2001

| | |
|---|---|
| 1/7 | Record Sunday School attendance: 1,742. |
| 1/21 | *Keyboard Festival of Praise* presented by Bob Cash, Glen Sloan and Glenn Crosthwait. |
| 2/4 | Dr. Self received W. Lee Arrendale Award for Vocational Excellence, Rotary Club of Johns Creek (the inaugural award for this chapter). |
| 2/12-14 | William L. Self Preaching Lectures at McAfee School of Theology. Guest lecturer: Dr. William Willimon, Dean of the Chapel, Duke University, Durham, North Carolina. |
| 4/1 | Chancel Choir and Orchestra presented *The Story of Easter*. |
| 5/4 | Dr. Self received W. Lee Arrendale Award for Vocational Excellence, Rotary Club District 6910 in Savannah, Georgia. |
| 5/6 | "Join the Church" Sunday (36 additions). |
| 5/20 | First "Experience the Tithe" Day. Dean Alan Culpepper presented Life Membership in President's Club of Mercer University to JCBC. |
| 6/24 | First annual *Celebrate America!* presented by Chancel Choir and Orchestra. |

| 7/11 | Michael McCullar's book, *Sessions with James*, published by Smyth & Helwys. |
| **7/25** | **Plans regarding Phase IV (sanctuary) presented (60,000 sq. ft.).** Tommy Boland, Chair of Building Committee. |
| 8/19 | 8:30 a.m. worship service resumes. |
| 8/21 | Trip to Holy Land, scheduled for March 2002, was cancelled (125 were enrolled). |
| 9/11 | Terrorist attacks on America. |
| 9/12, 14 | Special worship services for our country. (Highest attendance ever in Sunday School and worship the following Sunday.) |
| 9/13 | Hosted Georgia Baptist Developmental Disabilities Ministries meeting. |
| 9/30 | First New Member Orientation (4-week special elective for new Christians and those new to the Baptist faith; later became "Exploring JCBC;" held regularly). |
| 10/15 | First Baptist Women's Fellowship group began (morning and evening meetings). |
| 11/11 | Pastor Appreciation Day: Dr. Self's 10th Anniversary as Senior Pastor. |
| 12/8-9 | *Christmas at Johns Creek* presented by Chancel Choir and Orchestra (4 presentations). |

## 2002
**The church year changed from October 1 to September 30, to a calendar year beginning January 2002.**

| 1/13 | Record Sunday School attendance: 1,983. |
| 1/14 | New fellowship ministry for senior adults started called "Sixties Plus." |
| 1/20 | *Keyboard Festival of Praise* presented by Bob Cash, Glen Sloan and Glenn Crosthwait. |
| **1/23** | **Vote on *Faith Forward III* for additional funds for Family Life Center.** |

Goal: $4,000,000; June 2005 – May 2008. Tom Jack, Chair.

2/22    *Celebrating Marriage* banquet; speaker, Rev. Bill Coates.

3/1-2    JCBC hosted 10th Anniversary of Cooperative Baptist Fellowship.

3/4-6    William L. Self Preaching Lectures at McAfee School of Theology. Guest lecturer: Dr. Timothy L. Owings, Pastor, First Baptist Church, Augusta, Georgia.

3/10    First Christian College Fair for high school students and parents (with 5 Baptist colleges).

4/8    Dr. Self preached at International Congress of Preaching in Edinburgh, Scotland.

4/14    **Faith Forward III Information Sunday**.

4/20    Men's Ministry breakfast; speaker, Mark Richt, head football coach, University of Georgia.

4/28    Chancel Choir and Orchestra presented *Psalms, Hymns & Spiritual Songs*.

5/15    **Faith Forward III dinner**; entertainment, Oliver Sueing.

5/26    8:30 worship services discontinued.

6/12    Michael McCullar co-authored *Building Blocks for a Growing Sunday School*, published by Smyth & Helwys.

6/30    *Celebrate America!* presented by Chancel Choir and Orchestra.

9/14    First time to work with Habitat for Humanity.

10/6    First annual "Old-Fashioned Gospel" Sunday.

12/14-15    *Christmas at Johns Creek* presented by Chancel Choir and Orchestra (4 presentations).

## 2003

1/28    Dr. Self served as Chaplain of the Day in the Georgia State Senate.

February    *TWO* campaign (to encourage attendance for 2 hours each Sunday morning)

2/9    *Keyboard Festival of Praise* presented by Bob Cash, Glen Sloan and Glenn Crosthwait.

| | |
|---|---|
| 2/17-19 | William L. Self Preaching Lectures at McAfee School of Theology. Guest lecturer: Dr. Walter Brueggemann, Professor of Old Testament, Columbia Theological Seminary, Decatur, Georgia. |
| 2/21 | Marriage banquet. |
| March | First "Six Weeks of Commitment" (discipleship program: read Scripture, prayer, attendance, bring guest, tithe or increase contribution, share faith) |
| 3/19 | "Operation Uplift" started (service men and women added to Prayer List). |
| 3/30 | "Join the Church" Sunday (32 additions) |
| April | JCBC pictorial directory published. |
| 5/4 | Glenn Crosthwait recognized on 5th anniversary as Minister of Music. First Youth Year-End Celebration. |
| 5/11 | Dr. Self received Honorary Doctorate from Campbell University, Buies Creek, North Carolina. First "Muffins for Mom;" Mother's Day photos taken. |
| 6/15 | First "Donuts for Dad;" Father's Day photos taken. |
| 6/21 | Unveiling of *Journeys into Faith Vol. I*, Bob Lynn, editor (testimonies from 42 senior adults). |
| 6/29 | *Celebrate America!* presented by Chancel Choir and Orchestra. |
| 7/16 | New Preschool Steering Committee named. |
| 8/3 | "Best Years of Our Lives" reception celebrating 50th wedding anniversaries (later become the Golden Club). (See separate Appendix article.) |
| 8/17 | Record Sunday School Attendance: 2,043 (750% increase from fall 1993). |
| 9/28 | "Join the Church" Sunday (21 additions). |
| **10/19** | **Tenth Anniversary at Johns Creek location.** November Michael McCullar's book, *Basics of Theology*, published in-house. |
| 11/1 | First Singles' Conference; speaker Harold Ivan Smith. |
| 11/9 | "Join the Church" Sunday (18 additions). |
| 11/22 | Sean Smith in concert. |

12/13-14    *Christmas at Johns Creek* presented by Chancel Choir and Orchestra (4 presentations).

## 2004

January    JCBC went online with website: www.jcbc.org.

1/10    Glen Sloan recognized on 5th anniversary as Music Assistant/Pianist.

2/17    Roger Williams recognized on 5th anniversary as Minister of Pastoral Care.

2/29    "Six Weeks of Commitment" began.

March    Michael McCullar recognized for Outstanding Leadership in Christian Education by Congregational Life Department of Cooperative Baptist Fellowship.

3/8-10    William L. Self Preaching Lectures at McAfee School of Theology. Guest lecturer: Dr. William Hull, Research Professor, Samford University, Birmingham, Alabama.

3/14    Kathy Nichols Sanson ordained for ministerial service.

3/21    Chancel Choir and Orchestra presented Spring Celebration.

April    First started providing meals and fellowship at Memorial Drive Homeless Shelter.

4/4    "Demonstrate the Tithe" Day.

5/2    Youth Year-End Celebration becomes church-wide event. Unveiling of *Journeys Into Faith Vol. II*, Bob Lynn, editor (testimonies from 39 young adults).

6/27    *Celebrate America!* presented by Chancel Choir and Orchestra.

7/4    Dr. Self featured speaker on *Day1* radio program for first time; aired on more than 150 stations.

8/12    "Golden Club" Dinner (JCBC/Heritage Room).

8/15    Dr. Self featured speaker on *Day1* radio program.

**8/18    Building plans for Phase IV (Sanctuary) approved.** Tommy Boland, Chair of Building Committee.

9/12    Bob Cash recognized on 15th anniversary as Music Assistant/Organist.

| 9/19 | First annual "Spiritual Renewal" Weekend: Dr. Phil Lineberger, pulpit guest. |
| 9/26 | Michael McCullar recognized on 10<sup>th</sup> anniversary as Executive Pastor. Dr. Self featured speaker on *Day1* radio program. |
| 10/4 | Unveiling of *Journeys into Faith III*, Bob Lynn, editor (testimonies from 30 senior adults). |
| 10/6 | Michael McCullar's book, *Sessions with Corinthians*, was published by Smyth & Helwys. |
| 10/10 | "Mercer University" Day at JCBC; Guest speaker: Dr. Kirby Godsey, President. |
| 10/27 | First "Trunk or Treat" (church-wide annual event; supersedes Fall Festival). |
| 11/21 | "Join the Church" Sunday (16 additions). |
| 11/28 | Dr. Self featured speaker on *Day1* radio program. |
| 12/11-12 | *Christmas at Johns Creek* presented by Chancel Choir and Orchestra (4 presentations). |

## 2005

| 1/23 | Carl L. Tolbert, Jr., ordained for ministerial service. |
| February | Dr. Self and Everett Bennett selected as "Men of Forsyth" by *Forsyth County News*. |
| 2/21-23 | William L. Self Preaching Lectures at McAfee School of Theology. Guest lecturer: Rev. Joanna M. Adams, Pastor, Morningside Presbyterian Church, Atlanta, Georgia. |
| 2/26-27 | *Marriage Mechanics* Weekend. Guest speakers: Kirk & Gina Schreck. |
| **2/27** | ***Faith Forward IV* dedication service.** |
| 3/11-12 | First annual Women's Ministry Retreat at Brasstown Valley Resort with Kim Bolton, speaker. |
| **3/13** | ***Faith Forward IV* Information Sunday** Tom Jack, Chair. |
| 3/20 | Chancel Choir and Orchestra presentation: *Somebody's Praying Me Through*. |
| 3/27 | Easter: 3 morning services |

4/10, 17   Dr. Self featured speaker on *Day1* radio program, aired on more than 150 stations.

5/1   Jill Jenkins recognized on 10<sup>th</sup> anniversary as Minister to Children.

5/5   David White began as Minister of Pastoral Care.

5/12   ***Faith Forward IV* Special Event** (Capital Campaign).

5/24   Groundbreaking for Emory Johns Creek Hospital; Dr. Self led invocation.

**6/5**   ***Faith Forward IV* Commitment Day:** Goal: $10,000,000 (June 2005 – May 2008).

6/26   *Celebrate America!* presented by Chancel Choir and Orchestra.

6/26 - 7/1   Camp Rutledge (completed grades 8-12).

7/3   First "Casual Day" in church.

8/21   Unveiling of *Journeys into Faith IV*, Bob Lynn, editor (testimonies from 21 median adults).

8/24   *The Call* (church newsletter) went to 4-page format.

9/13   Ladies' Garden Club changed to JCBC Gardeners (to be more inclusive).

9/17-18   Spiritual Renewal weekend: Dr. Calvin A. Miller, pulpit guest.

**10/2**   **Steel beam-signing for Phase IV** (church members invited to sign one of two beams to go into new sanctuary; done in lieu of groundbreaking).

November   Series of Parenting Seminars. Ministerial staff prepared a CD titled *The Twelve Days of Christmas: Devotional Reflections for the Christmas Season* available free to church members and guests.

11/24   Georgia Baptist Convention severed relationship with Mercer University.

12/10-11   *Christmas at Johns Creek* presented by Chancel Choir and Orchestra (4 presentations).

12/18   Dr. Self featured speaker on *Day1* radio program, aired on more than 150 stations. Also, Dr. Self preached 13 weeks on Armed Forces Radio.

## 2006

| | |
|---|---|
| January | JCBC pictorial directory published. Senior Singers (senior choir) changed its name to The Master's Singers. |
| 1/21 | Men's Ministry Breakfast to kick-off Men's Small Groups (4 on different days of the week and in different locations. Study was *The Man in the Mirror* by Patrick Morley.) |
| 1/26-29 | First mission trip to Pearlington, Mississippi. |
| February | Jill Jenkins received CBF's 2006 Jack Naish Distinguished Christian Educator of the Year (national award), |
| 2/6-7 | William L. Self Preaching Lectures at McAfee School of Theology. Guest lecturer: Dr. Bryan Harbour, Pastor, First Baptist Church, Richardson, Texas. |
| 2/22 | Chancel Choir changed name to Sanctuary Choir. |
| 2/26 | "Six Weeks of Commitment" began. Debra Nolen Walters ordained for ministerial service. |
| March | Missions Liaison assigned from each adult Sunday School community. |
| 3/19 | *An Evening of Praise* presented by Sanctuary Choir and Orchestra. |
| 3/25-26 | 52 youth participated in March Missions Madness. |
| 4/30 | "Mercer Day" with pulpit guest: Bill Underwood, President-elect of Mercer University. |
| 5/7 | Unveiling of *Journeys into Faith V*, Bob Lynn, editor (testimonies from 36 median adults). |
| 5/23-26 | Helped host China Bible Exhibit at Second Ponce de Leon Baptist Church (one of three venues held in the U.S.) |
| 6/21-23 | 50 volunteers staffed registration at CBF General Assembly at World Congress Center. |
| 6/25 | *Celebrate America!* presented by Sanctuary Choir and Orchestra. |
| 7/2, 9 | Dr. Self featured speaker on *Day1* radio program, aired on more than 150 stations. |

8/22    Dr. Self attended McAfee's inaugural Founder's Day celebration.

9/10    Tammy Sullivan recognized on 5th anniversary as Minister to Preschool.

Jim Walls recognized on 5th anniversary as Minister to Youth.

9/16-17  Spiritual Renewal weekend: Dr. Calvin Miller, pulpit guest.

10/22   Tommy Boland recognized for serving 50 years as church treasurer.

10/28   David White recognized as Gardner-Webb Distinguished Graduate.

10/30   Michael McCullar's book, *Sessions with Timothy & Titus*, published by Smyth & Helwys.

**11/1    3:00 pm steeple and cross erected on new sanctuary.**

November Article in *Baptists Today*, "A Conversation with Bill Self."

11/4    Church-wide prayer event: 12 hours of prayer in Chapel.

11/5    Open House: Tour of new (unfinished) sanctuary; opportunity to sign walls and stage floor.

12/9-10  *Christmas at Johns Creek* presented by Chancel Choir and Orchestra (4 presentations).

12/17   Dr. Self recognized on 15th anniversary as Senior Pastor.

## 2007

From new mission statement: focus this year: worship

1/7     "The Gathering" began (Youth worship for grades 6-12 at 11:00 on Sunday morning).

1/21    Discipleship group for Youth began meeting on Sunday evenings.

1/28    R. David White ordained for ministerial service.

1/31    Mission Statement and Core Beliefs and Values approved in church conference.

2/10    Sweetheart Dinner.

| 2/19-20 | William L. Self Preaching Lectures at McAfee School of Theology. Guest lecturer: Dr. Thomas G. Long, Bandy Professor of Preaching, Candler School of Theology, Emory University. |
| 2/24 | Inspirational Breakfast with Ronda Rich, guest speaker. |
| March | Missions Month. $27,000 given for CBF Global Missions. |
| 3/8 | Blessing of the Cross (in the baptistry of new sanctuary). |
| 3/17 | All-day Scripture reading in new sanctuary. |
| **3/18** | **First Sunday in the new sanctuary.** |
| 3/25 | New Sunday School schedule with only one session (at 9:45) and no Express Sunday School. |
| 4/8, 15 | Dr. Self featured speaker on *Day1* radio program, aired on more than 150 stations. |
| 4/11 | First meeting with Susan Beaumont with Alban Institute (for church survey). |
| 4/16-20 | Dr. Self preached at International Congress on Preaching, Cambridge, England. |
| 4/28 | Special dinner concert with Kyle Matthews, Christian recording artist. Children's talent show held in conjunction with the concert. |
| 5/1 | Church address changed from 7500 to 6910 McGinnis Ferry Road. |
| **5/6** | **Open House for Phase IV.** |
| 5/12 | Mother/Daughter Tea. |
| 5/16 | Daniel Stockum ordained for ministerial service. |
| 5/27 | First Memorial Day recognition of church members who died since January 2006. |
| 6/18 | Fratelli Ruffatti pipe organ arrived from Italy. |
| 6/24 | *Celebrate America!* presented by Sanctuary Choir and Orchestra. |
| 7/15 | Unveiling of *Journeys into Faith VI*, Bob Lynn, editor (testimonies from 24 median adults). |
| 8/15 | First Strategic Planning Initiative Steering Committee Meeting (see separate Appendix article). |

| | |
|---|---|
| 8/23 | Golden Club now has 59 active couples. |
| 9/16 | Spiritual Renewal: Dr. Tom Long, pulpit guest. |
| 9/24-28 | First mission trip to Weimar, Germany. |
| 9/30 | Free concert with "In the Round." |
| 10/9 | Dr. Self received Distinguished Alumni Award from Candler School of Theology for most service to the profession (only non-Methodist to receive this award). |
| 10/21 | Dedication of Fratelli Ruffatti pipe organ with Dr. Joyce Jones, guest organist. |
| 10/28 | Barbara Brown recognized on 15th anniversary as Ministry Assistant/Senior Pastor. |
| November | First time to assemble shoe boxes for Operation Christmas Child, a ministry of Franklin Graham's Samaritan Purse |
| Nov/Dec | Response to severe drought (spaced baptism to conserve water, ceased coffee service during Sunday School, etc.) |
| 11/2 | Mark Lowry in concert. |
| 11/10 | Prayer vigil (8:30-5:00) with focus on drought and commitment (pledging). |
| 12/2 | First annual Advent Lunch. |
| 12/8-9 | *Christmas at Johns Creek* presented by Chancel Choir and Orchestra (3 presentations). |
| 12/12 | Full Strategy Planning Survey Report in *The Call*. |

## 2008

From new mission statement: focus this year: evangelism and missions.

| | |
|---|---|
| 1/26 | Men's Ministry Kick-off Breakfast with Jeremy Lewis, Director of CBF's Rural Poverty Initiative, guest speaker. |
| 1/27 | Dr. Self featured speaker on *Day1* radio program, aired on more than 150 stations. |
| 1/28 | Tammy Holland Sullivan ordained for ministerial service. |
| 1/30–2/1 | New Baptist Covenant Meeting: Georgia World Congress Center. Dr. Self was a speaker and church members volunteered to help with registration. Shuttle service |

|   |   |
|---|---|
|  | provided by the church. (Organizer and Chair, Dr. Jimmy Allen, a member of JCBC.) |
| February | *ONE* Campaign: each member encouraged to bring one guest to church. |
| 2/6 | Church vote to change Missions budget to be split between CBF Global Missions and various missions endeavors supported through our Missions Committee. |
| 2/7 | First time to serve monthly meals to No Longer Bound (later served twice a month). |
| 2/8-9 | First offered "Created by God" (grades 5, 6 with parent), a study of human sexuality, led by Jill Jenkins and Jim Walls. |
| 2/10 | Unveiling of *Journeys into Faith VII*, Bob Lynn, editor (testimonies from 26 single adults). First "Sweet Tea," ministry for cancer patients, survivors, and care-givers. |
| 2/11 | William L. Self Preaching Lectures at McAfee School of Theology. Guest lecturer: Dr. Amy-Jill Levine, Professor of New Testament Studies at Vanderbilt University Divinity School, Department of Religious Studies, and Graduate Department of Religion, Nashville, Tennessee. |
| March | Missions Month. Goal: $38,000. Total given: $60,263. |
| 3/6-9 | First of 12 mission trips to Perry County, Alabama. |
| **3/9** | **Dedication service of new sanctuary.** |
|  | Pulpit Guest:  Neville Callam, General Secretary of Baptist World Alliance. |
| 3/30 | First "Exploring JCBC," an on-going 4-week class, especially for new church members (formerly New Member Orientation). |
| 4/15 | Michael McCullar's book, *A Christian's Guide to Islam,* published by Smyth & Helwys. |
| 4/19-26 | First mission trip to Istanbul to assist Elam College in their new location of ministry training (14 participated). |
| 4/27 | *May Jesus Christ Be Praised* presented by Sanctuary Choir and Orchestra (JCBC'sfirst professionally recorded compact disc). |

| | |
|---|---|
| 5/1 | Glenn Crosthwait recognized on 10th anniversary as Minister of Music. |
| 5/2-3 | Strategic Planning Committee summit at Simpsonwood Conference Center (66 participated). |
| June | Article on Sweet Tea Ministry in *CountyLine* magazine. |
| 6/1-4 | Vacation Bible School had 550 participants! (Goal was to buy 1 water buffalo for India but offerings provided for 4 buffaloes, some pigs and chickens!) |
| 6/16 | Honey bee colony removed from church attic (approximately 10,000 bees!) |
| 6/29 | *Celebrate America!* presented by Sanctuary Choir and Orchestra. |
| 7/23 | First JCBC Job Networking group meeting (held every other week). |
| 8/10 | Fall Women's Ministry Kick-off Luncheon with guest speaker Grace Powell Freeman, Director of Global Missions Operations of CBF. |
| 9/6 | Prayer vigil (9:00-5:00) focus on personal spiritual growth. |
| 9/7 | Spiritual Renewal Sunday: Anne Graham Lotz, pulpit guest. |
| 9/20-27 | First mission trip to Brussels to assist the Arab Baptist Church in the Arab sector. |
| 9/28 | "Prove the Tithe" Sunday. |
| Sept/Oct | Interview with Drs. Bill Self and Dee Shelnutt, Pastor of Johns Creek United Methodist Church, in *CountyLine* magazine. |
| 10/4 | Collected 3,000 children's books for Marion (Perry County), Alabama. |
| 11/2 | Pulpit guest, Billy Kim (former President of Baptist World Alliance); Korean Children's Choir sang. |
| 11/22 | First time to collect bicycles for North Fulton Community Charities' Santa Shop. |
| 12/13-14 | *Christmas at Johns Creek* presented by Chancel Choir and Orchestra (3 presentations). |

12/17      Family Christmas Concert with Kyle Matthews.

**2009**
From new mission statement: focus this year: discipleship and personal spiritual growth.

1/10       Glen Sloan recognized on 10th anniversary as Music Assistant/Pianist.

1/11       Adult Sunday School now at 21 communities.

1/12       Michael McCullar & Rickey Letson's book, *Sessions with Mark,* published by Smyth & Helwys.

1/14-18    First mission trip to Presidio, Texas.

1/25       Strategy Planning Report presented to church (see separate Appendix article).

2/1        Weekly newsletter went monthly in print, still online weekly.

2/8        Unveiling of *Journeys into Faith VIII*, Bob Lynn, editor (testimonies from 26 median adults).

2/16, 17   William L. Self Preaching Lectures at McAfee School of Theology. Guest lecturer: Rev. Chuck Poole, Senior Pastor, Northminster Baptist Church, Jackson, Mississippi.

**3/1**    ***Faith for Future Generations*** (Capital Campaign for debt retirement) kick-off; Tom Jack, Chair. Goal: $3,900,000.

Spring     First time entire Adult Sunday School had single topic focus: Discipleship.

3/29       Spring concert *The Song of Easter* presented by Sanctuary Choir and Orchestra.

4/12       Easter attendance over 2,400.

May        Jill Jenkins featured in *Baptists Today* with article about children's Sunday School.

5/4        H1N1 virus rampant in U.S.; enhanced disinfecting of door handles, hand rails, children's equipment and restrooms.

5/12-17    First mission trip to Plaquemines Parish, Louisiana.

| | |
|---|---|
| 5/22 | Dr. Self preached at *Festival of Homiletics*, an annual national preaching conference. |
| 5/31-6/3 | VBS record attendance: 735. Raised $4,420 for Watering Malawi. |
| June | Michael McCullar's book, *Stewardship: A Way of Living,* published by NextSunday. |
| 6/28 | *Celebrate America!* presented by Sanctuary Choir and Orchestra. |
| 7/28 | "JCBC Reads" book club started. |
| 8/13 | Michael McCullar began his *FaithBlog*. |
| 9/13 | Spiritual Renewal: Bill Curry, guest speaker. |
| Fall | First offsite Sunday School session (at Alta Senior Living). |
| 9/17-18 | 20th annual Senior Adult Retreat at Georgia Baptist Conference Center in Toccoa. |
| 9/20 | Bob Cash recognized on 20th anniversary as Music Assistant/Organist. |
| 9/23 | Pastoral Succession Plan presented to church. |
| 9/27 | Michael McCullar recognized on 15th anniversary as Executive Pastor. |
| November | Second article on Sweet Tea Ministry in *CountyLine* magazine (also on cover). |
| 11/1 | First WidowCare luncheon (spawned *Connections* and WITs). |
| 11/17 | First weekly meeting of Hook & Needle Guild. |
| 11/22 | Dr. Self featured speaker on *Day1* radio program, aired on more than 150 stations. |
| 12/4 | Jim Walls graduated with a Doctorate of Ministry from Beeson Divinity School. |
| 12/12-13 | *Christmas at Johns Creek* presented by Chancel Choir and Orchestra (3 presentations). |

## 2010

| | |
|---|---|
| January | *Small Steps 2010* introduced to promote our commitment to our Christian walk. |

(Quarterly focuses: Scripture reading, Fruit of the Spirit, prayer, and stewardship.)

| | |
|---|---|
| 1/5 | First meeting of Bridge Club. |
| 1/27 | Pastoral Succession Resolution adopted. |
| | Comprehensive witnessing strategy called "The Force of 70" approved; Bob Lynn, coordinator. |
| 2/25 | First luncheon for Connections. |
| | Mark Lowry in concert. |
| 3/10-13 | First of 4 mission trips to Haiti. |
| | First of 12 mission trips to Dominican Republic. |
| 3/19 | Sean and Leigh Anne Tuohy, guest speakers (inspiration for movie *The Blind Side*). |
| 4/2 | Good Friday: Youth presented the first "Stations of the Cross," a 30-minute visual walk. |
| 4/5-6 | William L. Self Preaching Lectures at McAfee School of Theology. Guest lecturer: Dr. Robert Smith, Jr., Associate Professor of Divinity, Beeson Divinity School, Samford University, Birmingham, Alabama. |
| 4/21 | Discipleship Task Force 3-year plan adopted; Angie Kleckley, coordinator. |
| | Ben McDade licensed for Christian ministry. |
| 5/2 | David White recognized on 5th anniversary as Minister of Pastoral Care. |
| 5/3 | Ed Rivers began as Recreation Director. |
| 5/6 | Hosted Jubal Chorus, 250-voice choir of Ministers of Music and church musicians. |
| 6/6 | Jill Jenkins recognized on 15th anniversary as Minister to Preschool and Children. |
| 6/6-9 | VBS; missions offering over $4,500. |
| 6/27 | *Celebrate America!* presented by Sanctuary Choir and Orchestra. |
| August | Gym closed for installation of new floor. New prayer room opened daily (7:00 a.m. to 8:00 p.m.). |

| | |
|---|---|
| 8/8 | Sunday School year kick-off with Black Hawk Helicoptor landing on soccer field. Unveiling of *Journeys into Faith IX*, Bob Lynn, editor (testimonies from 30 young adults). |
| 9/10-12 | Spiritual Renewal: Dr. Charley Reeb, pulpit guest. |
| 9/29 | Plans presented for renovating the pre-school and children's area. |
| 10/20 | Online Pledging software fully operational. |
| 10/31 | First Spirit Day (wore favorite team colors to church in support of our Recreation Ministry). |
| 12/11-12 | *Christmas at Johns Creek* presented by Chancel Choir and Orchestra (2 presentations). |

## 2011

| | |
|---|---|
| January | JCBC members encouraged to read *The Story* during the calendar year. Books modified for adults, teens, and children were available. |
| 2/6 | First annual Super Bowl Breakfast; Clay Shiver, guest speaker. |
| 2/10 | Dr. Self featured in *Baptists Today* (newspaper). |
| 2/20 | Dr. Self announced his desire to initiate the church's pastoral succession plan. |
| 2/28-3/1 | William L. Self Preaching Lectures at McAfee School of Theology. Guest lecturer: Dr. Eugene Lowry, William K. McElvaney Professor of Preaching Emeritus, St. Paul School of Theology, Kansas City, Missouri. |
| March | JCBC pictorial directory published. |
| 3/7 | First "Blessing of the Children" ceremony in worship. |
| 3/20 | Unveiling of *Journeys into Faith X*, Bob Lynn, editor (testimonies from 30 young adults). |
| 4/22 | Good Friday: Youth presented "Stations of the Cross," a 30-minute visual walk. |
| 4/27 | Senior Pastor Search Committee approved: Tom Benberg, Phil Brown, Melissa Floyd, Danny Henderson, Tom Jack, Angie Kleckley, Sanford McAllister, Kirby Pate (chair), Trudy Woodard. |

| | |
|---|---|
| 5/4 | First JCBC Prayer Walk (self-guided, twelve stations, in conjunction with National Day of Prayer). |
| 5/22 | Prayer vigil for Pastor Search Committee. |
| 6/11 | First Biker's Club (motor cycles) ride; held twice a year. |
| 6/26 | *Celebrate America!* presented by Sanctuary Choir and Orchestra. |
| 9/4 | Jim Walls recognized on 10th anniversary as Minister of Youth. |
| 9/10 | Prayer vigil for Spiritual Renewal (10:00-3:00). |
| 9/11 | Spiritual Renewal: Dr. Robert Smith, pulpit guest. |
| 9/14 | Senior Pastor Survey distributed to membership. Beth Irwin began as Children's Music Director. |
| 9/25 | First "New & Expecting Parents" Breakfast. |
| October | Members solicited to write Advent devotional guide. Dr. Self's tenth book, *Surviving the Stained-Glass Jungle,* published by Mercer University Press. |
| 11/6-7 | Hosted CBF/Georgia Annual Meeting. |
| 11/17-19 | New Baptist Covenant meeting (at Second Ponce de Leon Baptist Church). |
| December | Michael McCullar's book, *2012 Annual Bible Study Guide for Moderate Baptists* (on Book of *James*), published by Smyth & Helwys. |
| 12/10-11 | *Christmas at Johns Creek* presented by Chancel Choir and Orchestra (3 presentations). |
| 12/11 | Dr. Self recognized on 20th anniversary as Senior Pastor. First "Angel Breakfast" for preschool families (over 250 attended). |

## 2012

| | |
|---|---|
| January | Testimonies of 12 members uploaded to YouTube channel named *JCBC video* (part of the Force of 70). |
| 2/12 | Children wore red for Valentine's Day and "Healthy Heart" month. |
| 2/22 | Devotional guides for season of Lent were made available for individual study. |

| | |
|---|---|
| 2/25 | Johns Creek Symphony Orchestra joins JCBC Sanctuary Choir for Beethovan concert. |
| 2/27-28 | William L. Self Preaching Lectures at McAfee School of Theology. Guest lecturer: Dr. Brian McLaren, noted author, speaker, activist, public theologian and former English professor and preacher. |
| March | Special prayer opportunities from 9:00-9:30 on Sunday mornings; focus: Pastor Search Committee and missions ministry. Annual Missions Month offering: $85,000+. |
| 3/9 | Hosted Ernie Haase and Signature Sound in concert. First Parents' Night Out (Youth fundraiser to raise money for mission trip to Dominican Republic). |
| 3/16-18 | JCBC hosted Georgia's *March Missions Madness* for youth (250+ participated). |
| 3/28 | Vote to approve Term Loan Modification for debt reduction. |
| 4/15-29 | First Peer Pressure seminar (grades 5). |
| 6/24 | *Celebrate America!* presented by Sanctuary Choir and Orchestra. |
| 7/16-20 | First JCBC Music Week (grades 1-6). |
| 8/1 | Preschool Weekday Program approved to begin in the fall 2013. |
| 8/12 | New Sunday School year kick-off, "Soaring to New Heights;" Drs. Self & McCullar went up in a hot air balloon! |
| Fall | Adult Small Groups: Men now have 5 groups; ladies have 4 groups. Adult Sunday School: 22 communities + 1 offsite. |
| 9/9 | Spiritual Renewal: Dr. Eugene Lowry, guest, presenting *Faith & Jazz*. |
| 9/23 | Rev. Shaun Michael King preached in view of a call; unanimous vote to approve. |
| 10/28 | World Series Breakfast, guest speaker Darrel Chaney. (Wear your team attire!) |

| 11/4 | Introduction of Karen Keyes, Preschool Director of new program beginning 2013. |
|---|---|
| 11/10 | Annual bike drive for NFCC; collected 600+ bikes, trikes and scooters. |
| 11/11 | 500+ shoe boxes filled for Operation Christmas Child, a ministry of Franklin Graham's Samaritan's Purse. |
| 11/16 | Rev. Shaun King began as Senior Pastor. |
| 12/2 | Dr. Self's final sermon: *It Is Finished* (John 19:30); promoted to Senior Pastor Emeritus. |
| 12/8-9 | *Christmas at Johns Creek* presented by Chancel Choir and Orchestra (3 presentations). |

## 2013

| January | Hospitality Hubs placed in church rotundas for guests' convenience. Newcomer Meal (quarterly) introduced; formerly "Guests' Luncheon." "4D" introduced; formerly "New Members Orientation." Parking lot attendants and portico point people used weekly. |
|---|---|
| January | Payment on long-term debt brought balance to below $10 million. |
| **1/6** | **Rev. Shaun King preached first sermon as Senior Pastor.** |
| 2/10 | Installation service for Rev. Shaun King as 22$^{nd}$ Senior Pastor. |
| 2/25-26 | William L. Self Preaching Lectures at McAfee School of Theology. Guest lecturer: Rev. Doug Dortch, Pastor of Mountain Brook Baptist Church, Birmingham, Alabama. |
| 3/3 | Youth Ministry Spaghetti Luncheon (fundraiser to support the third Dominican Republic team). |
| 5/12 | Glenn Crosthwait recognized on 15$^{th}$ anniversary as Minister of Music. Rev. King's first Parent/Child Dedication (Presley Tetterton was dedicated). |
| June | Michael McCullar's book, *Basics of Theology,* republished by Smyth & Helwys. |

| | |
|---|---|
| 6/23 | *Celebrate America!* presented by Sanctuary Choir and Orchestra. |
| 8/11 | Theme for the year: iMAGINEXT. |
| | JCBC website re-developed. |
| 9/3 | JCBC Preschool (Tuesday to Friday) opened. |
| 9/22 | Chris Moore began as Minister to Youth. |
| 10/20 | 20th anniversary celebration. |

# CHURCH OFFICERS

| | President | Vice President | Secretary | Asst. Secretary | Treasurer | Asst. Treasurers | Trustees |
|---|---|---|---|---|---|---|---|
| Oct 1991-Sep 1992 | Dr. Bill Self | Richard Eason | Norma King | | Tommy Boland | Claude Head | Bob Harris, Cora Lee Hyde, Lillian Henderson |
| Oct 1992-Sep 1993 | Dr. Bill Self | Robert McFarland | Norma King | | Tommy Boland | Claude Head | Cora Lee Hyde, Lillian Henderson, Richard Eason |
| Oct 1993-Sep 1994 | Dr. Bill Self | Grant Curtis | Barbara Brown | | Tommy Boland | Claude Head | Cora Lee Hyde, Lillian Henderson, Richard Eason |
| Oct 1994-Sep 1995 | Dr. Bill Self | Tom Jack | Barbara Brown | | Tommy Boland | Claude Head | Cora Lee Hyde, Lillian Henderson, Richard Eason |
| Oct 1995-Sep 1996 | Dr. Bill Self | Richard Eason | Barbara Brown | | Tommy Boland | Claude Head | Cora Lee Hyde, Lillian Henderson, Richard Eason |
| Oct 1996-Sep 1997 | Dr. Bill Self | John Dixon | Barbara Brown | | Tommy Boland | Claude Head | *Trustees were no longer needed after the property was sold.* |
| Oct 1997-Sep 1998 | Dr. Bill Self | Way Kidd | Barbara Brown | | Tommy Boland | Claude Head | |
| Oct 1998-Sep 1999 | Dr. Bill Self | Edwin Boland | Russell Graves | | Tommy Boland | Claude Head | |
| Oct 1999-Sep 2000 | Dr. Bill Self | Keith Compton | Russell Graves | | Tommy Boland | Claude Head | |

| By-Laws Revised August 23, 2000, to change to calendar year. | | | | | | |
|---|---|---|---|---|---|---|
| Oct 2000- Dec 2001 | Dr. Bill Self | Kirby Pate | Russell Graves | | Tommy Boland | Claude Head | |
| 2002 | Dr. Bill Self | Dale Stone | Russell Graves | | Tommy Boland | Phil Brown, Richard Eason, Claude Head | |
| 2003 | Dr. Bill Self | Norman Parker | Russell Graves | | Tommy Boland | Phil Brown, Richard Eason, Claude Head | |
| 2004 | Dr. Bill Self | Everett Bennett | John E. Hudson | | Tommy Boland | Phil Brown, Richard Eason, Claude Head | |
| 2005 | Dr. Bill Self | Ray Johnson | John E. Hudson | Barbara Brown | Tommy Boland | Phil Brown, Richard Eason, Claude Head | |
| 2006 | Dr. Bill Self | Danny Henderson | John E. Hudson | Barbara Brown | Tommy Boland | Phil Brown, Richard Eason, Claude Head | |
| 2007 | Dr. Bill Self | Robbie Hamrick | John E. Hudson | Barbara Brown | Tommy Boland | Richard Eason, Mike Ernst, Claude Head | |
| 2008 | Dr. Bill Self | Marsha Janofsky | John E. Hudson | Barbara Brown | Tommy Boland | Richard Eason, Mike Ernst, Claude Head | |
| 2009 | Dr. Bill Self | Bo Haywood | John E. Hudson | Barbara Brown | Tommy Boland | Richard Eason, Mike Ernst, Claude | |

| | | | | | | | |
|---|---|---|---|---|---|---|---|
| | | | | | | Head, Greg Kennedy | |
| 2010 | Dr. Bill Self | Kirby Pate | John E. Hudson | Barbara Brown | Richard Eason | Mike Ernst, Greg Kennedy, Bob Prator | |
| 2011 | Dr. Bill Self | John Zwald | John E. Hudson | Barbara Brown | Richard Eason | Mike Ernst, Greg Kennedy, Bob Prator | |
| 2012 | Dr. Bill Self | Bob Prator | John E. Hudson | Barbara Brown | Richard Eason | Mike Ernst, Bret Hegi, Bob Prator | |
| 2013 | Rev. Shaun King | Tom Waller | John E. Hudson | Barbara Brown | Richard Eason | Mike Ernst, Bret Hegi, Bob Prator | |

# PASTOR'S COUNCIL

The church by-laws, completely revised and approved on August 23, 2000, provided for a Pastor's Council which would assist the pastor in preparing and reviewing plans, special events, or other matters that impact the total church program or the future of the church. The Senior Pastor shall serve as chairperson of this council. The Pastor's Council shall be made up of persons who hold the following positions:

- ❖ Deacon Chairperson
- ❖ Stewardship Committee Chairperson
- ❖ Sunday School Director
- ❖ Church Treasurer

The Pastor's Council members are as follows:

| | Senior Pastor<br>Stewardship Chair | Executive Pastor<br>Sunday School Director | Deacon Chair<br>Treasurer |
|---|---|---|---|
| 2001 | Bill Self<br>Dean Rydquist | Michael McCullar<br>Tom Jack | Kirby Pate<br>Tommy Boland |
| 2002 | Bill Self<br>Nathan West | Michael McCullar<br>Tom Jack | Dale Stone<br>Tommy Boland |
| 2003 | Bill Self<br>Steve Pickens | Michael McCullar<br>Tom Jack | Norman Parker<br>Tommy Boland |
| 2004 | Bill Self<br>Mike Goodman | Michael McCullar<br>Tom Jack | Everett Bennett<br>Tommy Boland |
| 2005 | Bill Self<br>Mike Ernst | Michael McCullar<br>Tom Jack | Richard Eason<br>Tommy Boland |
| 2006 | Bill Self<br>Mike Ernst | Michael McCullar<br>Tom Jack | Danny Henderson<br>Tommy Boland |
| 2007 | Bill Self<br>Mike Goodman | Michael McCullar<br>Tom Jack | Robbie Hamrick<br>Tommy Boland |

| 2008 | Bill Self<br>Bob Prator | Michael McCullar<br>Tom Jack | Marsha Janofsky<br>Tommy Boland |
|------|-------------------------|------------------------------|--------------------------------|
| 2009 | Bill Self<br>Mike Goodman | Michael McCullar<br>Tom Jack | Bo Haywood<br>Tommy Boland |
| 2010 | Bill Self<br>Mike Goodman | Michael McCullar<br>Tom Jack | Kirby Pate<br>Richard Eason |
| 2011 | Bill Self<br>Phil Brown | Michael McCullar<br>Tom Jack | John Zwald<br>Richard Eason |
| 2012 | Bill Self<br>Phil Brown | Michael McCullar<br>Tom Jack | Bob Prator<br>Richard Eason |
| 2013 | Shaun King<br>Kevin Tolbert | Michael McCullar<br>Tom Jack | Tom Waller<br>Richard Eason |

# JOHNS CREEK BAPTIST CHURCH STATISTICS

| Year-end | Total Membership | Resident Members | Baptisms | Other Additions | SS Enrollment | Budget | Facilities Budget |
|---|---|---|---|---|---|---|---|
| 1991 | 1,744 | 889 | 8 | 14 | 983 | $575,000 | Debt Retirement $50,000 |
| 1992 | 1,790 | 943 | 19 | 99 | 906 | 501,000 | 50,000 |
| 1993 | 1,799 | 952 | 15 | 61 | 652 | 587,500 | JCBC New Bldg. Fund 150,000 |
| 1994 | 2,162 | 1,298 | 101 | 341 | 845 | 686,600 | 150,000 |
| 1995 | 2,363 | 1,499 | 53 | 220 | 1,251 | 1,000,000 | 200,000 |
| 1996 | 2,445 | 1,523 | 52 | 244 | 1,665 | 1,300,000 | 200,000 |
| 1997 | 2,677 | 1,696 | 101 | 211 | 1,783 | 1,700,000 | 200,000 |
| 1998 | 2,864 | 1,842 | 88 | 230 | 1,932 | 1,950,000 | 250,000 |
| 1999 | 3,105 | 2,018 | 103 | 249 | 2,109 | 2,400,000 | 250,000 |
| 2000 | 3,357 | 2,226 | 121 | 203 | 2,386 | 3,230,000 | 250,000 |
| 2001 | 3,572 | 2,381 | 111 | 238 | 2,888 | 3,400,000 | 250,000 |
| 2002 | 3,709 | 2,464 | 86 | 144 | 2,563 | 3,765,000 | 250,000 |
| 2003 | 3,893 | 2,590 | 122 | 162 | 2,546 | 3,990,000 | 250,000 |
| 2004 | 4,010 | 2,658 | 101 | 124 | 2,624 | 4,390,000 | 250,000 |
| 2005 | 4,071 | 2,637 | 64 | 88 | 2,340 | 4,640,000 | 250,000 |
| 2006 | 4,157 | 2,524 | 64 | 115 | 2,547 | 4,460,000 | 250,000 |
| 2007 | 4,266 | 2,580 | 54 | 103 | 2,592 | 4,640,000 | 250,000 |
| 2008 | 4,351 | 2,554 | 49 | 125 | 2,300 | 4,978,000 | 275,000 |

| 2009 | 4,441 | 2,619 | 73 | 95 | 2,227 | 4,550,000 | 275,000 |
| 2010 | 4,475 | 2,656 | 41 | 83 | 2,152 | 4,390,000 | 275,000 |
| 2011 | 4,650 | 2,722 | 76 | 73 | 2,220 | 4,390,000 | Facilities revitalization 250,000 |
| 2012 | 4,613 | 2,753 | 64 | 60 | 2,348 | 4,200,000 | Debt transition fund 250,000 |

# FACILITIES

**PHASE I (Chapel, Education space, Offices, parking lot and addition); completed 1993**

| | | |
|---|---|---|
| *Size: | 27,600 square feet Total cost: | $ 2,823,229 |
| Staff: | Dr. William L. Self, Pastor | |
| | Larry E. Jones, Minister of Education | |
| | Gregory K. Walton, Minister of Music | |

Building committee members:

| | |
|---|---|
| Thomas E. Boland, Chair | Melba Franklin, Vice Chair |
| T. Edwin Boland, Jr. | Chester C. King |
| Edith Bond | Robert L. Prator |

**PHASE II (Education space, additional parking, and additional 8 acres of land); completed 1997**

| | | |
|---|---|---|
| *Size: | 35,400 square feet    Total cost: | $ 4,445,707 |
| Staff: | Dr. William L. Self, Pastor | |
| | Dr. Michael D. McCullar, Minister of Education & Administration | |
| | Gregory K. Walton, Minister of Music | |
| | Donald B. Deavers, Minister of Youth | |
| | Jill A. Jenkins, Minister of Children | |

Building committee members:

Thomas E. Boland, Chair

| | |
|---|---|
| Keith L. Compton | Kirby E. Pate |
| Melba L. Franklin | Robert L. Prator |
| Tom E. Jack | Gail V. Sawyer |

**PHASE III (Family Life Center, Main Foyer, Offices); completed 2000**

| | | |
|---|---|---|
| *Size: | 78,000 square feet    Total cost: | $14,078,476 |
| Staff: | Dr. William L. Self, Senior Pastor | |
| | Dr. Michael McCullar, Executive Pastor | |
| | R. Clif Anderson, Minister of Recreation | |
| | Lee C. Bates, Associate Minister of Music | |
| | Glenn Crosthwait, Minister of Music | |
| | Jill A. Jenkins, Minister of Preschool & Children | |
| | Melissa P. Lewis, Associate Minister of Preschool & Children | |
| | Stephen B. Prevatte, Minister to Adults | |
| | Mark R. Sauls, Business Manager | |
| | Ben T. Vogler, Minister to Youth | |

Roger P. Williams, Minister of Pastoral Care

Building committee members:

| | |
|---|---|
| Thomas E. Boland, Chair | Robert W. (Butch) Nicholson |
| Keith L. Compton | Norman C. Parker |
| Tom E. Jack | Kirby E. Pate |
| Sue E. Kay | Carl W. Tolbert |

## PHASE IV (Sanctuary, Music Suite, Youth Suite); completed 2007

*Size:  62,050 square feet    Total cost:    $24,570,276 (including pipe organ)

Staff:    Dr. William L. Self, Senior Pastor
Dr. Michael D. McCullar, Executive Pastor
Glenn A. Crosthwait, Minister of Music
E. Michele Deriso, Church Administrator
Jill A. Jenkins, Minister to Children
Rickey A. Letson, Minister to Adults
Perry A. McCain, Associate Minister of Music
Tammy H. Sullivan, Minister to Preschool
Jim W. Walls, Minister to Youth
R. David White, Minister of Pastoral Care

Building committee members:
Thomas E. Boland, Chair

| | |
|---|---|
| W. Everett Bennett | Leslie C. Morgan |
| Tom E. Jack | Kirby E. Pate |
| Robert L. Lynn | D. Dale Stone |

**Total    203,050 square feet    Total cost:    $45,917,688**

* JCBC Summary of Building Projects (7/28/2009)

# MISSION STATEMENTS, CORE BELIEFS AND VALUES

In 1865 as Atlanta was recovering from the effects of the Civil War, a small group of Baptists in the Chamblee area formed the Corinth Baptist Church. In 1920 the church was renamed Chamblee Baptist Church and, in 1950, became the First Baptist Church of Chamblee. Forty-three years later the church relocated to a new ministry opportunity in the burgeoning area of Johns Creek. Through a grant of land and an invitation to begin a new ministry in the region, Johns Creek Baptist Church opened its doors on October 17, 1993. Since its inception in 1865, this church has, regardless of location, upheld the classic values and beliefs of Baptists. This document is a result of our commitment to those Baptist principles and to God's Kingdom.

The following sections outline the theological foundations and beliefs of Johns Creek Baptist Church. Included is a Mission Statement, plus the Core Beliefs and Core Values of the church. The Mission Statement succinctly expresses the aims of the church to promote worship, evangelism and personal spiritual growth. These will also provide annual themes for upcoming years. The Core Beliefs form the theological "absolutes" of the church and are held to be non-negotiable to basic Christian doctrine. The Core Values are the unique aspects of Johns Creek Baptist Church that combine to create a ministry distinctness among Christian congregations.

## MISSION STATEMENT

We exist to reach up through the worship of God
We exist to reach out through the sharing of our faith and our service to God
We exist to reach in through Bible study and building Christian community

# CORE BELIEFS

God is the loving Creator and deserves our worship;
Jesus Christ is God's Son and everyone needs to know Him as Savior;
The Holy Spirit is God's presence in every Christian;
The Bible is God's inspired word for our lives;
Christians should seek to grow in faith, practice their faith, and share their faith so that
others may know Jesus as both Savior and Lord;
Johns Creek Baptist Church is part of the body of Christ here on earth.

# CORE VALUES

We value meaningful worship through preaching, prayer, scripture reading, varied musical styles, and other expressions of our faith. Corporate worship at Johns Creek Baptist Church includes the following elements: choirs, orchestra, organ and piano, and congregational participation. Youth worship is also featured, as is a special Children's worship education tract.

We value life-changing spiritual growth through Christian education by providing Sunday morning and weekly Bible study and Christian growth options for all ages. These include age-appropriate opportunities for preschool, children, teenagers, and relevant studies for adults.

We value Christian community by creating and sustaining relationships in order to provide care and support for one another. We encourage involvement and participation in care-group ministries through the Sunday School, music ministry, age-group programs, and other established small groups.

We value the reality that all things belong to God and, as God's followers, we are to share generously our God-given resources through the church. This is done through Biblical stewardship principles that include one's time, abilities and material blessings. We value God's ability, as demonstrated in scripture, to call both men and women to any task in the work of God's Kingdom. This includes service through vocational ministry, the ministry of deacons, and other areas of ministry.

We value church membership as a sign of our commitment to God and the local church.

The primary way a person becomes a church member is through public profession of faith in Jesus Christ, followed by baptism. Christians may join by transferring  membership from another Baptist congregation, or by stating their faith experience through a non-Baptist Christian denomination, including baptism by immersion.

We value each person's freedom to take part in the theological journey and to share with
others their own perspective and ideas. As a church we seek to establish a safe environment through which learning and thinking about scripture, theology and faith practices combine for progressive personal spiritual growth.

We value sharing the love of God by word and deed throughout the world. To this end, we support missions through education, participation and financial support.

We value sharing the Gospel as individuals and as a church so everyone may have the opportunity to enter into a personal relationship with Jesus Christ.

# MISSION STATEMENT HISTORY

**May 19, 1993 (Date of approval by church in conference)**

The Mission of the Johns Creek Baptist Church is to proclaim the message of Jesus Christ in order to lead individuals to faith in Him as Savior, and to provide:

- celebrative worship and Christian growth opportunities;
- needs-oriented ministries and mission involvement through the community;
- wholesome regional fellowship of excellent spiritual nurture and support.

**February 22, 1995 (Date of approval by church in conference)**

The above mission statement was amended to add the underlined phrase: "…needs-oriented ministries and mission involvement through the community <u>and the world</u>…."

**January 31, 2007 (Date of approval by church in conference)**

We exist to reach up through the worship of God.
We exist to reach out through the sharing of our faith and our service to God.

We exist to reach in through Bible study and building Christian community.

# DEACONS AT JOHNS CREEK BAPTIST CHURCH

The New Testament word for "deacon" means "servant." The very meaning of the word "servant" gives the best statement as to the nature of the deacon role. Deacons are selected and called by God and chosen by the church. They are dedicated to the office by personal voluntary choice. They are elected to serve the members and assist the Senior Pastor in the serving role.

Our deacon bylaws state that the highest position of trust a layperson can ever receive from the church is to be elected as a deacon by their church. The position, however, should not be looked upon as a position of honor. The New Testament standards for deacons are as high as those for ministers. There are two principal passages which are used as a standard for the office of deacon. Even though no individual will ever attain perfection as to these qualifications, these should represent the standard to which every deacon is striving. See Acts 6:1-7 and 1 Timothy 3:8-12.

To be nominated as a deacon at Johns Creek Baptist Church, one must have been a member of JCBC for a minimum period of two years and attained the age of 21 prior to April 1 of the election year. Church employees and their spouses are not eligible for nomination or election. Once elected, deacons remain on the active body for a period of three calendar years. A deacon who has served for three years will become inactive and will not be eligible for re-election to active service until at least one year has transpired.

How does one nominate a member to be a deacon? Prayerfully consider those whom you feel are called to serve our church. Obtain a Deacon Nomination form, fill it out, and return it to the church. If the nominee meets the requirements (length of membership and age requirements), their name will be added to the ballot and voted on by the church membership.

# How Deacons Serve at Johns Creek Baptist Church

An ordained deacon serves our church in many ways. Some of the more visible of these would include attending monthly meetings, ushering during the weekly services, serving the Lord's Supper, and assisting the Senior Pastor in other needed capacities. All deacons are encouraged and choose to be involved in the various Mission opportunities in our church (whether international, national, community, local, or in our own church), guided by their own spiritual gift(s) in choosing their area of service. Deacons support the church monetarily by tithing. Another important aspect of accepting the call as a deacon at Johns Creek includes cultivating one's own spiritual development – through personal Spiritual Disciplines as well as collectively attending retreats and times of study.

In addition, a major responsibility of a deacon is to choose one or more of four Ministry groups in which to serve each year. The four areas are briefly described below.

> ➢ The New Member Ministry. When a guest joins JCBC, that new member is assigned a deacon for their first months of membership. The main function of the deacon during that time would be to assist the new member in the transition to becoming an active, thriving member of the church. Examples of activities might include answering questions, giving directions, helping them to find the right Sunday School class, helping them to plug in to ministries in which they have an interest, introducing them to other members, introducing them to staff members, and making sure they are aware of the ongoing 4-week *Exploring JCBC* class (the ongoing 4-week course open to all visitors and new members.)

> ➢ The Care Ministry. Any time any member finds themselves in need (illness, hospitalization, homebound, grief, crisis

situations) and the church is made aware, a member of the Care Ministry can and will assist. The ministry may take the form of a card, a phone call, a visit, transportation, a meal, or various other forms of assistance and prayer. While all deacons perform this kind of ministry on an ongoing basis, the Care Ministry has this as their official function. As well, the Care Ministry Team Leader maintains an ongoing email Prayer Ministry, ensuring that all members of the congregation have their needs lifted up through the prayers of all elected deacons.

➤ The Growth Ministry. When a guest visits JCBC, they are contacted after their initial visit and are made to feel welcome. During that contact, the deacon would answer any questions about the church, let them know of upcoming dates of interest, tell them the dates of the next Guest Luncheon (where they would meet with the Senior Pastor and other ministers and have the chance to get their specific questions answered,) and tell them about the *Exploring JCBC* class (the ongoing 4-week course open to all visitors and new members.)

➤ Homebound Ministry. "Homebound" will be defined as "individuals on our church and Sunday school rolls that are unable to attend services or activities regularly, due to illness, age, or physical disability, either short or long term." Homebound Ministry team members will be asked to select at least one, possibly two homebound persons to visit each month, as well as one other to be responsible for sending a card to monthly. This ministry serves the JCBC Homebound community, as well as reaches out to comfort and encourage their families. Ministry team members will add names to their personal care list until all names on JCBC Homebound list are selected and will be ministered to either by visits if welcomed or cards if visits are declined.

# DEACON OFFICERS

|  | Chair | Vice Chair | Secretary | Treasurer |
|---|---|---|---|---|
| 1990-91 | Phil Brown | Richard Eason | Bob Davis | Edwin Boland |
| 1991-92 | Richard Eason | Robert McFarland | Edwin Boland | Freeman Sanders |
| 1992-93 | Robert McFarland | Grant Curtis | Freeman Sanders | Jimmie Baggett |
| 1993-94 | Grant Curtis | Tom Jack | Jim Cook | Phil Brown |
| 1994-95 | Tom Jack | Richard Eason | Phil Brown | Wesley Flowers |
| 1995-96 | Richard Eason | Edwin Boland | Wesley Flowers | Paul Herrington |
| 1996-97 | John Dixon | Beth Ann Boland | Pete Brown | Kirby Pate |
| 1997-98 | Way Kidd | Kirby Pate | Dale Stone | John E. Hudson |
| 1998-99 | Edwin Boland | Tony Turpin | Bob Davis | Mike Jones |
| 1999-2000 | Keith Compton | Bob Prator | Marsha Janofsky | Ron Franks |
| 2000-2001 | Kirby Pate | Ray Johnson | Harold Hyde | Brad Roper |
| 2002 | Dale Stone | Norman Parker | John E. Hudson | Trudy Woodard |
| 2003 | Norman Parker | Edwin Boland | John Zwald | Brad Roper |
| 2004 | Everett Bennett | John Zwald | Marsha Janofsky | Jim Harrington |
| 2005 | Ray Johnson | Richard Eason | Richard Kay | Bill Dorris |
| 2006 | Danny Henderson | Cecelia Prator | John Wiley, Jr. | Alan McKnight |
| 2007 | Robbie Hamrick | Mike Jones | Charlie Darwin | Ken Berg |
| 2008 | Marsha Janofsky | Tom Waller | Jeff Quick | Bo Haywood |
| 2009 | Bo Haywood | Greg Kennedy | Sonia Hankins/ Richard Kay | Alan McKnight |

| 2010 | Kirby Pate | Phil Brown | Richard Kay | Mike Ernst |
|------|-----------|-----------|-------------|------------|
| 2011 | John Zwald | Kevin Tolbert | Bryan Self | Nathan West |
| 2012 | Bob Prator | Tom Waller | Rosanne Patton | Marsha Hunter |
| 2013 | Tom Waller | Edwin Boland | Angie Kleckley | Greg Fletcher |

# DEACONS EMERITUS

October 21, 2009          Thomas E. Boland, Sr.

August 22, 2010          John T. Wylie, Sr.

April 18, 2012          Jerry Hyde (died July 2, 2013)

November 7, 2012          Tom Jack

# DEACON ORDINATIONS

September 30, 1990
>Beth Ann Boland
>Edith Bond
>John E. Hudson
>Celeste Massey
>Cecelia Prator

August 8, 1993
>Wesley Flowers
>Jeff Quick

September 17, 1995
>Robert R. (Bob) Cash
>Kirby Pate
>Dale Stone
>Carl Tolbert

December 1, 1996
>Hugh E. Sawyer

October 5, 1997
>Keith Compton
>Marsha Janofsky
>Matthew Winn

October 4, 1998
>Ronald M. Barnes
>David Doverspike
>Gerald L. Knoedler
>Jeff Richardson
>Raul L. Rivero, Jr.

November 1, 1998
    Bradley R. Roper
    Samuel P. Gilliam
    Jean C. Albright

November 7, 1999
    Phil Herrington
    Richard Kay

September 24, 2000
    Jack Gillian, Sr.
    David Hyde
    Leslie Morgan
    Trudy Woodard

January 6, 2002
    Thomas C. Reese
    Bryan Self
    Thomas H. Waller
    Daniel N. (Nathan) West
    John H. Zwald

November 10, 2002
    Sue Bowron
    Todd Burkhalter
    David Gray
    Jim Majors

October 26, 2003
    Alan McKnight
    Sean Smith
    Todd Tibbetts
    John Wiley, Jr.

October 17, 2004
 Kenneth M. Berg
 Charles R. Darwin
 J. Robert Hamrick
 Kevin G. Hankins
 John M. Link
 Steven A. Pickens
 Brenda B. Turpin

October 23, 2005
 David (Lee) Derrick, Jr.
 Patricia B. Jones
 Gail V. Sawyer
 Don M. Walters
 Bryan R. Weaver

October 22, 2006
 David Bowen
 Greg Fletcher
 Sonia Hankins
 Greg Kennedy
 Ian Mercado
 Shan Pate
 Lynne Waller

November 4, 2007
 Colin Bryant
 Juliet Weaver
 Clayton Williams

October 19, 2008
 Jakki Royal Bryant
 Heidi Carr
 Mike Ernst
 Diane Haywood

Viki Shadoan
Kevin Tolbert

November 15, 2009
Molly Darwin
Bret Hegi
Angie Kleckley
Rosanne Patton
Taylor Sword

November 21, 2010
Jean Bowen
Bill Hamilton
Wayne Lawson
Patrick O'Donnell
Susan Tripp

January 19, 2011
Marsha Hunter

November 20, 2011
Tony Bligh
Deborah Peterson
DeWitt Weaver

October 28, 2012
Mary Bryant
Anil Gundugollu
Don Lott
Sanford McAllister
Paul Peterson

# DEACON ELECTION RESULTS

Deacons are elected for three-year terms. Until January 2002 when the church changed to a calendar year (January to December), Deacons served from October 1 to September 30. From time to time, a deacon will resign and, in accordance with the by-laws, another deacon may be elected to fill the unexpired term. Election procedures are defined in the church by-laws.

## TERM ENDING 1990

Cecil Bowman (unexpired term)
Marcus Canada (resigned 8/1989)
Jim Cook
Grant Curtis
Larry Dodson (unexpired term)
Jim Fambrough (unexpired term)
Fred Henderson
Harold Hyde
Jerry Hyde
Chester King
Joe Massey
George Parker (resigned 8/1989)
Norman Parker
Dave Rogers
Don Wiggs (resigned 9/1989)

## TERM ENDING 1991

Mike Brown
Phil Brown
Marvin Camp
Bob Davis
Monroe Dempsey
Jim Dill
Claud Eason
Jim Harrington
Claude Head (resigned 9/1990)
Tom Jack
Jim Newton (unexpired term)
Leland Thomas (resigned 5/1991)
Ed Waters

## TERM ENDING 1992

Edwin Boland
Tommy Boland
W. O. Brannan
Richard Eason
Warren Fields
Larry Hansard

Joel Herndon
Paul Herrington
Chester King (unexpired term)
Bob Prator
Wallace Randolph
Charles Skidmore (resigned 5/1991)
Tony Turpin

## TERM ENDING 1993
Beth Ann Boland
Edith Bond
Lee Bracewell
Wayne Carpenter
John Dixon
Fred Henderson (unexpired term)
John Hudson
Celeste Massey (resigned 9/1992)
Robert McFarland
Cecelia Prator
Freeman Sanders
Dan Sheppard (resigned 11/1992)
Rick Smith (resigned 5/1991)

## TERM ENDING 1994
Jimmie Baggett
Jim Cook
Grant Curtis
Jim Dill (unexpired term)
Harold Hyde
Jerry Hyde
Joe Massey (resigned 9/1992)

Larry Sessions
Al Stewart

## TERM ENDING 1995
Phil Brown
Bob Davis
Monroe Dempsey
Claud Eason
Jim Harrington
Tom Jack
Norman Parker
Ed Waters

## TERM ENDING 1996
Edwin Boland
Tommy Boland
Richard Eason
Wesley Flowers
Paul Herrington
Bob Prator
Jeff Quick
Tony Turpin

## TERM ENDING 1997
Beth Ann Boland
Edith Bond
Wayne Carpenter
John Dixon
Fred Henderson
Ray Johnson
Freeman Sanders
Steve Wright

## TERM ENDING 1998
L. E. (Pete) Brown
Bob Cash
Jim Cook
John E. Hudson
Harold Hyde
Jerry Hyde
Bob Kent
Kirby Pate
Cecelia Prator
Dale Stone
Carl Tolbert
Lane Watson

## TERM ENDING 1999
Rudy Bowen
Phil Brown
Robert Davis
Monroe Dempsey
Larry Hansard
Jim Harrington
Tom Jack
Mike Jones
Way Kidd
Norman Parker
Hugh Sawyer
John Wiley

## TERM ENDING 2000
Edwin Boland
Tommy Boland
Keith Compton
Wesley Flowers
Ronny Franks
Paul Herrington

Marsha Janofsky
Harry McElveen
Van Pease
Bob Prator
Tony Turpin
Matthew Winn (resigned 6/98)
Jean Albright (unexpired term)

## TERM ENDING 2001
Ronald M. Barnes
Beth Ann Boland
Edith Bond
Tom Cantwell (resigned)
John Dixon
David Doverspike
Richard Eason
Sam Gilliam
Ray Johnson
Jerry Knoedler
Jeff Quick
Bill Pemberton
Jeff Richardson
Raul Rivero
Brad Roper
Bill Dorris (unexpired term)

## TERM ENDING 2002
Wayne Carpenter
Doyle Chasteen
Russ Graves
Phil Herrington (resigned)
John E. Hudson
John T. Hudson (resigned)
Harold Hyde

Jerry Hyde
Richard Kay
Bob Kent
Kirby Pate
Cecelia Prator
Dale Stone
Carl Tolbert (resigned)
Ed Waters
Lane Watson

## TERM ENDING 2003
Bob Born
Rudy Bowen
Phil Brown
Jim Cook, Sr.
Bob Davis
Jim Dill
Jack Gillian, Sr.
Claude Head
David Hyde
Tom Jack
Mike Jones
Way Kidd
Leslie Morgan
Norman Parker
Hugh Sawyer
Trudy Woodard

## TERM ENDING 2004
Jean Albright
Everett Bennett
Edwin Boland
Tommy Boland
Wesley Flowers
Ron Franks (resigned 2002)

Woody Galloway
Paul Herrington
Marsha Janofsky
Bob Lynn
Ray Majors
Harry McElveen
Bob Prator
Tom Reese
Bryan Self
Tony Turpin
Tom Waller
Dave Woodard
Nathan West
John Zwald
Keith Compton (unexpired term; resigned 2003)
Jim Harrington (unexpired term)

## TERM ENDING 2005
Ron Barnes
Beth Ann Boland
Sue Bowron
Todd Burkhalter
John Dixon
Bill Dorris
Richard Eason
David Gray (resigned 6/2005)
Bo Haywood
Emmett Henderson
Ray Johnson
Jerry Knoedler
Jim Majors
Marion "Oogie" Ogden
Jeff Quick

Raul Rivero
Brad Roper
Carl Tolbert (resigned
12/2004)
David White (resigned
5/2005)
W.A. Whitten

## TERM ENDING 2006
Cecil Alford (resigned 9/2004)
Edith Bond (unexpired term 1
yr.)
Wayne Carpenter (resigned
6/2004)
Cliff Cordell
Joe Fannon
Danny Henderson
John E. Hudson
John T. Hudson
Harold Hyde
Jerry Hyde
Richard Kay
Alan McKnight
Kirby Pate
Cecelia Prator
Sean Smith
Dale Stone
Todd Tibbetts
Brenda Turpin (unexpired
term)
Lane Watson
John Wiley, Jr.
John Wiley, Sr.
Steve Wright

## TERM ENDING 2007
Ken Berg
Bob Born
Rudy Bowen
Phil Brown
Eddie Bugg, Jr.
Jim Cook, Sr.
Charlie Darwin
Bob Davis
Jim Dill
Robbie Hamrick
Kevin Hankins
David Hyde
Tom Jack
Mike Jones
Bob Kent
John Link
Norman Parker
Steve Pickens
Hugh Sawyer
Trudy Woodard

## TERM ENDING 2008
Jean Albright
Everett Bennett
Edwin Boland
Tommy Boland
Lee Derrick
Joe Fannon (unexpired term)
Wesley Flowers
Jim Harrington
Marsha Janofsky
Pat Jones
Bob Lynn
Bob Prator

Gail Sawyer (resigned 12/07)
Bryan Self
Tony Turpin
Don Walters
Tom Waller
Nathan West
Bryan Weaver
David Woodard
John Zwald

TERM ENDING 2009
Beth Ann Boland
David Bowen
Todd Burkhalter (resigned 12/2008)
Heidi Carr (unexpired term)
John Dixon
Greg Fletcher
Sonia Hankins (resigned 6/2009)
Bo Haywood
Emmett Henderson
Frank Holland (unexpired term 1 yr.)
Ray Johnson
Greg Kennedy
Bob Kent (unexpired term ½ yr.)
Jerry Knoedler
Ian Mercado
Oogie Ogden (resigned 2008)
Shan Pate
Jeff Quick
Raul Rivero
Brad Roper

Mark Sauls
Lynne Waller
Roger Williams (resigned 2008)

TERM ENDING 2010
Colin Bryant
Richard Eason
Danny Henderson
John E. Hudson
Harold Hyde
Jerry Hyde
Richard Kay
Angie Kleckley (unexpired term 1 yr.)
Alan McKnight
Kirby Pate
Cecelia Prator
Tom Reese
Charles Skidmore
Dale Stone
Todd Tibbetts
Brenda Turpin
Debra Walters (unexpired term 1 yr.)
Juliet Weaver
John Wiley, Jr.
John Wiley, Sr. (resigned 12/31/09)
Clayton Williams (resigned 12/31/09)

TERM ENDING 2011
Rudy Bowen
Phil Brown

Jakki Bryant
David Bugg
Heidi Carr – (unexpired term.
2-1/2 yrs.)
Jim Cook, Sr. (resigned
12/08)
Charlie Darwin
Jim Dill
Mike Ernst
Robbie Hamrick
Kevin Hankins (resigned
4/09)
Diane Haywood
Lamar Henderson
David Hyde
Tom Jack
Mike Jones
John Link
Norman Parker
Tres Rice
Viki Shadoan (unexpired term
3 yr.)
Kevin Tolbert
Trudy Woodard

## TERM ENDING 2012
Jean Albright
Jim Cook
Molly Darwin
Lee Derrick
James (Jim) W. Ellis, Sr.
Bo Godwin
Jim Harrington
Bret Hegi
Marsha Janofsky

Pat Jones
Bob Lynn
Oogie Ogden
Rosanne Patton
Bob Prator
Bryan Self
Taylor Sword
Tony Turpin
Don Walters
Nathan West
John Zwald

## TERM ENDING 2013
Doug Beck
Beth Ann Boland
Jean Bowen
Greg Fletcher
Bill Hamilton
Bo Haywood
Marsha Hunter
Ray Johnson
Greg Kennedy
Angie Kleckley
Jerry Knoedler
Wayne Lawson
Patrick O'Donnell
Jeff Quick
Raul Rivero
Brad Roper
Susan Tripp
Tom Waller
Lynne Waller
Bryan Weaver

## TERM ENDING 2014

Tony Bligh
Edwin Boland
Colin Bryant
Tim Clagg
John Dixon
Richard Eason
Danny Henderson
John Hudson
Harold Hyde
Richard Kay
Alan McKnight
Deborah Peterson
Cecelia Prator
Mark Sauls
Dale Stone
DeWitt Weaver
Juliet Weaver
Roger Williams
David Woodard
Steve Wright

## TERM ENDING 2015

Phil Brown
Jakki Bryant
Mary Bryant
David Bugg
Charlie Darwin
Jim Dill
Mike Ernst
Anil Gundugollu
Robbie Hamrick
Diane Haywood
Lamar Henderson
David Hyde
Mike Jones
Don Lott
Sanford McAllister
Kirby Pate
Shan Pate
Paul Peterson
Kevin Tolbert
Trudy Woodard

# THE GOLDEN CLUB

In 2003 when Dr. & Mrs. Self celebrated their 50th wedding anniversary, they invited those who had been married for 50+ years to celebrate with them. They wanted to serve as an example and inspiration to younger couples that long marriages are possible, that regardless of the problems and heartaches that come with life, couples can persevere and keep their marriages intact.

The couples of 50+ years completed questionnaires which were compiled into a booklet. We recognized these couples in church, along with those whose spouses of 50+ years had died, and had a reception after Sunday services on August 3, 2003, in the third floor rotunda. We had 50+ couples the first year! The local newspapers and a television news reporter gave us ample coverage.

Each year since then we have inducted new members–those who have reached the 50th year and those with a 50-year+ marriage who became members of our church during that year. The Golden Club has met for the annual dinner to celebrate long marriages, usually on the fourth Thursday in August. In honor and memory of those couples who are members of the Golden Club, we are listing them here.

| INDUCTED IN 2003: | Marriage date: |
| --- | --- |
| Ray & Nancy Batson | June 8, 1951 |
| Jack & Eunice Black | April 8, 1939 |
| Bob & Betty Born | April 18, 1953 |
| Lee & Angie Bracewell | September 7, 1946 |
| W. O. & Kathleen Brannan | April 12, 1946 |
| Marvin & Dot Camp | January 4, 1945 |
| Rev. Robert & Pauline Cash | December 21, 1952 |
| Doyle & Jan Chasteen | November 22, 1953 |
| Grant & Dot Curtis | November 2, 1945 |
| Ernest & Bebe Davis | January 10, 1946 |
| Monroe & Jeannette Dempsey | October 3, 1947 |

| | |
|---|---|
| Claud & Mary Catherine Eason | November 7, 1942 |
| Ted & Ann Echols | February 23, 1951 |
| Joe & Tommie Fannon | June 21, 1947 |
| Sam & Lib Gilliam | May 1, 1948 |
| Jack & Dolores Gillian | April 12, 1951 |
| Dr. Wiley & Virginia Greenway | December 20, 1946 |
| George & Edna Harlow | March 21, 1953 |
| Bob & Joyce Harris | March 23, 1951 |
| Carroll & Lee Harvey | August 1, 1953 |
| Bob & Betty Hash | October 25, 1951 |
| Claude & Sylvia Head | April 12, 1952 |
| Dr. Emmett & Margaret Henderson | September 7, 1945 |
| Fred & Lillian Henderson | October 10, 1946 |
| Terry & Peggy House | January 4, 1953 |
| Hugh & Ollie Johnson | July 5, 1936 |
| Jack & Dot Johnston | May 7, 1949 |
| Duey & Mary Ann Kuhn | September 2, 1950 |
| Clatie & Maxine Lewis | December 27, 1946 |
| Tom & Myrtis Maddux | February 11, 1951 |
| George & Margaret McCune | August 1, 1947 |
| Dan & Norma Nicolai | September 12, 1953 |
| Milton & Cathy Pate | November 27, 1952 |
| Bill & Martha Pemberton | March 19, 1952 |
| Rev. Bill & Frances Pittard | |
| Louis & Frances Rathke | August 10, 1950 |
| Zeke & Jean Rutherford | September 8, 1946 |
| Bill & Carolyn Self | August 2, 1953 |
| Charles & Edna Shafer | August 14, 1950 |
| Bob & Loretta Snyder | August 16, 1952 |
| Hershel & Katherine Stalvey | December 22, 1950 |
| Al & Sandy Stewart | September 3, 1949 |
| Myron & Syble Strickland | March 6, 1953 |
| Carney & Ann Walker | December 14, 1946 |
| Ed & Dot Waters | June 29, 1946 |
| Lane & June Watson | November 13, 1948 |

| | |
|---|---|
| Dr. W. A. & Lucille Whitten | June 6, 1948 |
| John & Louise Wiley | June 27, 1953 |
| Carl & Lucille Wrenn | February 14, 1948 |
| Joe & Ellie Wynne | February 17, 1951 |

## INDUCTED IN 2004:

| | |
|---|---|
| Everett & Teresa Bennett | May 8, 1954 |
| Wayne & Norma Carpenter | May 30, 1954 |
| Harry & Doris Chance | October 16, 1954 |
| Jim & Carol Dill | November 24, 1954 |
| Ed & Anne Jones | March 20, 1954 |
| Jim & Sallye Nisewonger | February 2, 1954 |

## INDUCTED IN 2005:

| | |
|---|---|
| Ralph & Lily Alewine | September 6, 1945 |
| Paul & Dorothy Herrington | December 23, 1955 |
| Wesley & Betty Medford | November 26, 1955 |

## INDUCTED IN 2006:

| | |
|---|---|
| Reese & Jeanette Chappell | June 8, 1956 |
| Burley & Fleeta Davis | |
| Herb & Iris Goolsby | July 30, 1956 |
| Tom & Elizabeth Jack | July 19, 1956 |
| Ray & Dixie Majors | September 1, 1956 |
| John & Camely Mayfield | April 23, 1950 |
| Dan & Mary Sherrill | March 31, 1956 |
| Dick & Sue Shoemaker | May 4, 1956 |
| Chan & Alice White | February 12, 1956 |

## INDUCTED IN 2007:

| | |
|---|---|
| Lon & Dorothy Bush | March 2, 1957 |
| Jim & Billie Ellis | May 16, 1953 |
| Jimmy & Annie Faye Gardner | September 28, 1956 |
| Bill & Teeny O'Kelley | March 28, 1953 |
| Cliff & Faye Powers | June 19, 1954 |

| | |
|---|---|
| Charles & Rose Rigdon | April 25, 1953 |
| Dick & Pat Roberts | October 20, 1957 |
| Charles & Nancy Skidmore | June 15, 1957 |
| Bob & Carole Smith | December 26, 1957 |
| Eugene & Janie Thornton | |
| Kyle & Della Wilcutt | December 18, 1954 |

**INDUCTED IN 2008:**

| | |
|---|---|
| Jim & Barbara Foster | June 15, 1958 |
| Burton & Doris Johnson | May 16, 1944 |
| Don & Peggy Schroer | November 1, 1951 |
| David & Betty Sullivan | March 1, 1954 |

**INDUCTED IN 2009:**

| | |
|---|---|
| Don & Julie Amerson | February 21, 1959 |
| Tommy & Beth Ann Boland | May 23, 1959 |
| Don & Margaret Braswell | August 22, 1959 |
| Don & Jackie Brown | December 17, 1955 |
| Tommy & Donna Chupp | August 4, 1956 |
| Gaylord & Sandra Coan | November 28, 1957 |
| Dick & Carol Gastley | June 27, 1959 |
| Jack & Barbara Hiers | |
| Harry & Sylvia McElveen | August 11, 1959 |
| Oogie & Darlene Ogden | June 12, 1959 |

**INDUCTED IN 2010:**

| | |
|---|---|
| Gary & Nancy Rush | August 23, 1958 |
| Harry & June Bobeng | April 15, 1955 |
| Frank & Glenda Crumpler | June 25, 1960 |
| Jack & Doris McGaha | June 6, 1953 |

**INDUCTED IN 2011:**

| | |
|---|---|
| Charles & Rose Adams | April 29, 1961 |
| Jim & Imogene Cook | July 1, 1961 |
| Don & Ruth Ann Nast | October 14, 1961 |

| | |
|---|---|
| Ken & Marian Eugea | November 26, 1960 |
| Lee & Sandy Holland | December 18, 1961 |
| Richard & Audrey Killmon | February 13, 1954 |

## INDUCTED IN 2012:

| | |
|---|---|
| Harvey & Oclla Fletcher | December 15, 1962 |
| Gerald & Barbara Gibson | June 24, 1961 |
| J.W. & Joyce Hutchens | June 22, 1962 |
| Harold & Kaye Hyde | December 28, 1962 |
| Norman & Barbara Parker | April 22, 1962 |
| Lloyd & Barbara Parrish | November 18, 1960 |
| Gary & Carol Sandlin | May 26, 1962 |

## INDUCTED IN 2013:

| | |
|---|---|
| Robert (Bob) & Anne Bell | April 12 1963 |
| Pete & Barbara Brown | October 5, 1963 |
| Bobby & Sarah Couch | June 29, 1963 |
| R.G. & Sue Crump | March 10, 1963 |
| Charles (Bo) & Diane Haywood | June 8, 1963 |
| Gerald (Jerry) & Janet Knoedler | June 16, 1963 |
| Patrick (Pat) & Janice Vinson | December 14, 1963 |
| Victor & Milly Wu | June 18, 1960 |

# MISSIONS

*The church exists by missions, as fire exists by burning* (Emil Brunner). Quoted by Dr. Self in the April 27, 1994 issue of *The Call*.

## Our History

Johns Creek Baptist Church has been a missions-oriented congregation from its earliest incarnation. After First Baptist Church of Chamblee voted to relocate, several ministries were transferred or diminished to facilitate the move. Because of the strong emphasis the church has always placed on missions, that ministry continued throughout the relocation process.

As a Baptist Church, we support our local, state and national organizations. These would include the Atlanta Baptist Association, the Georgia Baptist Convention, the Southern Baptist Convention, and the Cooperative Baptist Fellowship. Percentages of the general budget go to support these organizations, and these percentages change from time to time. The percentage we give to each organization is not important for this article.

In preparing to relocate a sub-committee of the Strategic Task Force was to establish and support the Chamblee-Doraville Ministry Center. During the relocation process, much work was done behind the scenes to establish this Center. This Center was also supported by First Baptist Church of Doraville, Dunwoody Baptist Church, and Wieuca Road Baptist Church. The dedication service of the facility was held on October 11, 1999. Included on the Board of Directors from Johns Creek Baptist were John Dixon, Beth Ann Boland, Monroe Dempsey and Robert Prator. Our church supported this Ministry Center with leadership, manpower and money for more than ten years after its establishment. This later became Atlanta Intercultural Ministry Center, and Richard Kay and Tom Jack served on that Board of Directors.

First Baptist Church of Chamblee owned the house on Hood Avenue that was adjacent to the church. "Missionary Manor" was refurbished and redecorated to provide comfortable lodging for missionaries or denominational workers on a temporary basis. Even after our relocation, the residence was used by missionaries. Because of its location, it was not practical for our church to maintain the facility so it was sold.

In the early years at Johns Creek we invited missionaries to speak to our church many times, usually on Wednesday evenings. However, we have had special pulpit guests for Sunday morning worship services. These include:

Dr. Karl Heinz Walter, General Secretary of European Baptist Federation (worldwide mission endeavors), in 1993;

Dr. Keith Parks, Global Missions Coordinator of CBF, in 1994;

Dr. Harlan Spurgeon, Associate Global Missions Coordinator of CBF, in 1994;

Dr. Cecil Sherman, Coordinator of CBF in 1995;

Dr. Denton Lotz, General Secretary of Baptist World Alliance, in 2000;

Dr. Daniel Vestal, Coordinator of Cooperative Baptist Fellowship, in 2000;

Rev. Neville Callam, General Secretary of Baptist World Alliance, in 2008;

Rev. Billy Kim, former President Baptist World, in 2008.

### *The Missions Committee*

In January 1995 the church voted to redefine the By-Law concerning membership of the Missions Committee. In addition to six members elected at large, the following leadership positions are represented: Director of Women's Missionary Union, Director of Sunday School, President of Baptist Women, Chair of Women's Ministries, Chair of Men's Ministries, Chair of Seniors Ministries, and a Johns Creek representative of the Chamblee-Doraville Ministry Center. The by-laws dated June 29, 2005, were changed again. This defines our current Missions Committee:

## 5.4 MISSIONS COMMITTEE

### *Function*

The Missions Committee shall lead the church's mission involvement, coordinate the total missions framework of the church, recommend to the Stewardship Committee the annual missions budget, review and recommend to the Stewardship Committee any/all requests for missions spending including the annual missions budget, assist the various missions groups within the church with their programs and along with the Senior Pastor and the Executive Pastor, develop the overall missions strategy for the church.

### *Membership*

The Missions Committee shall consist of eight members elected by the church, one of whom shall be a youth member representing the youth ministry. Each person selected shall serve for a term of two years. The Missions Committee shall also include the following ex-officio members who represent ministry areas in the church.

- ❖ Women's Ministry Chairperson
- ❖ Men's Ministry Chairperson
- ❖ Senior Ministry Chairperson
- ❖ Sunday School Director
- ❖ Adult Sunday School Director

## *After the Relocation:*

Long a supporter of denominational cooperative missions, JCBC created a unique model that would soon be emulated by many other churches. JCBC has continued impressive support of global missions through the Cooperative Baptist Fellowship, while implementing opportunities for members to become directly involved locally, nationally and internationally. During these twenty years, missions giving and participation has increased exponentially. JCBC has fielded mission teams in eight states, ten countries and countless local endeavors.

This is not a comprehensive list of missions activities but, hopefully, it will provide a comprehensive overview of the mission work of JCBC to date.

**Abbreviations used throughout this article:**
AIM = Atlanta Intercultural Ministry
CDMC = Chamblee-Doraville Ministry Center
CBF = Cooperative Baptist Fellowship
GBCH = Georgia Baptist Children's Home
JCBC = Johns Creek Baptist Church
NLB = No Longer Bound
NFCC = North Fulton Community Charities
VBS = Vacation Bible School

## Our Involvement
### Children's missions:

The second week after relocating the preschool/children's missions program resumed on Wednesday evenings, and continues to run during the school year. The theme of the first VBS (August 1-5, 1994) at Johns Creek was *A Heart for Missions*. The children have had several special missions studies, such as "Around the World with Missions" in the fall of 2001.

Some of the annual projects our children participate in are:

Christmas Stockings in conjunction with the Salvation Army (started 1994). This became a church-wide project. By 1998 over 365 stockings were filled. Starting in 2001 teddy bears and Barbie dolls were also collected.

Collection of coats/hats/scarves/gloves in the fall (started 1994).

Birthday Party for Jesus; preschoolers bring baby supplies for local charities (started 1996).

Collection of school supplies and backpacks (1997).

Trick or Treating at Noble (now Belmont) Village Assisted Living (started 2001).

Vacation Bible School always has a mission emphasis for their nightly collection. Also, leftover VBS snacks are sent to Jesse's House, an emergency children's shelter, in Cumming.

Several of the special children's mission projects include:

60 Easter baskets prepared for CDMC;
Collection of books and school supplies for areas hit by natural disasters;
Collection of toys for local charities;
Prepared care packages for our college students;
Collected coins to support an orphan in Africa;
Decorated bird houses for House Calls;
The Gospel for Asia: Bridge of Hope schools;
Collection of ChapStick and candy for soldiers (2 years);
Collection of hygiene items (sample/travel sizes) for Haiti;
Collection of toys for the children who live in "The Dump" in Ecuador (2004);
"Living the Green Life;" (in 2008);
"Eggs for Ghana;" (in 2011)

### Middle School and Youth missions:

As early as the summer of 1995, our youth had a mission project in Atlanta, and in October went on a Mission Retreat in Birmingham, Alabama. In the summer of that year college students, Clay Chatham and Steven Wright, were named summer missionaries by the Georgia Baptist Convention. They were the only two from Georgia Southern University and both were members of JCBC!

Our youth participated in missions weekends around the state and in contiguous states doing yard work and house repairs: Griffin, Decatur, Macon, Hartwell, Warm Springs, Rome, Manchester, and Morrow, Georgia; Smyrna, Tennessee; Stetson University in Deland, Florida; Hilton Head, South Carolina; Awanita, South Carolina;

Wherry Housing Development, Smyrna, Tennessee; Camp Lee at Anniston, Alabama; and Wingate University in Wingate, North Carolina. They also made a mission trip in 2003 to Bellarmine University in Louisville, Kentucky.

They have sponsored projects for Noble (now Belmont) Village Assisted Living. They have participated in collections of various supplies including socks, book bags and school supplies, have provided manpower to assist local charities at Christmastime, and have made several mission trips to inner-city areas and those hit by natural disasters. Our youth also participate in some of the adult projects and trips, including a trip in 2012 to Dominican Republic where they distributed Spanish New Testaments. Another mission trip is planned for October 2013.

In March 2012, JCBC hosted March Mission Madness for more than 250 youth and adults from churches through the state.

### Adult Missions:
### Local

JCBC has celebrated each year with one month designated as "Missions Month," typically in March, called "March Missions Madness," during which we have a special collection for missions and provide various opportunities for service. As early as November 1993, we had a goal of $3,000 for CBF's "Doing Missions in a World without Borders" (foreign missions offering). In 1997 our goal was $15,000. In 1999, we collected over $26,000. In 2008, our goal of $38,000 was surpassed with a total collection of $62,539. In 2013, our goal was $100,000, and we surpassed that goal!

In December 1993, Baptist Women resumed meeting. In September 1994, Baptist Women were renamed/redesigned as Women on Missions. Their projects included sewing blankets and gowns for newborns at Grady Hospital; donating clothing for the needy in the Chamblee-Doraville area; preparing and serving refreshments, and bagging grocery donations for the Stewart Center; and collected un-iced, suitable for freezing cakes for the Baptist

Children's Home to be used throughout the year for birthdays. Starting in 2001, they made quilts for abused and neglected children.

Our Men's Ministry has been involved for many years in supporting the Atlanta Union Mission for homeless men in Atlanta. That support continues to this day. On occasion the women of the church and the Seniors' Ministry have provided cakes for the Atlanta Union Mission for Thanksgiving.

In1994, we started an "Adopt-a-Family for Christmas" in which each adult Sunday School Community would be assigned a family available through the Missions Committee in conjunction with CDMC or NFCC.

In 1995, every 5$^{th}$ Sunday was designated as Food Pantry Collection Sunday for CDMC or NFCC. This later occurred the last Sunday of each month.

In March 2000, we had a new missions program over a seven-week period called "ONE" where each member of JCBC was challenged to bring one person into the life of our church, especially for those we know who are not part of a family of faith. We did this again in February 2008.

The Men's Ministry started supporting House Calls International and Habitat for Humanity in 2002, by providing manpower in building homes for needy families. The Men's Ministry has also provided assistance with home repairs for individuals. The Women's Ministry or Sunday School Communities provided lunch for most of these "builds."

In 2003, Baptist Women's Fellowship had a baby shower for the CDMC Pregnancy Center.

We have provided ministry to Belmont Village, an assisted living facility adjacent to the back of our back yard. We have led computer literacy training, and weekly vespers services on Sunday evenings. We have been volunteer partners with the residents, and have provided drivers for their van.

In conjunction with Atlanta Baptist Association, we provided meals four or five times a year and other special needs for residents of

Memorial Drive Shelter for homeless families in inner city Atlanta, starting in 2004. We prepared, delivered and served the meals, then spent some time in fellowship with these families. We continued this ministry until the Shelter closed in 2009.

In 2006, the Missions Committee proposed that each Sunday School community have a Missions liaison to help promote missions awareness.

Beginning in 2007, the Progressive Sunday School class (senior adults) sent monthly care packages to soldiers serving in the Middle East.

In 2007, we participated for the first time in Operation Christmas Child, a project of Franklin Graham's "Samaritan's Purse" whereby local churches and other ministries fill shoeboxes with gifts for children in over 130 countries. We also served as a collection site. This has become an annual project.

In 2008, we collected and repaired bicycles for the Santa Shop Bike Drive in conjunction with NFCC. This has become an annual project. As we became aware of No Longer Bound, a men's addiction rehabilitation program in our geographic area, we started supporting them. We have provided monthly meals since 2008, prepared and served by Sunday School communities on a rotating basis. We currently serve meals twice monthly to approximately 35 men. Rickey Letson also led a Bible study for them twice a month. We have collected various items for their thrift store. They often attend our worship services.

Other local Missions/Ministries that we have supported are:

Atlanta Union Mission;
Georgia Baptist Developmental Disabilities Ministries;
Stewart Center (after-school program) in inner-city Atlanta;
Moncrief Center;
Techwood Baptist Center;
Georgia Baptist Medical/Dental Fellowship;
Gideon's International;

Canine Assistants;
American Red Cross (hosted several emergency blood drives and encouraged participation);
Morningstar (for severely emotionally disturbed youth)
Brookhaven Baptist Church;
Park Avenue Baptist Church near Grant Park;
Thanksgiving meals for numerous needy families.

## National missions:

During the past twenty years, various areas of our country have been devastated by several natural disasters. When Hurricane Katrina hit New Orleans on August 29, 2005, several church members provided immediate relief by collecting emergency supplies and delivering them directly to New Orleans. Many adults have taken numerous trips since then to various locations hit hard by the Katrina. Pearlington, Mississippi was totally destroyed, and CBF adopted this community. We organized and made several trips to Pearlington. We have also provided assistance within the State of Georgia hit by tornadoes and affected by floods.

In 2006, we supported a church-planting effort by CBF with Texas Baptists. Other areas we helped were Presidio, Texas; Plaquemines Parish, Louisiana; Chalmette, Louisiana; and Bluegrass, Iowa.

We have worked in conjunction with CBF's Rural Poverty Initiative, and have made several trips to Perry County, Alabama, one of the poorest counties in America. The first trip was in 2008 to deliver 3,000 children's books we had collected, and to build bookshelves. We continue our support today.

## International missions:

In May 1995, eight adults made a mission trip to Prague to help renovate the new quarters for the International Baptist Seminary that had recently relocated from Ruschlikon to Prague.

Also in 1996, adults made a mission trip to Curacao, Netherlands, Antilles.

In August 1998, ten members assisted the Canadian Baptist Seminary in Langley, British Columbia.

Starting in 1999, several of our members went to southern England on its first of numerous missions trip to Elam College and Ministry Center which is a Christian school dedicated to educating and training individuals for evangelistic work among Muslims in the Middle East and around the world. Many of the students are former Muslims. David Yeghnazar, Vice President of Elam College, has presented special seminars at our church. Four additional trips have been made since then to refurbish their facility. We have also made three trips to Istanbul, Turkey, to assist with Elam College there. We distributed Farsi Bibles on their behalf, and provided financial assistance and manpower. This relationship has continued to date.

In 2000, we assisted with the renovation and refurbishment of Spurgeon's College in London, England, as they prepare people to serve God in Europe.

In 2002, eleven adults took a missions trip to South Wales Baptist College at Cardiff, Wales.

When CBF wanted to send a missionary to Brussels, Belgium, we were instrumental in providing manpower and funds. Two trips were made to Brussels. We also assisted the Baptist Church in Weimar, Germany. Since 2008, we have made three trips to Weimar.

The Haiti/Dominican Republic was hit by an earthquake in 2010. We have made four trips to Haiti, and twelve trips to Dominican Republic, taking various supplies. Flip flops were especially needed early on. We then collected first aid items, crutches and other medical equipment. Buildings needed to be constructed. Fresh water is a necessity so emphasis was placed on building wells. Our church has provided manpower and financial aid to aid this impoverished nation.

On March 11, 2011, Japan was struck by an earthquake and tsunami. We sent an emergency check to CBF for their effort to assist the Japanese.

## *Our Legacy*

Our mission involvement begins with educating our children and encouraging their participation. We have held several church-wide Missions Fairs to educate all of our church family. We have had missionaries speak to our congregation on Wednesday nights and Sunday mornings.

We see no borders in our involvement, whether it is in our community, state, nation or the world. Our Missions Committee is flexible in that they can act on immediate needs, and our members are always ready to meet those needs.

# STRATEGIC TASK FORCE: RELOCATION

[**Note:** *At the time of relocation, several people mentioned that we should document the process our church went through as a model for other churches who may find themselves in the position of needing to relocate. This chronology, taken from the minutes of the church business meetings, is an attempt to record the process.*]

The Deacons of the First Baptist Church of Chamblee presented to the church membership on February 21, 1990, to be voted on at the next business conference, the following recommendation:

*It is increasingly apparent that the future of First Baptist Chamblee will be determined by our ability to adapt to changes in our community. To help us minister effectively and responsibly in light of these changes, and to help us become a landmark Christian institution, we recommend the appointment of a strategic task force with the following responsibilities:*

- *To assess ministry opportunities in light of community change.*
- *To study staff and lay leadership needs for the future.*
- *To research the advantages and disadvantages of various location options, such as continued ministry at our present site or possible relocation.*
- *To develop a comprehensive strategic plan and report to the church within six months.*

*This task force would give periodic progress reports to the church and would be comprised of the following persons:*

| | |
|---|---|
| Tommy Boland | Sandra Eason |
| Jim Cook | Melba Franklin |
| Grant Curtis | Colin Harris |
| John Dixon | Fred Henderson |

*Ruth Howell*             *L. H. Johnson*
*Tom Jack*                *Suzanne Tolbert*


This recommendation was approved unanimously on March 21, 1990. The task force was under the leadership of Dr. David Sapp, Pastor.

On May 23, 1990, reports were heard from the Strategic Task Force sub-committees:

International Ministries – Sandra Eason reporting. Group consisted of Sandra Eason, Jim Cook and Tommy Boland.
Church Relocation – Fred Henderson reporting. Group consisted of Fred Henderson, Grant Curtis and Suzanne Tolbert.
Church Dual Location – Ruth Howell reporting. Group consisted of Ruth Howell, Melba Franklin, Colin Harris and L. H. Johnson.

At a called business meeting on December 2, 1990, Deacon Chair Phil Brown, representing the Deacon Body, made a motion that the following recommendation of the Strategic Task Force be adopted:

- *That we choose to live for a long and active ministry.*
- *That we plan for a continued ministry in this community.*
- *That we plan for a relocation to a site which is both conducive to growth and accessible to our present.*
- *That the Strategic Task Force be asked to continue its service and to develop a specific plan which would be presented to the church at the earliest possible date.*

Tom Jack seconded the motion; motion carried. A motion was presented from the Strategic Task Force that the vote be conducted by written ballot. Motion was seconded by W. O. Brannan; motion carried. Discussion followed.

Several deacons distributed, collected and counted the ballots. Results were as follows:

In favor of motion          168
Against motion               69
Blank Ballots                 9

On March 10, 1991, members of the Strategic Task Force discussed the possible relocation of First Baptist Chamblee to a 15.8-acre site located in the Johns Creek area of North Fulton/Forsyth counties. The following recommendation was presented for consideration:

- *That the First Baptist Church of Chamblee accept the gift of the McGinnis Ferry land as a site for our church's relocation.*
- *That the First Baptist Church of Chamblee become a co-sponsor with Dunwoody Baptist Church of the Johns Creek Mission Church until such time as we relocate. Chamblee would not be expected to contribute to the financial support of the mission. At the time of relocation, the mission would be merged into Chamblee and the name of the total group would become the Johns Creek Baptist Church.*
- *That the First Baptist Church of Chamblee, through its Strategic Task Force, take these steps to facilitate the sale of our present site (excluding the cemetery):*
  - ○ *Begin marketing the property.*
  - ○ *Ask the Task Force to submit plans to the church for attractively enclosing the cemetery, providing better vehicular access and maintaining the property in perpetuity.*
- *That the majority of the proceeds from the sale of Chamblee's property be designated to fund a building on the McGinnis Ferry land, with a substantial portion reserved for funding the Chamblee ministry.*
- *That the Task Force be asked to pursue discussions with Dunwoody, the Atlanta Baptist Association, and other interested parties about developing a major ministry in the*

*Chamblee area. A recommendation about this should be brought to the church for approval as soon as feasible.*

The recommendation was discussed in detail by Strategic Task Force members. Questions and comments from members of the congregation were solicited and addressed.

It was announced that printed material regarding the proposal had been mailed to all members of First Baptist Chamblee and that small group meetings to discuss the matter would be held on March 17, 18 and 20. The recommendation was to be voted on at a special called business meeting on March 24, 1991. It was also announced that escorted tours of the property and surrounding community would be made available to the congregation on March 23 with transportation provided from the present church location.

The called business meeting on March 24, 1991, was called to order by Dr. David Sapp, Pastor. The recommendation of the Strategic Task Force was presented in writing to the membership. The recommendation included a synopsis of the proceedings to date regarding the acceptance of the gift of land from Technology Park/Atlanta, starting with the presentation on March 10, 1991, by the Strategic Task Force. Motion to adopt the resolution was made by Deacon Chair Phil Brown, seconded by W. O. Brannan; motion carried.

A motion was made and seconded that the vote be conducted by written ballot; motion carried. After discussion, ballots were distributed and collected. The following people tabulated the ballot results: Bob Davis, Edwin Boland, Richard Eason, and Norma B. King. Balloting results were as follows:

| | | |
|---|---|---|
| In favor of motion | 173 | 78% |
| Against motion | 49 | 22% |
| No response | 4 | |

The deacons joined the Strategic Task Force also recommending the addition of the following church-at-large members to the listed sub-committees of the Task Force:

## Chamblee Ministry:
Task Force Members: John Dixon, Grant Curtis and Ruth Howell.
Church-at-large Members: Terri Clark, Monroe Dempsey, Tom Jack, Kristen Prator, Frances Hudson, Doris Sears, Dorothy Latham, Joel Herndon.

## Building/Property Disposal:
Task Force Members: Tommy Boland and Melba Franklin.
Church-at-large Members: Edith Bond, Edwin Boland, W. O. Brannan, Bob Prator, Chester King.

## Cemetery/Memorial:
Task Force Members: Jim Cook and Fred Henderson.
Church-at-large Member: Frank Stovall.

## Transportation:
Task Force Members: Harold Hyde and Richard Eason.
Church-at-large Members: Wayne Carpenter, Jim Baggett, Aubrey Martin, Jim Harrington.

## Relationship with Johns Creek and Program Planning:
Task Force Members: Tom Jack, Sandra Eason, Suzanne Tolbert, L. H. Johnson, Jim Cook and Grant Curtis.
Church-at-large Members: Doris Sears and current staff to include interim staff members.

The Church-at-large Members were approved at the business meeting on April 24, 1991.

Beginning in May 1991 the Strategic Task Force invited Richard Eason, Deacon Vice Chair and Chair-Elect, to become an ex-officio member. Richard was asked to lead the Property Acquisition

Committee's efforts in the transfer of title on the Johns Creek property to the First Baptist Church of Chamblee.

A special business meeting was held on September 4, 1991 for the purpose of presenting a progress report of the Strategic Task Force sub-committees to the church membership. L. H. Johnson served as Chair of the Strategic Task Force. The following committee chairs reported:

| | |
|---|---|
| Acquisition of Property | Richard Eason |
| New Building/Property Disposal | Tommy Boland |
| Programming and Building Requirements | Tom Jack |
| Chamblee Ministry | John Dixon |
| Transportation | Harold Hyde |
| Cemetery | Jim Cook |

Strategic Task Force at this time consisted of the following church members:

| | |
|---|---|
| Tommy Boland | Sandra Eason |
| *Phil Brown | Melba Franklin |
| Jim Cook | Fred Henderson |
| Grant Curtis | *Harold Hyde |
| John Dixon | Tom Jack |
| *Richard Eason | L. H. Johnson |
| | Suzanne Tolbert |
| *Ex-officio | |

At the meeting on August 21, 1991, the Task Force presented a recommendation regarding the incorporation of the church. For the 100+ year history of our church, the church had operated as a non-incorporated association which was historically the organizational structure of a Baptist church. In recent times, however, churches have tended to be incorporated as non-profit corporations since that legal structure is more well-defined in law and many times makes the day-to-day operational procedures easier and more well-defined. Legal counsel recommended that a non-profit Georgia corporation known as Johns Creek Baptist Church, Inc., be used as the legal structure for our church after the move to the new site. The title to the Johns Creek property would then be taken by our church in the name of the new corporation, and changes would not then be required at the time of the actual relocation. The following structure was recommended for our use:

President           Pastor (in the absence of the Pastor, the Chair
of the Deacons)

Vice President Deacon Chair (in the absence of a Pastor or Deacon Chair, the Vice Chair of the Deacons)

Secretary           An elected member of the church

Assistant Secretary    An elected member of the church

Treasurer           An elected member of the church

Assistant Treasurer    An elected member of the church

Under this arrangement, trustees would no longer be needed and the officers of the corporation would become the directors of the corporation as well.

There seemed to be no reasons not to change to this form of organizational structure, and the timing of the change would seem to be appropriate, as it would be appropriate to change the name of the church at the time of the move.

Therefore, the Task Force and Deacons recommended (on August 21, 1991) that a corporate organizational structure be adopted effective with the acquisition of the land for the purpose of taking title to the land, any transactions relative to the new buildings, the relocation, and, for all purposes, when the move to the Johns

Creek site takes place. The recommendation was approved in a meeting on September 18, 1991.

The organizational meeting of the Sole Incorporator of Johns Creek Baptist Church, Inc., was held on December 9, 1991. The Constitution and By-Laws of the First Baptist Church of Chamblee were adopted as the By-Laws of the Corporation subject to certain following stipulations in accordance with the terms of the Georgia Nonprofit Corporation Code.

At the business meeting on December 18, 1991, the moderator informed the members that Johns Creek Baptist Church, Inc., and the First Baptist Church of Chamblee were separate organizations with interlocking members and essentially interlocking officers, and that both organizations would continue in operation until such time as the First Baptist Church of Chamblee was dissolved and its assets transferred to the Corporation. A discussion was also held regarding the development of the proposed new church facility and the need to complete certain organizational matters with respect to the Corporation. The vote to accept the resolutions regarding the corporation was unanimous. This included qualifying the Corporation as a member of the Southern Baptist Convention and thereby obtained a 501(c)(3) tax exempt status.

Tom Jack, Chair, Johns Creek Relationship/Program Services sub-committee of the Strategic Task Force, reported that the Johns Creek Mission Church would meet for their last service on January 26, 1992. Members of the Mission Church would decide as individuals where they would participate. The Johns Creek Steering Committee made up of representatives from Roswell Association, Johns Creek, Dunwoody Baptist and First Baptist Chamblee would hold their final meeting in February 1992. The merger would then be accomplished.

John Dixon, Chair, Chamblee Ministry Sub-Committee of the Strategic Task Force, reported that the Sub-Committee gave an overview of its goals regarding ministries we would leave behind when we move to Johns Creek. One of the goals was the relocation of the Kindergarten. Doraville First Baptist had been contacted, and their deacons voted unanimously to accept the kindergarten as part of their church programs. If the membership approves the recommendation at their business meeting in January 1992, the Sub-Committee will make a recommendation at First Baptist Chamblee's business meeting in January.

The New Buildings-Property Disposal Sub-Task Group asked to be authorized to execute a contract with the architectural firm Chegwidden-Dorsey-Holmes Architecture & Planning for the design of facilities to be constructed for the church on the McGinnis Ferry site.

The property on McGinnis Ferry Road in Forsyth County, a gift from Technology Park/Atlanta, was deeded to the Johns Creek Baptist Church, Inc., on December 27, 1991, for the purpose of establishing a church on that site in accordance with a resolution adopted by the corporation at its regular December meeting. During the morning worship service on January 5, 1992, L. H. Johnson, Chair of and acting on behalf of the Strategic Task Force, presented to the church through Deacon Chair Richard Eason the title to 15.84 acres of property.

At the January 22, 1992 business meeting, the Strategic Task Force recommended that the Weekday School Program be discontinued at Chamblee and relocated to the First Baptist Church of Doraville, effective the beginning of the 1992 school year. We would provide assistance in the form of furniture, fixtures, supplies and/or equipment. Motion was made, seconded and approved.

At the February 19, 1992 meeting, the Strategic Task Force recommended that a Steering Committee be formed for the purpose of developing a Chamblee Ministry Center. The recommendation called for nine members, comprised of three each from Atlanta Baptist Association, Dunwoody Baptist Church, and First Baptist Church of Chamblee. It was further recommended that the Steering Committee members from First Baptist Chamblee be Beth Ann Boland, Monroe Dempsey and John Dixon. The members from the other two organizations would be selected by those institutions.

A recommendation was presented on April 29, 1992, by the New Buildings-Property Disposal Sub-Task Group. The architect had proposed a master plan which has four completely connected and integrated main structures which would accommodate around 1100-1200 people for education and worship, and could include both fellowship and recreational facilities if desired. Phase I would accommodate our beginning needs at the new location, including space for 400 in the educational facilities and about 550 for worship. A kitchen would also be provided. Phase I would be about 25,000 square feet with an estimated cost of $2,500,000. The Sub-Task Group also recommended arrangements for financing the new building, in the event the Chamblee property is not sold and closed by the date funds are needed for construction. The final plans, construction contracts, and pricing would be approved by the church prior to any commitments being made for construction. These recommendations were approved unanimously at the church business meeting on May 20, 1992.

Also, on May 20, 1992, the Strategic Task Force made a recommendation for a restructuring to be known as Strategic Task Force II. The recommendation was approved on July 1, 1992.

I.   Coordinating Council
   A. Structure
      - Dr. Bill Self, Pastor:
        Serves as Chair of Strategic Task Force II;
        Also serves as Chair of the Coordinating Council.
      - 8 Members of Coordinating Council to be comprised of the Chair and Vice Chair of "Strategic Task Force II" committees as described below.
   B. **Responsibilities**:
      - Forum for Pastor and staff on matters related to relocation;
      - Coordinate plans and procedures related to relocation;

- Evaluate progress toward relocation and report to the church;
- First level of approval for recommendations to be taken to the Deacons and the church;
- Refer proposals and recommendations a necessary to the entire Strategic Task Force II.

## II.   Committee Structure & Responsibilities:

### A.  New Building/Property Disposal Committee:
- Structure

| | | |
|---|---|---|
| Chair | - | Tommy Boland |
| Vice Chair | - | Melba Franklin |
| Members | - | Edwin Boland |
| Edith Bond | | |
| W.O. Brannan | | Chester King |
| Bob Prator | | |

- Responsibilities:
  - Property sale;
  - Building plans, contractor selection, construction, furnish & equip;
  - Cemetery enclosure, memorial & perpetual care.

### B.  Community Missions Ministry Committee:
- Structure

| | | |
|---|---|---|
| Chair | - | John Dixon |
| Vice Chair | - | Beth Ann Boland |
| Members | - | Monroe Dempsey |
| All Current Missions Committee Members | | |

- Responsibilities:
  - Transfer of Week Day Schools, ESL, Blessing Room, Citizenship Classes and International Sunday School;

o Mission Center Project (FBC, DBC &
Atlanta Baptist Association);
o Transition of responsibilities to Steering
Committee & FBC Missions Committee
– Remain liaison, provide oversight;
o Liaison with Hispanic Mission regarding
its relocation;
o Community Missions budget planning.

## C. Johns Creek Advance Planning Committee:

- Structure

| | | |
|---|---|---|
| Chair | - | Tom Jack |
| Vice Chair | - | L.H. Johnson |
| Members | - | Sandra Eason |
| Fred Henderson | | |
| Harold Hyde | | Suzanne Tolbert |

Other members to be determined.

- Responsibilities:
  o Special events to create visibility and
  identify with the Johns Creek community;
  o Leadership for high profile/premier
  quality events;
  o Transportation logistics and planning;
  o Resource to Building Committee on new
  building issues;
  o Working relationship with existing FBC
  structure to assure orderly transition and
  make the best use of resources;
  o Liaison with Public Relations Committee;
  o Liaison with church staff and church
  council in matters of program planning
  and transition.

## D. "Together We Move" Committee:

- Structure

Chair            -        Richard Eason
Vice Chair       -        Phil Brown
Members          -        Jim Cook
                          Other members to be
determined.

- Responsibilities:
  o New building financial requirements (i.e., work with New Building/Property Disposal Committee on ascertaining and procuring necessary funds);
  o Programming financial requirements (i.e., work with staff on ascertaining and procuring necessary funds);
  o Community Missions financial requirements (i.e., work with Community Missions Ministry Committee on ascertaining and procuring necessary funds);
  o Determine appropriate fund raising strategies and arrange for implementation;
  o Liaison with the Stewardship Committee.

III.  **Role of Current Church Leadership and Organizations**
(Staff, Deacons, Church Council, Music Ministry, Sunday School, WMU, Stewardship, Nominating, Personnel and other existing committees)

A. **Strengthen and maintain program and organization in readiness for transition to new location.**

B. **Staff configuration and recruiting.**

C. **Use of space in new facility.**

D. **Special services in current location.**

On August 19, 1992, the New Building/Property Disposal Committee recommended that Holder Construction Company be employed as the general contractor for the construction project of the new church building at Johns Creek at a guaranteed maximum price not to exceed $2,400,000. The recommendation was approved on August 19, 1992.

On September 23, 1992, the following church members were added to the Task Force Committees:

Johns Creek Advance Planning Committee:

Brenda Bowman          Robert McFarland
Ray Johnson            Jeff Quick
Traci Johnson          Tony Turpin

"Together We Move" Committee:
Jim Harrington         Debi Sessions
Jerry Hyde             Kathy Wilson
Kirby Pate             Steve Wright
Cecelia Prator

On September 23, 1992, the New Building/Property Disposal Committee recommended approval of the design of the new facility at Johns Creek and execution of the contract with Holder Construction for construction. This recommendation was approved at the church business meeting on October 14, 1992.

Also at the October 14, 1992 meeting, the New Building/ Property Disposal Committee presented a recommendation to obtain a loan from Wachovia Bank of Georgia, NA, in the amount of $2,400,000 for construction of the facility. Motion was made, seconded, and approved unanimously. A recommendation from the "Together We Move" committee was made that a building fund, along with a structured campaign, be approved for the purpose of soliciting the congregation for pledges and contribution to the building of the church's new facilities at Johns Creek. The committee requested that the campaign be approved for $300,000 over a two-year period (1993, 1994). Motion was made, seconded, and approved unanimously.

Ground-breaking for the new facility took place on Sunday, October 25, 1992. Prior to the ceremony, a worship service was held at the Northeast Atlanta Hilton where pledges for the "Together We Move" campaign were also received.

On January 20, 1993, the Community Missions Ministry Committee of the Strategic Task Force II recommended that an amount equal to ten percent of the net proceeds of the sale of the Chamblee property be designated for use in ministries in the Chamblee/Doraville area. The funds would be paid over a period of time in a fashion recommended by the Stewardship Committee and approved by the church so long as such a ministry continues to successfully carry out programs and ministries considered by the Missions Committee and by the church to be meaningful, viable, productive, and in concert with the mission of our church. The recommendation was approved.

On March 28, 1993, a homecoming was held. Many former members attended the morning worship service, followed by "dinner on the ground."

On March 31, 1993, Larry Jones, Minister of Education, reported that with the relocation to Johns Creek some changes would be made in our current Sunday School format. Every division (preschool through adults) was being evaluated. Some areas would see more immediate change than others. Plans to implement the Sunday School transition model would begin in Adult 3 in May. Basically, adults would have an opportunity to select from some half dozen or more topics (modules) to study, most for eight weeks at a time. An Advisory Council would address any concerns that arise with this change. Tom Jack and Larry Jones would co-chair the Advisory Council. John Dixon, Jerry Hyde and Marsha Janofsky would serve as representatives "at large." The Preschool/Children's Minister would represent those two areas when that person is hired. Then Traci Johnson, Bill Jinks, L. H. Johnson, Greg Walton, Vivian Gay and Carolyn Self would be part of the Advisory Council, giving input on youth, single adults, young adults, median adults, senior adults, and special/entry events respectively.

On May 19, 1993, a new telephone system was approved that would be installed and used at the Chamblee location then moved to Johns Creek. The Mission Statement (see separate Appendix article) was also approved, and the maximum amount of the construction contract was increased to $2,450,000.

On June 16, 1993, the Properties Committee was authorized to throw away, set price of and sell, move, and/or arrange for storage of such items as it deemed in the best interest of the church. The church also approved a recommendation to proceed with the search for and employment of a Pre-School & Children's Minister whose duties would include, among other things, the establishment of a day care center in the church at Johns Creek.

On July 21, 1993, after consulting with the New Building Sub-Committee, the "Together We Move" Sub-Committee of the Strategic Task Force II recommended the church establish a "Memorial & Honorary" gift campaign for the new facilities at Johns Creek. A list of specific items, included quantities and price, would be provided. Only items on this list would be a part of this campaign and no other campaigns were to be recommended nor would they be recognized. This would be a low key promotion with no pressure on anyone to make a gift, however it would be promoted as gifts over and above the General and Building Funds. Both committees recommended that we do not allow plaques on pews and other furnishings, and that recognition of gifts be confined to a single memorial plaque or book. This campaign would free up other funds for the purchase of larger items. Another item of business was the presentation of a new Facilities Use Policy for the church.

At the September 22, 1993 church business meeting, a Special Ministries Program was presented and approved for the purpose of providing attractive and meaningful programs designed to reach and nurture adults. Three councils would be established: Women's Ministries Council, Men's Ministries Council, and Senior Adult

Ministries Council. The membership and chairpersons would be nominated by the ministerial staff and elected by the church. The Councils would serve from October 1, 1993, through December 31, 1994, at which time a permanent structure would become effective. The chairperson of each council would serve on the Church Council.

A resolution was recommended that effective October 11, 1993, the facilities of the church at the Chamblee site be closed as to use for weekly worship and activities of the church and maintained thereafter for the use of the Hispanic Mission of the church until the properties are sold, and that effective October 11, 1993, the location of our church be moved to the Johns Creek site at 7500 McGinnis Ferry Road, Alpharetta, Georgia, for weekly worship and other church activities, which will begin on Sunday, October 17, 1993. It was also resolved that the church discontinue public use of the name First Baptist Church of Chamblee, though the real property which the church owns at 5303 New Peachtree Road, Chamblee, Georgia will continue to be owned by the Trustees for First Baptist Church of Chamblee until sold. It was further resolved that henceforth the church shall be known as Johns Creek Baptist Church (incorporated as a Georgia non-profit corporation).

During this entire process, the catch-phrase was "If we build it, will they come?," (from the movie *Field of Dreams*). A ribbon-cutting occurred and the first worship service at Johns Creek Baptist Church was held on October 17, 1993. The sanctuary overflowed, with chairs in the aisles and in the hallway to the main foyer. An estimated 600 persons were in attendance. "If we build it, will they come?" Yes! We did, and they did!

# STRATEGIC PLANNING INITIATIVE: CHURCH SURVEY

Having completed our four-phase church campus development plan, the Pastor's Council presented a recommendation at the church business meeting on July 18, 2007. They felt that it was time to make both short and longer term plans for the future and to develop a vision for the coming years. It would be easy to become lax following the completion of the construction of the church's buildings. We would utilize the services of The Alban Institute, located in Herndon, Virginia, which at that time was the leading ecumenical church and clergy support organization in the country for three decades. The Institute would conduct a written survey of church members to help understand our current perceptions, spiritual needs and desires. They would do demographic research on the larger community of people who live and work in the area surrounding the church. Discussion groups with church members would be held. The outcome would be the development of a three- to five-year plan for the church.

The Pastor's Council recommendation was that our church enter into a strategic planning initiative, employing the Alban Institute to assist in the effort. The budgets of 2007 and 2008 would be revised in the aggregate amount of $55,000 to accommodate the amounts required to fund this initiative. The steering committee was composed of the Senior Pastor Dr. Self, Executive Pastor Dr. McCullar, Greg Kennedy as Chair, Tom Jack, Deborah Peterson, Tommy Boland and Carole Smith. The vote passed unanimously. (Greg Kennedy had to resign later because of the time commitment required. Kevin Tolbert was elected September 26, 2007, to serve as chair.)

This assessment and planning process included four distinct phases:

- Phase I – Preparing to Plan: July 2007 – October 2007 was primarily the gathering of historical data through the creation of a small steering committee to work closely with the consultant.
- Phase II – Assessment: October 2007 – March 2008 involved the assessment of our present status and would include at least three data gathering devices.
    - The U.S. Congregation's Survey to be administered on a Sunday morning during Sunday School, and the goal was for approximately 700 people to undertake this survey, typically age 15 and above.
    - Precept, the Church Information Leader, would provide demographic data as to the composition of our local mission field.
    - A series of twelve listening sessions composed of about twelve members each would be held, under the direction of our Alban consultants.
- Phase III – Shaping the Future: April 2008 – September 2008 would involve the shaping of future plans. A steering committee appointed by the church would engage in a study and understanding of all of the data and information provided by the consultants that resulted from the surveys and the listening sessions. This data, along with information gleaned from the Precept demographic study, would be synthesized and strategic needs, priorities, and possibilities of the congregation would be placed into a strategic long range plan.
- Phase IV – Ownership and Implementation: October 2008 – December 2008 would be the presentation of the strategic planning to the church for its approval and implementation The steering committee would generate a written plan that includes three to five overall strategic priorities: one-, two- and three-year goal statements and measures for each of the strategic priorities; and an outline of expected budgetary requirements to support the strategy planned.

The process started in late 2007 and proceeded over several months with 882 members participating in the U.S. Congregational Life survey, followed by 185 participants in 19 listening sessions, and 70 participants in a planning retreat. The result was a comprehensive report which outlined the current strengths that the congregation believed needed to be preserved and five new strategic priorities to pursue vigorously for the future. This report was given at a Special-Called Business Meeting on January 28, 2009.

Those strengths the congregation wished to maintain and preserve are:

- We value the format and focus of our Sunday School program. We seek to preserve the community model of our program with its strong emphasis on care groups. We value Bible-based, age-appropriate and inclusive teaching formats in our group programs, preschool, children, youth and adults.
- We continue to nurture our identity as a warm and loving, family-oriented community of care. We value knowing one another and being known by one another. We foster an environment of intimacy and warmth in spite of our large church identity.
- We have experienced and continue to expect world class, visionary preaching and teaching from integrity-filled pastoral leaders.
- We value excellence in our worship experience, a traditional worship format and a quality music program.

Those strategic priorities to pursue and accomplish over the next three to five years are:

- Leadership Development: We operate with depth of leadership of strength at all levels of the congregation. Our decision-making processes are transparent and open, encouraging the involvement and development of future leaders. We have a succession plan in place for our senior pastor and other key leaders.

- Christian Witness and Mission Outreach: We offer an integrated, intergenerational program of Christian witness and missions that actively engages a broad base of our members. We are known for our Christian witness and mission influence in the area immediately surrounding the church, in the greater Atlanta area, and throughout the world.
- Discipleship: Our membership is strengthening the practice of faith as evidenced by deepening commitment to Christian study, participation and application.
- Children's Ministry: We operate vibrant preschool and children's ministry programming, hosted in dedicated, appealing and child-friendly environments.
- Debt Reduction: We are focused on healthy, balanced program growth while actively reducing our debt load.

The recommendation passed unanimously.

At the October 21, 2009 church business meeting, the Pastoral Succession Resolution was presented. Dr. Self explained that when a pastor retires, a congregation can lose a large amount of momentum during the interim time between pastors. Though he has no retirement date in mind, he thought of ways to make the process go more smoothly and discussed the issue with a few church leaders. Then the church launched the strategic planning initiative, and during the listening groups, members mentioned the topic of pastoral succession. So it is appropriate to address this topic in a positive, forward-looking way.

This Pastoral Succession plan would relate only to the retirement of our present Senior Pastor, Dr. William L. Self, and would include the following:

- Once Dr. Self, following God's leadership and with the ongoing support of the Pastor's Council, decides that the timing is appropriate to initiate the process for transition, the process will begin.

- Dr. Self will inform the church in writing that he wishes to begin the transition to retirement, which starts the church's process for searching and calling a new Senior Pastor, following the church's By-Laws.
- The church will be called into a season of prayer through the search and transition process.
- Dr. Self will continue as Senior Pastor throughout the search process.
- After the search committee completes its task and the church calls a new Senior Pastor, a period of up to three months will allow for the transition of duties from Dr. Self to the new Senior Pastor.
- At the conclusion of the transitional period, Dr. Self will retire and the new Senior Pastor will continue in the role.

If adopted, the plan would give the church's ministerial staff members a greater sense of security. Retaining our team of ministers will ensure continuity and progress in the church's programs and ministries before and after a pastoral transition. Also, the proposed succession plan would not change the way the search committee interacts with church members. Vote was taken at the church business meeting on January 27, 2010, and was approved.

At a special-called business meeting on December 2, 2009, Kevin Tolbert, chair of the strategic planning task force, said that in reference to one of the five strategic priorities identified by the task force is "Christian witness and missions outreach," the task force recommends the creation of a position of church witnessing coordinator. This person would be responsible for coordinating the outreach and witnessing efforts that are undertaken by multiple groups within the church such as Sunday School communities, deacons, missions groups, and staff members. The plan calls for the implementation of programs that would result in 70 people actively engaged in outreach and evangelism. The coordinator would oversee this effort, and would see that church members receive training in evangelism, and that resources are shared effectively among the groups that do outreach. Bob Lynn was recommended for this position. Dr. Lynn was elected unanimously.

At the January 27, 2010 business meeting, a comprehensive witness strategy called "The Force of 70," was presented. This would be an answer to another strategic priority identified in the initiative which was to organize, enlist and train members for effective sharing of the gospel through Christian witness and missions outreach. Dr. Bob Lynn said the recommendation was based upon the passage in Luke 10 where Jesus sends 70 disciples as an advance team to the villages of Galilee to announce that He is coming to proclaim the Good News. Members of the evangelism task force were Polly Cloud, Lamar Henderson, Ray Johnson, Carol Smith, Steve Wright, Bob Lynn, Dr. Self and David White.

The strategy calls for the force of 70 to serve on nine teams:

- Prospects Mining Team would develop a greatly expanded prospect master list for the church. Steve Wright would head the team.
- The Corps of 25 would serve as counselors, available for one-on-one witnessing to people with spiritual needs. Danny Henderson would lead this team.
- Sunday School Outreach Coordinators would enlist and train an outreach coordinator for each adult Sunday School community who would lead class members to be witnesses for Christ. Ray Johnson would head this team.
- Telephone Witness Team would coordinate the reaching and follow-up of prospects by telephone among various groups, including ministers, deacons, Sunday School communities, and church-wide phone committees. Jeff Quick would lead the team.
- Communication and Emerging Technology Team would train and encourage church members to use innovative methods to spread the gospel via the internet, online

publishing, video and audio production, Facebook, Twitter, etc. Kay Brinson would head the team.

- Worship Hosts Team is an existing group which would expand its ministry as official hosts during worship services. Lamar Henderson leads this team.

- Events Witness Team would design, plan, coordinate and host special events at JCBC as outreach and witness to the community. Sarah Durham would head this team.

- Neighborhood Work and Outreach Team would encourage and train church members on innovative ways to witness within their neighborhoods and work settings. Polly Cloud would lead this team.

- Outside Groups Team is an outgrowth of a special deacon ministry, and would serve as the church's ambassadors to outside groups who hold events at our facilities. They would greet guests and provide assistance and information to them while they are here. Jean Watson would head this team.

To support the witnessing effort, a witnessing coordinating council would be formed and would be composed of the Senior Pastor, a staff liaison, the church witnessing coordinator, the witnessing training coordinator, and the chairs of the nine teams. This council would administer the overall witnessing strategy. By unanimous vote, the church approved the comprehensive witnessing strategy.

At the church business meeting on April 21, 2010, the Strategic Planning Task Force recommended the approval of the Discipleship Task Force Three-Year Plan. The members of the Discipleship Task Force who developed the plan are Angie Kleckley, Heidi Carr, Bo Godwin, Alan McKnight, Kirby Pate, Charles Skidmore and Trudy Woodard. The two goals were (1) to review the present discipleship curriculum and programs; (2) to create a three-year plan to focus on deeper discipleship for all age groups. Themes were recommended for each year:

(1)  Year One (2011) – Grow -- Spiritual Growth;

(2)   Year Two (2012) – Give -- Investing in our church and community;

(3)   Year Three (2013) – Go -- Missions.

The "Small Steps" program of 2010 is prelude to initiating this discipleship plan. The first quarter emphasis was on scripture reading. The second quarter was on fruits of the spirit. The third quarter focus was on prayer. The fourth quarter was on sharing our faith. The vote on this plan was unanimously approved.

At a special-called business meeting to approve the 2011 ministry budget on September 29, 2010, Mike Goodman explained that an item called "building fund" in past budgets is renamed "facilities revitalization fund" to reflect the nature of the planned expenditures. The majority would be spent on renovations to the educational space for children's and preschool ministries. Tom Jack presented plans that had been developed to renovate the children's and preschool areas. The objective is to update and refresh the education space, and to create an overall theme for the area. The theme is "creation." New colors, murals and three-dimensional graphic elements would be used to communicate the Biblical stories of creation in ways that are both educational and entertaining to children. Scripture verses would also be used. Completion date was estimated as August 2011. The 2011 ministry budget was unanimously approved.

At a special-called business meeting on March 28, 2012, Richard Eason reported on a plan for debt reduction. He explained that the current loan with Wells Fargo Bank (formerly Wachovia Bank) was initiated in 2005, and the proceeds were used to fund construction of the church's sanctuary that opened in 2007. The original loan amount was $25 million, and we have paid the balance down to $11.2 million. This good payment record has allowed us to secure a favorable modification to the terms of the loan with the bank. We hope to pay down the debt aggressively in the next few years, which will reduce the amount of interest, thus reducing the total amount we will pay out to the bank.

The new interest rate we would be getting will be 4.24% for five years beginning on July 1, 2012. However, when the principal balance is paid below $10 million, the rate will be further adjusted down to 3.99% with no penalty for prepayment. These are excellent rates.

The modification also provides for a new annual principal payment of approximately $880,000 with interest payments due monthly. The final maturity date of the loan does not change. Also, the loan covenants are amended, which regulates how the church spends and saves over the life of the loan. The loan should be paid in full in about seven years or so. The church may conduct a new capital fund-raising campaign at some point, and that would assist in paying off the loan. The motion in favor of the recommendation concerning the term loan modification passed.

With these actions of the church, all five priorities defined by the Strategic Planning Initiative had been or are in the process of being satisfied.

# CHURCH MEMBERS WHO MOVED FROM CHAMBLEE TO JOHNS CREEK

(This list is of resident church members only; it does not include non-resident members or members of Sunday School only.)

ADAMS, Buford & Hazel
ADAMS, Fannie
ADAMS, Charlotte
ALBRIGHT, Jean
ALEXANDER, Jack & Meta
ALEXANDER, Jacob
ALLISON, Ben & Pauline
ANGLIN, Mildred
ARNETT, Gerson & Martha
ASH, Richard & Pauline
AUSTIN, Jackie
AYERS, Martha
BACON, Darrell
BAGGETT, Jimmie & Sue
BAGWELL, Dalene
BAGWELL, Clarice
BAILEY, Sue
BAKER, Virginia
BALKCOM, Nell & Suzanne
BALLEW, Claude & Lois
BARKER, Johnnie
BARNETT, Gerald, Nina & Dina
BARRINGER, Jewell
BARRINGER, Robert
BARTON, Margie
BATTIE, Oscar & Margaret
BAXTER, Camille
BEARD, David
BEAVERS, John, Mary, Craig & Jeffrey
BENFORD, M. C. & Faye
BENNETT, Jackie
BENNINGTON, Betty
BENTON, Mary
BERNSTEIN, Velda
BERNSTEIN, Michael

BLACK, Jeanette
BLACKSTONE, Sara
BLANKENSHIP, David & Jan
BOGGS, Grace
BOLAND, Tommy & Beth Ann
BOLAND, Edwin
BOND, Edith
BOND, George, Sara & Gina
BOWMAN, Brenda
BOWMAN, Kim
BOWMAN, Greg & Carlene
BOZEMAN, Mabel
BRACEWELL, Lee & Angie
BRACEWELL, Thomas
BRADFORD, Mary Lou, Morris & Thomas
BRAMLETT, Irvin & Estelle
BRAMLETT, Michael & Colleen
BRANCH, JAMES
BRANNAN, W. O. & Kathleen
BRASWELL, Don, Margaret & Brad (Bo)
BRAY, Hazel
BRAY, Larry
BREWER, Jason & Elaine
BROOKS, Margie
BROWN, Phil & Tamra
BROWN, L.E. (Pete), Barbara & Sandra
BROWN, Bill & Chris
BUCHHEIT, Ethel
BUCHHEIT, Wynne
BULLARD, Mona
BURNAM, Mable
BURRELL, Rita
BURRY, David & Evelyn

BUTLER, Wayne & Laura
CALDWELL, Jane
CAMP, Marvin & Dorothy
CAMP, Michael
CANTRELL, Martha
CARLSON, Lynn & Cindy
CARPENTER, Wayne & Norma
CARPENTER, M. W. & Foy
CARTER, Frances
CARVER, Rosario
CASH, Inez
CASH, Bob
CASH, Conrad
CAUSEY, Shirley
CHAMBERS, Carl & Peggy
CHASTEEN, Doyle & Jan
CHASTEEN, Will
CHATHAM, Martha
CHAUVIN, Christa
CHILDRESS, Roy & Frankie
CHILDRESS, Rick
CLARK, Donna
CLARK, David & Sandie
CLARK, Bob, June, Caryn & Taylor
CLEMENT, Charles & Willye Mae
CLIFTON, Angela
CLINTON, Adena
COKER, Teresina
COLEMAN, Rhea
CONWAY, Charlie & Sharon
COOK, Charlene
COOK, Jim, Imogene, Jim & Julie
CORNELISON, Edra
COSPER, Marvis & Jackie
COULTER, Mertie
COX, Evelyn
COX, Lisa
CRAVEY, Carol
CREDILLE, Carol & Chuck
CREIGHTON, Joe
CRIDER, Freddie & Debbie
CROWFOOT, Rebecca & Byron
CURTIS, Grant & Dot
CURTIS, Paul

DABBS, Trez
DANIEL, Herbert & Barbara
DANIEL, Frank
DANIEL, Joan & Melissa
DAUGHERTY, Ed, Susan, Brad & Benjy
DAVIS, Ersie
DAVIS, Burley & Fleeta
DAVIS, Ernest & Bebe
DAVIS, Bob, Vickie & Brad
DAVIS, Frances
DAVIS, Robin
DAWS, Marge
DeANGELIS, Bobbi
DEAL, Deborah
DECKER, Dean, Patricia & Scott
DECKER, Howard & Alma
DEEGAN, Peggy
DEEN, Jo
DEMPSEY, Monroe & Jeannette
DEMPSEY, Mark
DENNEY, Lynn
DEVEREAUX, Bill, Joyce & Steve
DEVORE, Jere, Donna & Jon Paul
DICKEY, Calvin, Fran, Scott & Kenneth
DILL, Jim, Carol & Greg
DILL, Tom
DIXON, John, Linda, Drew & Courtney
DODD, Merle
DODSON, Larry, Olivia, Michael, Scott & Keith
DODSON, Wayne
DOERLICH, Angie
DONALDSON, Candace
DONALDSON, Don & Deborah
DOTSON, Harold
DOWLING, Chris
DOWLING, Ronnie
DUFNER, Mark & Jane
DULIN, Katherine
DUNCAN, Eleanor
DUTTON, Deborah

DWYER, Christy & Stephanie
EASON, Claud & Mary Catherine
EASON, Richard, Sandra, Richard & Keith
EDWARDS, A. W. (Happy)
ELLER, Margaret
ELLIS, Mary
ELLIS, Evelyn
ELLIS, Robert & Linda
ELLIS, Jim, Dolores & Jamie
ENTREKEN, Nancy
FAMBROUGH, Jim, Jan, Jamie & Jonathan
FAULKNER, Donna
FIELDING, Clarence & Kay
FIELDS, Warren & Bobbie
FLOWERS, Wesley & Gina
FORD, Bobby
FORD, Velma
FORRESTER, Jeremy
FRANCIS, Jimmy
FRANCIS, Johnny
FRANKLIN, Don, Melba, Nicole & Sheli
FROST, Dan & Joan
FUJII, Brian
GADDY, Betty
GALLOWAY, Harry & George
GARRETT, James & Helen
GARRETT, Kelli
GAULT, Scott
GAUT, Lisa
GAY, Vivian
GENTRY, Tammy
GILBERT, Randy
GILBERT, Richard & Sally
GILLIAM, Sam & Lib
GILLIAN, Jack Jr.
GILLILAND, Billy & Carolyn
GLISSON, Patrick, Janie, Patrick, Ryan & Paige
GOBER, Frances & Denise
GOODMAN, Mary
GOUGE, Agnes

GRAZIOSA, Allan & Patti
GREENWAY, Bradley
GREENWAY, Wiley & Virginia
GRIFFIN, Dale & Pat
GRINNELL, Carolyn
GULLICK, Bobbie
GUNN, Pamela
HALFORD, Robert
HALL, Brenda
HALL, Tom & Linda
HALTERMAN, Arnold, Susan & Kelli
HANCOCK, Jo Ann
HANCOCK, Eddie
HANSARD, Larry, Judy & Ivey
HARE, Shelly
HARRINGTON, Jim & Sue
HARRIS, Martha
HARRIS, Bob & Joyce
HARRIS, Betsy
HARRIS, Carla
HARVEY, Carroll & Lee
HAWKINS, Ralph & Jay
HEAD, Claude & Sylvia
HEGWOOD, Gene, Helen, Kirk & Amy
HENDERSON, Fred & Lillian
HENDERSON, Beulah
HERRINGTON, Paul & Dorothy
HERRINGTON, Phil & Lynn
HESTER, Lillian
HESTER, Troy
HIBBETTS, Hazel
HICKEY, Bertha
HICKS, Steven
HILL, Shari
HODGES, Joe &, Ann
HOLBROOK, Lewis
HOLBROOK, Wade
HOLCOMB, Norma
HOLCOMB, Mitchell
HOLLAND, Henry
HOMER, Lucile
HORNSBY, Sue

HORTIN, Sara
HORTON, Heyward
HOSICK, Marguerite
HOWELL, Denise
HOWINGTON, Jackie
HUDSON, Frances
HUDSON, John & Elizabeth
HUDSON, Karen
HUIE, Jason
HUMPHRIES, D. P.
HYDE, Cora Lee
HYDE, David & Wanda
HYDE, Jerry, Brenda & Michael
HYDE, Harold & Kaye
HYDE, Mona
IM, Aun
IRVIN, Beth
IVES, Bootsie
JACK, Tom & Elizabeth
JACK, Susan
JACKSON, Don
JACKSON, Cindy
JACKSON, Helen
JACOBSON, Maria
JAMES, Don, Ann & Matthew
JANOFSKY, Marsha
JENKINS, Bill & Betty
JENKINS, Katherine
JENKINS, B. L. & Joy
JENKINS, Gary, Linda, Steven & Jonathan
JINKS, Bill
JOHNSON, Buddy & Christen
JOHNSON, Hugh, Ollie & Dorsey
JOHNSON, L. H. & Charis
JOHNSON, Ray, Beverly, Kim & Jennifer
JOHNSON, Ron
JOHNSON, Traci
JOHNSON, David
JOHNSON, Gale
JOHNSON, Kevin
JONES, Larry, Karen, Meghan & Mallory

JONES, Mike & Pat
JONES, Tom & Kathryn
JONES, Martin
JORDAN, Randy & Denise
KAY, Richard & Sue
KENT, Bob, Susan & Susie
KIDD, Way & Marybeth
KIM, Kon, Susie, Audrey & Caroline
KING, Chester & Norma
KINNARD, Betty
KRAUSE, Robert, Shirley & Diana
KUGLAR, Willie
LAMB, Rebecca
LANE, Juanita
LANKFORD, Patti & Matt
LATHAM, Dot
LAW, Steve & Jennifer
LAWSON, Bobby & Matt
LEDBETTER, Tim & Teresa
LEGG, Eddie & Bette
LEWIS, Maxine
LEWIS, Sybil
LEWIS, Nancy
LITTLE, Betty
LORD, Juanita
LOUDERMILK, Bessie
LOUDERMILK, Winfred & Carrie
LOWE, Gary & Ricky
LUCARELLI, Melissa
MACY, Lorrene
MADDOX, Michael
MADDUX, Tom & Myrtis
MADREN, Paul & Kelly
MALONE, Paula
MARTIN, Aubrey & Mary
MARTIN, John, Diane, Jim & Linda
MARTIN, Shirley & Belle
MASSEY, Jim
MASSEY, Joe
MASTERS, Montine
MAULDIN, Juanita, Len & Cheryl
MAXEY, Nick & Gerry
MAYO, Tom & Ann
McCALL, Steve & Janice

McCLESKEY, William
McCOLLUM, Deborah
McDANIEL, Kelly
McDONALD, Robert & Donna
McFALL, Joe
McFALL, Kay & Morgan
McFARLAND, Robert & Helen
McNEELY, Edward & Vi
MILES, Gloria
MILLER, Laura & Dara
MILLER, Mary
MINTON, Elsie
MITCHELL, Verna
MOORE, Mary Ann
MORGAN, Jason
MORPHY, Dorothy
MORRELL, Tabitha
MORRISON, Redina
MURPHY, Emory
MYERS, Nellie
NAGY, Joan
NASWORTHY, Grace
NELMS, Jennifer
NEWMAN, Emily
NIX, Dortha
NOLAN, Ted
NOON, Robin
OBARR, Louis & Christopher
OLIVER, Charles & Margaret
OWENS, James & Gail
PADGETT, Kathleen
PARHAM, Jerome & Arnette
PARKER, Faye
PARKER, Norman & Barbara
PARKER, Cindy
PARTRIDGE, Dollie
PASSMAN, Paul
PATE, Kirby & Shan
PATEL, Husna
PATTERSON, Gail
PAVLIC, Michael, Mary & Beth
PERKINS, Sandra
PERRY, Charles & Allene
PERRY, Christina

PETTEPHER, Matt
PETTEPHER, Jon
PIERCE, Paul
PINSON, Scott
POLLOCK, Dorothy
POLLOCK, William
PRATOR, Bob, Cecelia, Kristen & Nancy
PRESNELL, Jean
PRESNELL, Jeffrey
PRUITT, Agnes
PURCELL, Allene
QUICK, Jeff & Karen
RAFIZADEY, Majtaba & Hedye
RAMSEY, Lowell & Patty
RANDOLPH, Wallace & Thelma
RAY, G. N.
REESE, Gene
REESE, Tom & Iris
REESE, Joe
REEVES, Frank & Dolle
REYNOLDS, Robert
REYNOLDS, Kathy
REYNOLDS, Lee & Janice
RIDDLE, Nell
RILEY, Minnie
RIMMER, Basil & Lucy
RIMMER, David
RIVERS, Nell
RODGERS, C. D. & Audrey
ROE, Tommy, Diane, Stephanie & Melissa
ROGERS, Elise
ROGERS, Scott
ROGERS, Shelly
ROUTT, Joe, Marlene, Dana, Scott & Greg
SANDERS, Freeman, Sue & Nancy
SANDERS, Jeannie
SANDERS, Richard
SANDERS, Casey & Christi
SAPPINGTON, Howard
SCHULTZ, Margaret
SCHWAB, Michele

SCOTT, Roy, Diane, Matt & Clarke
SCROGGINS, Evella
SEARS, John & Doris
SELF, Bryan & Karen
SELF, Bill & Carolyn
SESSIONS, Larry, Debi, Alex & Lisa
SEXTON, Bobby
SEXTON, Susan
SHANKWEILER, Marilyn
SHANNON, Joel
SHEAD, Swannee
SHEALY, Elsie
SHEFFIELD, Herman & Nancy
SHELLHORSE, Agnes
SHEPARD, Sharry & Shellee
SHEPHERD, Oscar & Dorothy
SHEPPARD, Sheree
SHERMAN, Cecil & Dot
SHULL, Adam & Stacie
SIMMONS, Walter
SIMS, Paul, Kathleen, Jennifer, Maggie & William
SKIDMORE, Kent
SMELLEY, Rachel
SMITH, Harold & Elizabeth
SMITH, Edna
SMITH, Robbie
SMITH, John
SMITH, Kathleen
SMITH, Donna & Randy
SMITH, Shirley
SMITH, Philip & Sherrie
SNYDER, Jim & Pam
SPENCE, Dinah
SPRUELL, Paul, Ruth & Todd
SPRUELL, Scott
SPRUILL, David
SPURGEON, Harlan & Joann
SPURLIN, Baxter, Ruth & Shelia
STARLING, Wayne
STEED, Craig & Sheri
STEPHENS, Matthew & Alston
STEPHENS, Meta
STEVENS, Ted & Agnes

STEVENS, Tommy
STEWART, Al & Sandy
STEWART, Linda
STEWART, Paul & Jennie
STEWART, Billy
STEWART, Debbie
STEWART, Kenny
STEWART, Steve
STINNETT, Kim & Sarah
STITH, Martha
STOCKBRIDGE, Derry & Cheryl
STONE, Dale & Renee
STOVALL, Frank & Bootsy
STOWE, Pam
STRAIN, William, Dora & Mary
STRICKLAND, Myron & Syble
TATUM, Paul & Era
TAYLOR, Cooper
TAYLOR, Ann
TAYLOR, John C., Nancy & John W.
TEMPLETON, Dan
THAXTON, Mickey & Sara
THOMAS, David
THOMAS, Janet
THOMAS, Lamar, Jr.
THOMAS, Lamar, Sr.
THOMAS, Ruth
THOMASSON, Chris
THORNTON, Eugene & Janie
TIENCKEN, Shann
TILLERY, Chris & Jessica
TOLBERT, Carl & Suzanne
TOLLISON, Debbie
TOLSON, W. E. & Ruby
TOMLIN, Daisy
TOMLIN, Evelyn
TURPIN, Tony & Jan
ULATOWSKI, Robyn
UPDEGRAFF, Don & Susan
USHER, Bill, Lois & Stacey
VISMOR, Nettie
VONTILLIUS, Alun
VONTILLIUS, Kay
WAGNER, K. A. & Flonnie

WAGNER, Richard
WAGNER, Donald
WAGNER, Michael
WALKER, Anne (Bunny)
WALKER, Carney & Ann
WALLACE, Anne & Debbie
WALLACE, Cannon
WALTON, Jay & Gail
WALTON, Greg & Terry
WAMSLEY, Bryan & Paula
WATERS, Ed & Dot
WATERS, Carol
WATERS, Carolyn
WATERS, Douglas
WATERS, John
WATSON, Lane & June
WEATHERSBEE, Eldon & Patti
WEATHERSBY, Rise
WEAVER, Gerald
WELDEN, Lori
WESTERLUND, Tammy
WHEELER, Eva
WHITE, Doug & Mary
WHITE, Winnie
WHITE, Joan, Joe & Billy
WHITTEN, W. A. & Lucille
WIGGS, Tom
WILBUR, Bea
WILEY, Ruby

WILEY, John & Louise
WILLIAMS, Alma
WILLIAMS, Patti
WILLIAMS, Jenni
WILLIAMS, Vicki, Butch, David &
Dennis
WILLIAMS, Sandra
WILLIS, Eddie & Rhonda
WILLIS, Julian & Katherine
WILSON, Monica
WILSON, Brad & Kathy
WILSON, Vicki
WINGATE, Ken
WINN, Matthew & Karen
WISE, George & Marion
WOLFE, Julie
WRIGHT, Steve, Virginia, Susan,
Steven & Paul
WRIGHT, Daniel & Patricia
YATH, Pak, Savoeun & Kim
YOUNG, Ashleigh
YOUNG, Rebecca
YOUNG, Thelma
YOUNGBLOOD, Mary


855 resident church members

# JCBC 2013 History Committee Members

*(L-R) Mary Lou Parrish, Barbara Brown (Chair), Dave Brown, Nancy Skidmore*

CPSIA information can be obtained at www.ICGtesting.com
Printed in the USA
LVOW06s0208260913

354067LV00004B/4/P